The Concept of Justice in Judaism, Christianity and Islam

# Key Concepts in Interreligious Discourses

Edited by
Georges Tamer

## Volume 4

# The Concept of Justice in Judaism, Christianity and Islam

Edited by
Catharina Rachik and Georges Tamer

DE GRUYTER

ISBN 978-3-11-056062-6
e-ISBN (PDF) 978-3-11-056169-2
e-ISBN (EPUB) 978-3-11-056066-4
ISSN: 2513-1117

**Library of Congress Control Number: 2025933615**

**Bibliographic information published by the Deutsche Nationalbibliothek**
The Deutsche Nationalbibliothek lists this publication in the Deutsche Nationalbibliografie; detailed bibliographic data are available on the internet at http://dnb.dnb.de.



www.degruyterbrill.com
Questions about General Product Safety Regulation:
productsafety@degruyterbrill.com

# Preface

This volume in the book series *Key Concepts in Interreligious Discourses* (KCID) is based on a conference on the concept of justice in Judaism, Christianity, and Islam, held at the Friedrich-Alexander-Universität Erlangen-Nürnberg on May 11–12, 2017. I would like to thank the Hanns-Seidel-Foundation for helping to fund this conference.

The conference and the book series *Key Concepts in Interreligious Discourses* (KCID) are central projects of the Bavarian Research Center for Interreligious Discourses (BaFID). The main goal of the Center is to study the fundamental ideas and central concepts of Judaism, Christianity, and Islam with the aim of uncovering their interconnectedness and highlighting the similarities as well as the differences between these three religions. By sharing the results of our research, BaFID seeks to promote peaceful relations among religious communities and to foster mutual understanding and social cohesion in pluralistic societies. In addition to the published volumes, selected highlights from each volume are also made available online on the BaFID website.

BaFID aspires not only to engage a small group of academic specialists in reflecting on central religious ideas but also to disseminate these ideas in a manner that is accessible and appealing to the broader public. Academic research that serves society is crucial for counteracting the contemporary trend of segregation rooted in ignorance and for strengthening mutual respect and acceptance among different religions. This aspiration is fulfilled through the discursive investigation of concepts, as exemplified in this volume on the complex concept of justice.

BaFID could not fulfill its mission without the generous support of the Bavarian State Ministry of the Interior, for Sport and Integration. Their support has been instrumental in advancing our research and outreach efforts, and I extend my deepest gratitude to Minister of State Joachim Herrmann and his team for their unwavering commitment to promoting interreligious understanding and social integration.

I would like to express my gratitude to Walter de Gruyter Publishers for their competent management of this volume and the entire book series.

Georges Tamer — Erlangen, April 2025

https://doi.org/10.1515/9783110561692-001

# Table of Contents

**Preface —— V**

Aryeh Botwinick
**The Concept of Justice in Judaism —— 1**

Elisabeth Gräb-Schmidt
**The Concept of Justice in Christianity —— 59**

Sabri Ciftci
**The Concept of Justice in Islam —— 115**

Catharina Rachik and Georges Tamer
**Epilogue —— 183**

**List of Contributors —— 213**

**Index of Persons —— 215**

**Index of Subjects —— 217**

Aryeh Botwinick

# The Concept of Justice in Judaism

## 1 Introduction

Justice is one of the most central concepts in the monotheistic religions. In Judaism, especially the active pursuit of justice is underscored: "He has told you, O man, what is good; and what does the Lord require of you, but to do justice, to love kindness, and to walk humbly with your God?" (*Micah* 6:8). But what exactly does it mean "to walk humbly with your God" given God's infinite distance from the human world as it is held by negative theology?

This article aims to explore how the notion of justice is articulated within Jewish tradition. *Section* 2 analyzes one of the most central verses of the Bible in regard to pursuing justice, namely *Deuteronomy* 16,20 and its interpretation in Jewish tradition. In close connection with the pursuit of justice stands the human vision of God and the accessibility of divine knowledge. The conceptualization of God's nature and the complex relationship between divine and human justice will be elaborated on in *Section* 3 which serves as a theoretical framework for further analyses of the concept of justice throughout the article. *Section* 4 focuses on the history of the concept of justice within the text of the Hebrew Bible. Especially the Covenant and its meaning for the human-divine relationship will be illuminated. *Section* 5 offers a comparative perspective on how these ideas resonate with or diverge from those found in Christianity and Islam. *Section* 6 portrays the perception of justice within Jewish mysticism where the possibility of re-literalization of the Divine-human encounter – without in any way directly diminishing the inaccessibility of God – is found. After a brief outline in *Section* 7 of the current state of the concept in Judaism and its relevance for future development, *Section* 8 interprets the practical dimensions of the concept of justice by focusing on Maimonides' view on the judge.[1]

---

1 This version of the article contains additions and revisions by the editors.

https://doi.org/10.1515/9783110561692-002

# 2 The Basic Terminology and the Sources of the Concept of Justice in the Sacred Texts of Judaism

Perhaps the best place to start in inquiring how the concept of justice is understood in traditional Judaism is by examining the verse in the Bible that most explicitly and melodramatically admonishes us to practice this virtue – namely, the verse in *Deuteronomy* 16,20 which says, "Justice, justice shalt thou pursue." The immediately perplexing feature about this verse is the repetition at the start of the verse of the noun, "justice." On the surface, the sentence "pursue justice" has the same cognitive content as "pursue justice, justice." The appropriate English translation of *tsedeḳ, tsedeḳ tirdof* is no different from the appropriate English translation of the sentence, *tsedeḳ tirdof.* In both cases, we would translate the sentences as "pursue justice." What is the second "justice" in the verse coming to add?

An approach adopted by several rabbinic commentators is to say that the second "justice" in the verse qualifies the first listing of the term by implicitly emphasizing that a noble end of justice must be pursued through equally noble means to qualify as "justice." How one gets to where one wants to go is as crucial (or more crucial) for determining the justice-quotient present in the end one is pursuing as the end itself. There is no moral judgment that determines the moral caliber of what one is doing. There must be continual assessments and reassessments of the means one is adopting to reach one's goals to ensure that they never fall too radically out of sync with the ends one is seeking.[2]

What this reading of the verse immediately insinuates is the anti-perfectionist stance of Jewish ethics. A valuable goal by itself does not guarantee very much. It is the continual efforts invested in shoring up the imperfections that are disclosed in translating into practice the means of getting there that determine the qualitative level of the end reached. One must relentlessly pursue justice many times over in painstakingly adjusting and re-adjusting means to ends for an action to qualify as just. If the end must be re-outfitted and re-conceptualized in the light of the means that on moral grounds were adopted for getting there, then so be it. Justice does not have to be known a priori to be attained. It needs to represent a coherent, satisfactory unit of human intervention, that considers all the successive moves and countermoves that went into the crystallization of the result.

2 *Sanhedrin* 32b:6; *Midrash Tannaim* on *Deuteronomy* 16:20:1.

In this reading, there appears to be an infinite distance between the mobilization of human activity to achieve justice and the actual attainment of justice. The actual grammatical construction of the Biblical text in Deuteronomy almost suggests that justice is most acutely realized in the "pursuit." The claim upon us as human beings is to pursue justice — to engage in activities that in our judgment and experience are most likely to bring it about. We are not bidden to achieve justice — but just to go after it.

In Judaism, the pursuit of human justice is always relational to the divine. The justice discourse in the Bible very strikingly resembles the God discourse that pervades the Bible as a whole.[3] The first systematic collective human encounter with God is contained in the Tower of Babel narrative found at the beginning of the Book of Genesis:

> And the whole earth was of one language and of few words. And it came to pass as they journeyed from the east that they found a deep valley in the land of Shinar and they abode there. And they said one to another "Come let us make bricks and burn them thoroughly." And they had brick for stone and bitumen had they for mortar. And they said "Come we will build for us a city and a tower whose head may reach unto heaven and we will make for us a name lest we be scattered upon the face of the whole earth." And the Eternal came down to see the city and the tower which the children of men had built. And the Eternal said "Behold it is one people and they have all one language and this they begin to do and now shall they not be precluded from anything which they have devised to do? Come we will go down and there confound their language that they may not understand one another's speech." So, the Eternal scattered them from thence upon the face of all the earth and they ceased to build the city. Therefore, is the name of it called Babel because the Eternal did there confound the language of all the earth and from thence did the Eternal scatter them upon the face of all the earth.[4]

One possible reading of the Tower of Babel story is that the sin of the builders consisted in their desire to appropriate God – to bring Him down to earth – to make

3 In the Bible, God is portrayed as just and righteous: "For all His ways are justice; a God of faithfulness and without iniquity, just and right is He," (Deut 32,4), demanding just retribution by rewarding the righteous and punishing the wicked. A number of stories serve as examples: Adam and Eve disobeyed God and were therefore banished from the Garden; the builders of the Babel Tower were scattered because they attempted to "wage war against God". However, there are also many examples where divine just retribution could be called into question, as in the story of Jonah where the wicked prosper and the righteous suffer, cf. Weiss, Shira, *Ethical Ambiguity in the Hebrew Bible: Philosophical Analysis of Scriptural Narrative*, Cambridge: Cambridge University Press, 2018, 46 f. These and related questions create a tension between knowing God, resp. understanding his justice and pursuing his path (walking in the ways of God as a famous Jewish teaching conveys), and the fact that God is inaccessible and unreachable for humans, as traditional Judaism teaches (see Section 3).

4 Genesis 11:1–9.

Him literally and figuratively a part of themselves. From this perspective, the human beings building the Tower of Babel were quintessential Gnostics. Early in the development of Western religion, in the writings of Marcion and others, it seemed jarring that the Creator God, who fashioned what turned out to be a faulty and defective universe, should also be the author of redemption. Unlike negative theology which argues that given God's infinite distance from the human world there are no analogues between our finite vocabularies and any term we might want to project unto God and therefore the whole divine vocabulary has to be construed as being unwaveringly metaphoric, Gnosticism ends up literalizing the concept of God. Gnosticism seeks to resolve the tension between religion's creative and redemptive moments by assigning each vocation to different gods, thereby irrevocably breaching the absolute distance negative theology posits between God and man. Gnosticism thus originates as a remodeling of God to make Him answerable to a human intellectual need of reconciling God's power with His goodness.

This gnostic reading of the motivations of the tower-builders is reinforced by the Bible's emphasizing that both in order to thwart their plans and as a punishment for even formulating and pursuing them God fragments their universal language into a multiplicity of languages as if to drive home the point that human beings are doomed to endless paraphrasing – to a spinning of metaphors without end – without arriving at the reality that their paraphrases and metaphors are ostensibly about. Theologically speaking, the builders of the Tower of Babel express a deep revulsion against the ever-expanding middle of human life, and God, as it were, reaffirms that middle. A pursuit of justice that is forever preoccupied with means seems to be human destiny.

There are affinities between this construal of the Tower of Babel story and Maimonides' (1138–1204) reading of the transgression of Adam and Eve in the Garden of Eden. Such a juxtaposition is reflected by Rashi (1040–1105) in his commentary on the text suggesting that the Bible itself is intimating to us its illuminative force. In the verses cited above, the Bible refers to the builders of the tower as the "children of men". Following a hermeneutical principle of radical parsimony (that the Bible opts for the tersest formulation compatible with the meaning it seeks to convey), Rashi raises the question "But whose children could they have been (except the children of man, i.e. human beings) – perhaps the children of donkeys or camels? But it means the children of 'Adam Harishon (the First Man – the word "Adam" in the text which means literally man, i.e., generic man, is now understood to refer to Adam, the first human being that God had created)."[5]

5 Pentateuch with Rashi's Commentary: Genesis, trans. M. Rosenbaum/A. M. Silbermann, Jerusalem, 1972, 45.

According to Maimonides, the pre-expulsion state enjoyed by Adam and Eve in the Garden of Eden was defined by their ability to distinguish truth from falsehood:

> Through the intellect one distinguishes between truth and falsehood, and that was found in [Adam] in its perfection and integrity. Fine and bad, on the other hand, belong to the things generally accepted as known, not to those cognized by the intellect [...]. However, when he disobeyed and inclined toward his desires of the imagination and the pleasures of his corporeal senses – inasmuch as it is said: that the tree was good for food and that it was a delight to the eyes (Genesis 3:6) – he was punished by being deprived of that intellectual apprehension. He therefore disobeyed the commandment that was imposed upon him on account of his intellect and, becoming endowed with the faculty of apprehending generally accepted things, he became absorbed in judging things to be bad or fine [...]. With regard to what is of necessity, there is no good or evil at all, but only the false and the true.[6]

According to Maimonides, the story of the expulsion from Eden amounts to convention being substituted for truth. Man can no longer know anything beyond what convention sanctions and decrees. "Good" and "bad", which are conventionalist terms, are substituted for "true" and "false", which are ostensibly essentialist terms.[7] Maimonides' reading of Adam and Eve reflects a shift from intellectual apprehension of truth to moral conventions. For the discussion of justice, this would suggest that the pursuit of justice, like knowledge, is subject to the limitations of human experience.[8]

Following Rashi's lead in making sense of the Tower of Babel story in the light of the story concerning the expulsion from Eden, we are now able to appreciate the deep thematic continuity linking the two stories. The generation of the Tower of Babel were seeking to recoup Adam's loss. They were trying to recapture the idiom of truth which Adam had lost and to throw overboard the idiom of approximation which was already their fate. If the lesson to be derived from the expulsion from Eden is that we cannot aspire to a truth beyond convention, then there is never a point in our theoretical imaginings and projections or in their practical and technological translations where we can safely drop anchor upon

6 Maimonides, *Guide*, Part One, Chapter 2, 24–5. Cf. the discussion in my book, *Skepticism, Belief, and the Modern: Maimonides to Nietzsche*, Ithaca: Cornell University Press, 1997, 32–33.

7 A similar interpretation of the Garden of Eden story is found in Thomas Hobbes's *Leviathan*, chapters 20, 29, and 35. Compare Harvey, Zev, "The Israelite Kingdom of God according to Hobbes," *Iyyun*, 30 (1981), 27–38.

8 In the *Guide*, Maimonides poses the question if it was a punishment at all that Adam and Eve gained moral knowledge because of their disobedience, Cf. the discussion in Goodman, Lenn E., "Is Maimonides a Moral Relativist?" in: Curtis Hutt/Halla Kim/Berel Lerner, *Jewish Religious and Philosophical Ethics*, London: Routledge, 2017, 87–106.

a reality beyond our verbal constructions. The generation of the Tower of Babel sought to reestablish such a secure point of anchorage and are rebuffed, as it were, by God Himself who jealously and zealously safeguards His negative theological identity.

A second reading of the Tower of Babel text would explore its affinities with the Netsiv's (Naftali 'Tsevi Yehudah Berlin's, 1816 – 1893) interpretation of Amalek's military confrontation with Israel soon after their exodus from Egypt. The Bible's narrative surrounding Amalek is found in the Book of Exodus:

Then came Amalek and fought with Israel in Rephidim. And Moses said unto Joshua, "Choose us out men and go out fight with Amalek, tomorrow I will stand on the top of the hill with the staff of God in mine hand." So, Joshua did as Moses had said to him to fight with Amalek and Moses, Aaron, and Hur went up to the top of the hill. And it came to pass when Moses lifted up his hand that Israel prevailed and when he let down his hand Amalek prevailed. But Moses's hands were heavy and they took a stone and put it under him and he sat thereon and Aaron and Hur stayed up his hands the one on the one side and the other on the other side and his hands were steady until the going down of the sun. And Joshua discomfited Amalek and his people with the edge of the sword. And the Eternal said unto Moses, "Write this for a memorial in the book and rehearse it in the ears of Joshua for I will utterly blot out the remembrance of Amalek from under heaven." And Moses built an altar and called the name of its Hashem-nisi. For he said, "Because the hand is on the throne of Yah, war from the Eternal with Amalek from generation to generation."[9]

The Netsiv raises the following interrelated questions about this text: How do we make sense of the Bible's vehement, everlasting denunciation of Amalek? If the Bible is referring to the historical, political kingdom called Amalek, why did the Rabbis command the Jewish community to remember Amalek throughout all the generations when the original historical kingdom has long since been destroyed? Even if a few paltry descendants are left in the world, why should this matter? If the intention in perpetuating the Biblical hostility against Amalek is to blot out his name and memory, then an important issue of reflexivity arises. Normative Judaism postulates it as axiomatic that the Bible endures forever (that its relevance never ceases). By incorporating the "blotting out" of the remembrance of Amalek into the text of the Bible, we are virtually guaranteeing that Amalek will never be forgotten. The Bible's dictum about the "blotting out" of Amalek is reflexively unsustainable in the light of the Bible's eternity.

9 *Exodus* 17:5 – 16.

In grappling with these perplexities, the Netsiv takes the "blotting out" to refer to Amalek's national mission and collective identity. In identifying this mission and identity, the Netsiv takes his cue from Balaam's description of Amalek in the Book of Numbers. Balaam refers to Amalek as "the beginning of nations."[10] Again, "beginning" cannot refer to first in power and prestige because Amalek – assessed geopolitically – was never more than a second-rate power. In terms of historical chronology, Amalek was also not the first nation. So, the Netsiv interprets "beginning" in this context to refer to *Geist.* Amalek constitutes the premier embodiment of anti-monotheistic nationhood. What does it mean to have an anti-monotheistic set of values? It signifies to be committed to inveterate naturalism – to the abolition of mystery and the eradication of uncertainty. It is presumably this attitude that empowers Amalek in its destructive mission against Israel at a time when, in accordance with the Biblical account, Israel was the object of multiple Divine miracles.[11] Amalek's metaphysics denies that there is any phenomenon both inside and outside the self that is not thoroughly permeable and transparent to the light of reason. In a special but still fully recognizable sense, we could say that Amalek is a gnostic nation whose overwhelming need and desire to make the cosmos answerable to the requirements of reason does not lead him to multiply Gods but to deny God altogether. However, the underlying impulse in the two cases – classical Gnosticism and the Amalekite variation – is the same, to make the universe answerable to human reason.

We are now able to read the Tower of Babel events as an Amalekite gnostic denial of God rather than as a classical gnostic attempt to proliferate Him through His intimate bonding with each of the builders. We might say that the generation of the Tower of Babel were promoters of a scientistic ideology. They wanted to push God out of the picture by laying claim to a technological mastery that made the world utterly transparent to their goals and purposes. Classical Marcionite Gnosticism rejects the negative theological focus upon God as Creator because it finds the evil and suffering that abound in the world too jarring with the idea that God created the world. To make the conception of Divinity compatible with and answerable to the claims of human reason, Gnosticism posits a second God of Redemption which it juxtaposes to the first God of Creation. The builders of the Tower of Babel – and Amalek – are Gnostics in the sense that they believe that the cosmos, nature, and history are permeable to human reason and its aspirations toward mastery without the additional postulation of a God. Where Marcionite

**10** Numbers 24:20.

**11** Tsevi Yehudah Berlin, Nafhtali, *Sefer Shemot (Book of Exodus).* With the Commentary Ha'Ameḳ Davar, Jerusalem: El Hameḳorot, 1966, 17:14; 149.

Gnosticism to rationalize God adds a second God to the pantheon of divinity, the Gnosticism of the builders of the Tower of Babel and of Amalek leads them in response to a similar need to rationalize God to take God out of the picture altogether. Marcion abolishes – or at least diminishes – mystery by bifurcating the Godhead and assigning the disparate provinces of creation and redemption to two different gods. The builders of the Tower of Babel —and Amalek – get rid of mystery —or at least contain it – by not allotting space to God altogether in their vision of the cosmos. The proliferation of divinities is functionally equivalent to the obliteration of Divinity. Either way from a negative theological perspective, the imperatives of human reason have tampered with the penumbra of uncertainty that hovers over the category of God as it hovers over all of our other concepts and categories and have dualistically dislodged the world (and the phenomena within it which man seeks to control) from that penumbra and made them susceptible to human rational resolution either by rejecting God or by proliferating Him.

The paradox emerges that it is only negative theological monism (that is to say, a monism that locates skepticism and God on the same ontological plane by identifying analogous problems of reflexivity regarding the formulation of both positions) that can sustain a place for God. Only an approach that emphasizes that attempts to formulate skepticism coherently confront the same self-defeating prospects as attempts to formulate the principles of monotheism coherently – those efforts to sustain an intellectual universe without God founder in much the same way as efforts to sustain an intellectual universe with God – manage in this crucial negative sense to keep the prospect of God alive. To emerge as properly consistent, skeptical doctrine must encompass a reflexive maneuver whereby skeptical critical canons are turned against the tenets of skepticism themselves – forcing them into a movement of recoil and thereby inhibiting their adequate formulation. Analogously, the utter conceptual removal of the monotheistic God, which renders Him totally unlike anything human, requires some kind of grammatical subject concerning whom the continual divestiture of predicates can take place. Skepticism is a doctrine of radical critique that both presupposes and denies a stable subject (in a grammatical sense): tenets of skepticism. Monotheism is also a doctrine of radical critique that simultaneously presupposes and denies a stable grammatical subject, namely, God.

Michael Oakeshott[12] (1901–1990) in his two essays on "The Tower of Babel"[13] provides us with yet a third approach for locating this Biblical narrative within the

12 Cf. also Botwinick, Aryeh, *Michael Oakeshott's Skepticism*, Ukraine: Princeton University Press, 2010, esp. 140; 149; 179. The ideas of the British political philosopher Michael Oakeshott are tied to his skepticism of ideological politics and his preference for what he called a "civil asso-

thematic of the negative theology versus Gnosticism categorial dichotomy. In *The Tower of Babel I*, Oakeshott distinguishes between two forms of the moral life: The moral life as "a habit of affection and behavior; not a habit of reflective thought, but a habit of affection and conduct"[14] and the moral life as "determined, not by a habit of behavior, but by the reflective application of a moral criterion. It appears in two common varieties: as the self-conscious pursuit of moral ideals, and as the reflective observance of moral rules."[15] In both essays on *The Tower of Babel*, Oakeshott favors a morality grounded in tradition and habit rather than a morality fashioned out of rules. *The Tower of Babel* symbolizes for him how a too heightened self-consciousness is ruinous for human life. Since this theoretical understanding is elaborated upon in relation to a distinct Biblical text, I think that it is fair to say that according to Oakeshott the God of the Bible is in crucial ways denied by an excessive self-consciousness. The paradox emerges that God who vouchsafes to us ultimate coherence is only available to us if we renounce the quest for ultimate coherence. It is only in the series of never-ending emotional and intellectual displacements that constitute tradition (tradition as a tissue of

---

ciation" as opposed to an "enterprise association." For Oakeshott, the state is understood as a non-purposive association, where individuals follow agreed-upon laws without being coerced into achieving a collective purpose. In the theory of Oakeshott, religion means life itself or living in the present, unburdened by any concern for worldly success. In his two essays about the tower of Babel he criticizes the perfectionism and obsession with success that are in fact harmful to modern life. He retells the myth of Babel and fashions it as a modern Western city "full of the bustle of getting and spending". The moral conveyed by this story is a strong critique of modern societies of all-consuming projects which they agreed upon. The end of the story is death and destruction caused by pursuing an all-consuming purpose. Both essays about the story of Babel emphasize "the irreligious quality of pursuing an unattainable goal at the expense of a lived life." cf. Franco, Paul/Marsh, Leslie (eds.), *A Companion to Michael Oakeshott*, USA: Penn State University Press, 2015, 8; 134–38. Cf. also Oakeshott, Michael, *On Human Conduct*, Kiribati: Clarendon Press, 1975.

**13** Oakeshott's first essay on this topic was included in *Rationalism in Politics*, which first appeared by Methuen in 1962 and has since been republished in a new and expanded edition: Indianapolis: Liberty Press, 1991. His second essay on the subject appeared in *On History* (Indianapolis: Liberty Fund, 1999). I shall be referring to these essays as *Tower of Babel I* and *Tower of Babel II*, respectively.

**14** Oakeshott, *Tower of Babel I*, 467.

**15** Oakeshott, *The Tower of Babel I*, 472. Haym Soloveitchik partially inspired by Oakeshott's distinction between a traditionally grounded morality and a rule-based morality (which he cites at Note 21) situates modern militant Orthodoxy along the latter axis: "Performance is no longer, as in a traditional society, replication of what one has seen, but implementation of what one knows. Seeking to mirror the norm, religious observance is subordinated to it. In a text culture, behavior becomes, inevitably, a function of the ideas it consciously seeks to realize." Soloveitchik, Haym, "Rupture and Reconstruction: The Transformation of Contemporary Orthodoxy," *Tradition* 28,4 (1994), 72.

endlessly receding displacements) that human life finds its highest level of repose and stability.

Oakeshott is devastated in his analysis of the moral flaw of the builders of the Tower of Babel. He says, "But whether the identity [of the builders] was that of Heaven-Seekers, or merely of Tower-Builders, remained obscure."[16] These captures in one sentence the problem of seeking Heaven. One can never conclusively verify or validate even for oneself that that is what one is after. To act in good faith given the limitations of human reason and the untrustworthiness of our emotional responses requires us to invert our understanding of the relationship between "purposes" and "activities" —between human reason and human will:

It is a favorite theory of mine that what people call "ideals" and "purposes" are never themselves the source of human activity; they are shorthand expressions for the real spring of conduct, which is a disposition to do certain things and a knowledge of how to do them. Human beings do not start from rest and spring into activity only when attracted by a purpose to be achieved. To be alive is to be perpetually active. The purposes we attribute to particular kinds of activity are only abridgements of our knowledge of how to engage in this or that activity.[17]

The optimal self for Oakeshott is one characterized by a reduced self-consciousness that allows for the play of different impulses and an ongoing process of self-discovery. For Oakeshott, ideals and principles are inductive extrapolations out of propensities and abilities that only after the fact are codified as a set of moral dicta that sanctify the actions that fall under them.[18]

Keeping the level of self-consciousness low is what enables the Oakeshottian inversion between "purposes" or "ideals" and "activities" to take place. Purposes and ideals take a back seat to abilities because the center of gravity for the self is in what it does – and not in how it makes sense of what it does. Making sense of the self is always derivative and after the fact. For Oakeshott, as for classical Jewish sensibility, the "doing" precedes the "knowing."[19]

---

**16** Oakeshott, *The Tower of Babel II*, 197.

**17** Fuller, Timothy (ed.), *The Voice of Liberal Learning: Michael Oakeshott on Education*, New Haven: Yale University Press, 1989, 95.

**18** For Oakshott, religion is what we do and is not restricted to what humans believe or think, cf. Botwinick, *Michael Oakshott's*, 140.

**19** *Exodus* 24:7.

# 3 The Theological and Philosophical Principles that Serve as the Background of the Concept in Judaism

My central contention is that God's programmatic statement in the Tower of Babel narrative in the *Book of Genesis* foreclosing direct access to Himself and indicating that pluralistic routes grounded in the disparate languages and disparate linguistic cultures of humankind are the only way to approach Him becomes paradigmatic for both the elusiveness of a substantive conception of God and a firmly delimited enumeration of the contents of justice within Jewish tradition. Because of his tremendous influence on later philosophical formulations and codifications of the law in Judaism after his own *Guide of the Perplexed* and *Mishneh Torah*, Maimonides becomes a pivotal figure for comprehending the later fate of both God and justice in Judaism. Regarding Maimonides' *Guide*, the historical and philosophical scholarship of modernity has concentrated very heavily on his Greek and Islamic predecessors. However, it is very important to note that within central Rabbinic sources themselves there is a very strong predisposition toward skeptical readings of both God and justice. I would like to trace in brief outline some key sources from the Rabbinic canon that prefigure and legitimate Maimonides' negative theological conceptualization of God and his radically individualistic conception of the role of the judge in the administration of justice.[20]

One of the chief architects of the Oral Law of Judaism is Rabbi Akiva (Aḳiva ben Yosef) who was a Tanna of the third Tannaitic generation, living from the latter part of the 1st century to the first third of the 2nd century. Rav Yochanan says in the Babylonian Talmudic tractate of *Sanhedrin* 86a that "The author of an anonymous Mishnah is Rebbie Meir; of an anonymous Tosefta is Rebbie Nehemiah; of an anonymous dictum in the Sifra, Rebbie Yehudah; in the Sifre, Rebbie Shimon; and all are taught in accordance with the views of Rabbi Akiva." Rabbi Akiva is referred to in the Talmud as Rosh laHakhamim (Chief of the Sages).[21]

Rabbi Akiva advances *halakhic* positions and arguments in virtually all areas of Jewish law and engages in homiletical exegeses across the whole stream of the Biblical canon from Genesis to Chronicles. Scholars have been disputing for centuries what if any are the overarching principles governing his legal dicta and Bib-

20 This latter subject will be treated in section 7.

21 Parts of this section previously appeared in Botwinick, Aryeh, "Machiavelli's Theorizing of Power Juxtaposed to the Negative Theological Conceptualization of God: Implications for Mideast Peace," *Journal of Ecumenical Studies* 57.1 (2022), 40–57.

lical interpretations. In the 19th century one of the great modern canonizers of Jewish law, Rabbi Yeḥiel Mikhel Epstein (1829–1908), advanced in his masterwork, the *'Arukh HaShulḥan* (1884–1893), a conception of his own. Rabbi Epstein attributes to Rabbi Akiva a conception of the relationship between the possible and the impossible that reinforces and further legitimates the theological understandings we have been considering.[22] Rabbi Epstein claims that Rabbi Akiva subscribes as a general principle to the view that one cannot infer or deduce the possible from the impossible and that this shapes his understanding of the subject-matters dealt with in both the legal and homiletical and philosophical portions of the Talmud. This idea of the non-inferable of the possible from the impossible represents a kind of methodological condensation and translation of the principles of negative theology to render them applicable for the fashioning and construing of *halakhic* rules and *aggadic* (homiletic, non-legal) material. Negative theology comes up against the limit that for God to serve as our ultimate "explanatory" concept, He must embody a principle of difference so radically dissimilar to things human that He cannot explain anything at all in a literal sense. The theological upshot of monotheism (according to the critique offered by negative theology) is that we cannot make sense of the possible (our daily familiar selves and world) by invoking the impossible (God). Rabbi Akiva applies this principle of not drawing inferences to the possible from the impossible as a general meta-*halakhic* norm and decision-making rule – as well as a hermeneutical principle for interpreting non-legal formulations in the Talmud. Rabbi Epstein adduces two examples in support of this reading of Rabbi Akiva – and I would like to add several more:

A *braita*[23] cited in the Talmudic tractate of *Sukah* 11b says the following: "'For I made the children of Israel to dwell in booths'[24]: These [the booths] were clouds of glory, so Rabbi Eliezer. Rabbi Akiva says, "They made for themselves real booths."[25] Apparently, according to Rabbi Akiva, the physical artifact called "booth" can in no way be compared to the "divine artifact" called "clouds of glory." Since there is no way to close or to traverse the space between the possible and the impossible, the Biblical model for the *halakhic* requirement that Jews should build and reside in a

22 Epstein, Yeḥiel Mikhel, *'Aruch Ha-Shulḥan*, New York: Jonathan Publishing Company, 1961; Orakh Ḥayim, vol. 3, Siman 625, Paragraph 2, 63.

23 A *braita* is a Tannaitic statement that was not codified by Rabbi Judah the Prince (the editor of the Mishnah) in the Mishnah.

24 *Leviticus* 23,43.

25 The Babylonian Talmud: *Sukkah*, trans. Israel W. Slotki, London: Soncino Press, 1984. In the Tannaitic Midrash *Torat Kohanim*, the version of the dispute cited there lists the protagonists as Rabbi Eliezer and Rabbi Shimon – with Rabbi Eliezer holding that "booths" refers to real booths and Rabbi Shimon believing the term connotes clouds of glory.

booth during the festival of *Sukot* has to be the physical booths that the Jewish community constructed for themselves during their sojourn in the desert, rather than the "impossible" "clouds of glory" which we cannot comprehend, and therefore cannot duplicate. Rabbi Eliezer, by contrast, permits inferences across the chasm that separates the possible from the impossible. He could conceivably be adhering to a realist position in comparison with Rabbi Akiva's implicit nominalism – so that a general term and concept like God need not be answerable to the rationalistic constraints on patterns of derivation from discrete particulars to universals that might inhibit Rabbi Akiva from extrapolating from "clouds of glory" (which cannot be deconstructed into discrete, humanly accessible particulars) to literal, physical booths. From Rabbi Eliezer's perspective, as rationally incomprehensible as the term God is, it can still be realistically (in the sense of philosophical realism) postulated, and we can draw whatever inferences we deem appropriate.

The Mishnah in *Menaḥot* 82a states that "Everything [e.g., animal sacrifices] that is obligatory may be offered only from what is unconsecrated." The *halakhah* stated in the Mishnah comes to preclude fulfilling one's ritual obligations to slaughter and eat certain prescribed animals by utilizing animals that had been previously consecrated as "Second Tithe Animals" which one has to consume in Jerusalem, and the consecrator might be tempted to think that he could use this animal both to meet his Second Tithe obligation and for whatever additional ritualistic requirement he wanted to use the animal for. The Mishnah states that the Biblical source for the notion that obligatory sacrifices can only come from what is unconsecrated is the paschal lamb sacrificed on the day preceding Passover. The Talmud immediately goes on to ask:

> And whence do we know it [this principle] for the Passover-offering itself? – It was taught [in a *braita* in *Yevamot* 46a]: Rabbi Eliezer said: A Passover-offering was ordained to be brought in Egypt and a Passover-offering was ordained for later generations; as the Passover-offering that was ordained in Egypt could be brought only from what was unconsecrated [For at that time the law of the Second Tithe had not been promulgated, and even later, when this law was given, it was not to come into force until the Israelites entered the Holy Land], so the Passover-offering that was ordained for later generations may be brought only from what is unconsecrated. Said to him Rabbi Akiva: Is it right to infer the possible from the impossible? [The Passover-offering in Egypt could not possibly have been brought from Second Tithe items whereas that of future generations could.][26]

As in the case of the Biblical model for *Sukot* (booths), Rabbi Akiva again invokes the principle that it is illegitimate to infer the possible from the impossible. The Passover-offering tendered at the time of the Exodus from Egypt could not possibly

26 The Babylonian Talmud: *Menahoth*, trans. Cashdan, Eli, London: Soncino Press, 1989.

have come from a consecrated Second Tithe animal. Therefore, we are not entitled to draw any inferences from that unique event to later phases of Jewish history when the law of the Second Tithe had already been promulgated and the Jews had already come to inhabit the land of Israel which made this law obligatory. It is important to note that Rabbi Akiva interprets the principle that one cannot infer the possible from the impossible in exactly the same way when the subjects of comparison are God and man (as in the case of *Sukah*) and when the subjects of comparison are two different phases of Jewish history (as in the case of the ruling that everything that is obligatory may be offered only from what is unconsecrated). Apparently, Rabbi Akiva seeks to stay within the parameters of the rational and the humanly sustainable whether he is dealing with God-data or human-data. The God-data, also, must be assimilated and rendered coherent within a human context.

The Talmud in *Pesaḥim* 22b informs us that,

> Simeon Imsoni – others state, Nehemiah Imsoni – interpreted every *et* in the Torah [as an extending particle]; [but] as soon as he came to, Thou shalt fear [et] the Lord thy God[27], he desisted [holding it impossible that this fear should extend to another]. Said his disciples to him, 'Master, what is to happen with all the *etin* [plural of *et*] which you have interpreted?' 'Just as I received reward for interpreting them,' he replied, 'so will I receive reward for refraining from interpreting them.' [Since the *et* in one verse does not signify extension, it cannot do so elsewhere.] Until Rabbi Akiva came and taught: 'Thou shalt fear [*et*] the Lord thy God' is to include scholars. [Hence the verse exhorts obedience to religious authority.][28]

Apparently, again according to Rabbi Akiva, since fearing God is an impossible demand to sustain because we cannot grasp what the epithet "fear" means in relation to God, we renounce the effort to deduce the possible from the impossible and we extend the reference of this verse to include the fear (i. e., reverence and compliance) owed Rabbinic leaders. Rabbi Akiva does not displace God as the reference of this verse (the verse is still referring to God even according to Rabbi Akiva). He merely extends the scope of the verse to include human sources of religious authority while leaving untouched and un-translated (except in the mediated sense of holding in awe the promulgations of rabbinic expositors of the Divine word) the literal requirement to fear God.

In *Baba Mezia* 62a, we find the following *braita:*

---

27 *Deuteronomy* 6:13.

28 The Babylonian Talmud: *Pesahim*, trans. Freedman, H., London: Soncino Press, 1967. I have introduced two emendations into the Soncino Press translation.

> If two are travelling on a journey [far from civilization], and one has a pitcher of water, if both drink, they will [both] die, but if one only drink, he can reach civilization. – The Son of Patura taught: It is better that both should drink and die, rather than that one should behold his companion's death. Until Rabbi Akiva came and taught: 'that thy brother may live with thee': thy life takes precedence over his life. ['With thee' implies that thy life takes first place, but that he, too, has a right to life after thine is assured.][29]

The assured death of two parties when one party (the party that is the official owner of the life-sustaining resource) could have survived represents for Rabbi Akiva the condition of the impossible. Death is in this sense like God that it constitutes a limit to the human condition which suspends the applicability of the traditional human logical and rational "operators" such as reasoning by way of analogy or direct inference. (My traveling companion is exactly like me. If I have a right to life, so does he). In such a context, Rabbi Akiva advocates a rational and moral "regrouping" from the perspective of the possible – from the perspective of life. On a sheerly pragmatic basis, since the pitcher of water is owned by only one person, he becomes the person who is entitled to stay alive in a climate defined by limits and impossibilities of all sorts: Limits of resources (an amount of water that can only keep one person alive); limits to knowledge of self and other (we cannot indubitably attest who of the two traveling companions is the more morally virtuous person); limits to knowledge of the Divine will or perspective (we have no way of knowing how God evaluates these people – and what fates he has decreed for them).

Rabbi Akiva's refusal to draw any inferences across the boundary that separates the possible from the impossible can be interpreted as reflecting certain logical scruples. To draw such inferences would be to deny skepticism and the idea that there are limits to rationality. However, to reject the category of the impossible would also not be an acceptable alternative because that would involve illegitimately transforming limits to knowledge into a spurious knowledge claim: The impossible does not exist. Rabbi Akiva opts for a position that can be construed as being a counterpart to a generalized agnosticism, or a mysticism that is responsive to a generalized agnosticism. What we cannot talk about, we cannot claim to know, without impugning its reality. Rabbi Akiva does not take a decisive position against the idea of the impossible – and refrains as assiduously from rejecting it as he does from affirming it by debarring the conceptual and logical apparatus of the possible from regularly interacting with it. The "impossible" remains intact as a "possibility" that is neither literally affirmed nor denied – and the regular operations of mind are restricted to the domain of the possible.

---

29 The Babylonian Talmud, *Baba Mezia*, trans. Freedman, H., London: Soncino Press, 1986.

Maimonides' position on the question of the relationship between the possible and the impossible is extremely arresting. In the very same chapter in *The Guide of the Perplexed* where Maimonides vigorously asserts the finality of the category of "the impossible," he retraces his steps and suggests a countervailing position: "the point with regard to which there is a disagreement concerns the things that could be supposed to belong to either of the two classes – whether they belong to the class of the possible or to the class of the impossible."[30] The reason why the subsumption of a particular notion or phenomenon under the rubrics of either "the possible" or "the impossible" remains contestable is that there is no prima facie, mechanical test for distinguishing between the operation and products of reason and the imagination. Maimonides formulates his attack on the distinction between reason and the imagination as a series of cumulatively structured rhetorical questions:

> Would that I knew whether this gate is open and licit, so that everyone can claim and assert with regard to any notion whatever that he conceives: This is possible; whereas someone else says: No, this is impossible because of the nature of the matter. Or is there something that shuts and blocks this gate so that a man can assert decisively that such and such a thing is impossible because of its nature? Should this be verified and examined with the help of the imaginative faculty or with the intellect? And by what can one differentiate between that which is imagined and that which is cognized by the intellect? For an individual sometimes disagrees with someone else or with himself with regard to a thing that in his opinion is possible, so that he asserts that by its nature it is possible; whereas the objector says: This assertion that it is possible is the work of the imagination and not due to consideration by the intellect. Is there accordingly something that permits differentiation between the imaginative faculty and the intellect? And is that thing something altogether outside both the intellect and the imagination, or is it by the intellect itself that one distinguishes between that which is cognized by the intellect and that which is imagined?[31]

In this passage, Maimonides not only points to the circularity attached to the task of achieving an unequivocal description of a series of data as either "rational" or "imaginative," he also suggests that the circularity extends even toward attaining a non-controversial designation of the faculties from which the data spring as being either "reason" or the "imagination." If it is "by the intellect itself that one distinguishes" between reason and the imagination – and if one supports one's claims by adducing evidence consisting in the products produced by the respective faculties of the intellect and the imagination – then one's mode of reasoning becomes

---

**30** Maimonides, Moses, *The Guide of the Perplexed*, trans. Shlomo Pines, vol. 3, Chicago: University of Chicago Press, 1963, III:15:461.
**31** Maimonides, *Guide*, III:15:460–461.

eminently circular. The presence of a rational faculty is attested to by rational arguments, and the existence of the imagination is corroborated by imaginative formulations – but since the invocation of the one (product or faculty) is cited in an endlessly circular manner to confirm the validity and autonomy of the other (product or faculty), the identity of both remains everlastingly indeterminate. Maimonides tantalizingly insinuates that perhaps there is something that falls outside of the confines of both reason and the imagination that is responsible for the way we classify our verbal and textual artifacts as being either "rational" or "imaginative": "Is there accordingly something that permits differentiation between the imaginative faculty and the intellect? And is that thing something altogether outside both the intellect and the imagination?" Perhaps where there is enough convergence surrounding a particular conception, we pragmatically label it "rational," and where a sufficient degree of divergence still prevails, we call it "imaginative."[32]

In conclusion, both Rabbi Akiva's skepticism and Maimonides' philosophical reflections demonstrate a shared concern in Jewish tradition: the limitations of human understanding in matters of divine justice and theology. This tension between the possible and the impossible remains a characteristic theme of Jewish legal and philosophical thought.

# 4 The Historical Development of the Concept

## 4.1 Abraham's Struggle: Justice and Divine Command

The centrality of the thematic of justice in the collective identity of Judaism is captured in the colloquy between God and the patriarch Abraham concerning the destruction of the cities of Sodom and Gomorrah. Sodom is the first target of God's wrath after the Flood, and God notifies Abraham of his intention to destroy the city.[33] Abraham immediately summons God to account concerning the fate of the people of Sodom. He becomes their advocate in arguing that perhaps there is enough of a "saving remnant" to justify preserving the city. He goes down to as low a figure as "ten righteous people" and then withdraws. Staking out the claims of human justice, he says: "It is unworthy of thee to do after this manner to put to death the righteous with the wicked, so that like as the righteous so the wicked; it is unworthy of thee: Shall the Judge of the earth not do judgment?"[34]

32 Hampshire, Stuart, "A New Way of Seeing," *New York Review of Books* 13 (1995), 48.
33 Genesis 18, 17–21.
34 Genesis 18:25.

Three chapters later in the Book of Genesis, we have the account of the *aḳedah* – Abraham's binding of Isaac or Ishmael (depending upon whether one follows Jewish or Muslim tradition) on the altar ready for sacrifice to God, and his withdrawal only in the last minute. There is an intense tension (if not overt contradiction) between the two episodes. How is it possible that Abraham who so eloquently confronts God over a group of strangers – the inhabitants of Sodom – is not able to muster the determination and language to plead before God to spare his beloved, long-awaited son (either Isaac or Ishmael) and withdraw the command to sacrifice him?

Reading the *aḳedah* in an interreligious perspective, Shaikh ʿAbd al-Qādir al-Jīlānī (1078–1166/471–561)[35] provided interesting annotations on the *aḳedah*. Building on his thought we might conceive of Abraham's struggle in the *aḳedah* as representing a milestone in his working through the relationship between human others and the unconditional, absolute Other – namely, God. Does the love of God preempt and even circumvent human love – or are human relationships the venue in which love of God is most fully expressed and realized? Al-Jīlānī construes the immediate import of the *aḳedah* as requiring one to set aside all forms of competitive love, such as for one's family, for the sake of focusing exclusively on the love of God.[36] Yet, one could say that the *aḳedah* highlights how monotheistic teaching generally confronts the believer with a stark contrast between two routes to follow in actualizing its content. On the one hand, given the augustness and incomparability of God, it can be viewed as requiring its adherents to decathect from all human attachments for the sake of a total immersion in contemplation of and communion with God. On the other hand, given God's unbridgeable transcendence, a relationship with God can by default only proceed through the organization of the human spheres.[37] To state more succinctly Abraham's dilemma

---

**35** Was a Sufi, and founder of the Qadirīya-order. His biographers considered him the greatest saint of Islam, cf. Braune, W., "ʿAbd al-Ḳādir al-Djīlānī," in EI², published online: /referenceworks.-brill.com/display/entries/EIEO/SIM-0095.xml?rskey=1p3LB4&result=10 (accessed on 18.10.2024).

**36** al-Jīlānī, Shaikh ʿAbd al-Qādir, *The Sublime Revelation: A Collection of Sixty-Two Discourses*, trans. Muhtar Holland, Houston: Al-Baz Publishing, 1992, Forty-Sixth Discourse, 294. Compare al-Jīlānī, Shaikh ʿAbd Al-Qādir, *The Removal of Cares: A Collection of Forty-Five Discourses*, trans. Muhtar Holland, Ft. Lauderdale: Al-Baz Publishing, 1997, Forty-First Discourse, 242, n. 303.

**37** The history of Jewish thought shows, that the *aḳedah* has produced multiple answers – including critical and cynical ones, cf. Koller, Aaron J., *Unbinding Isaac*, Lincoln, Nebraska: University of Nebraska Press, 2020, 4 ff. A common view was to consider it as a foundation for faith. For example, Nissim of Gerona (Nissim ben Reuven, 1290–1376) states that several theological principles can be detected from Abraham's willingness to sacrifice his son. First and foremost the love for God is shown by this story, cf. *Derashot HaRan* 6:25. In the work of Abraham Yitsḥak HaCohen Kook (1865–1935) the tension between the love of the father for his son and the love for God is ad-in the *akedah:* What is the role of human others in relation to the primal Other connoted by God? Does God nudge all others aside from Himself out of place or is it mainly in relation to other people that traces of the Supreme Other (in some never fully redeemed metaphoric sense) can be experienced? With regard to the understanding of justice, the *akedah* records Abraham's wrestling with the limits of the monotheistic prophetic vision, and registers in the second half of the narrative (commencing with the angel's intervening to halt the sacrifice of his son, Genesis 22, 10–19) Abraham's resistance to the allurements of divine embeddedness in favor of a broader domain of freedom and responsibility carved out for human beings, itself grounded in negative theology.

## 4.2 Justice and Covenant

There are rabbinic commentators on the Bible who emphasize that even the laws that seem most straightforwardly rational and compelling must be understood as emanating from Divine command and are not merely a function of their intrinsic intelligibility and coherence. For example, the laws of damages and torts elaborated upon in the Book of Exodus which are eminently grounded in reason as a recognition of the need to maintain peace and order in the human community need to be acknowledged by the Jew as harboring an irrational foundation.[38]

This constitutes one reading of the verse in the middle of Exodus (21:1) which states, "And these are the laws which thou shalt put before them." The "And" at the beginning of the sentence is a translation of the Hebrew letter "Vav," which is a conjunction translatable as "And." Rashi in his commentary on this verse quotes the Tannaitic Midrash *Mekhilta* which says that everywhere in the Bible where you find the word "these," it introduces a discontinuity to that which precedes it. Where you find the phrase "And these," its purpose is to reinforce a continuity with the text that precedes it. The earlier text in question is the *Ten Commandments.* The *Mekhilta* goes on to add that just as the Ten Commandments are from Sinai, so, too, are these universal civil laws with which Chapter 21 of the

dressed, but there is not seen a conflict between the two: "For the mercy and love of the father in a pure soul is precisely the flame of a holy fire which proceeds directly from the pure love of God and His mercy upon all of His creatures, the appearance of which in the world magnifies the majesty and beauty of the systematic supernal holiness that raises life and all of existence to their great heights." Cf. *Olat Reiyah, Akedah* 40, all sources published online: Sefaria.org, https://www.sefaria.org/topics/binding-of-isaac?tab=notable-sources (accessed on 18.10.2024).

38 Schorr, Gedalia Halevi, *Ohr Gedalyahu,* vol. 2, Brooklyn, NY: 1984, 101–2.

Book of Exodus deals from Sinai.[39] One way of interpreting Rashi and the *Mekhilta* is that Sinai is not just a place name for the geographic location where Moses received the Ten Commandments to communicate to the Jewish community but has distinct metaphysical connotations as well. The first of the commandments, after all, begins with the phrase, "I am the Lord your God." It announces the existence of God as the source of both life and law. The monotheistic God as infinite is beyond the scope of reason to both comprehend and justify. According to this reading, the laws of tort which are among the most intuitively self-evident of the laws that we can come up with also have to be viewed as lodged in a source that is beyond our comprehension, namely, God. Having recourse to a different dimension of explanation – the infinite, rather than the finite – enables us to achieve repose in our search for the primary factors that account for the ways that we organize and structure our world. Presumably, the reason for this is that if we did not invoke the monotheistic God, the search for explanation and justification of any particular law would issue forth in an infinite regress, every invocation of texts and reasons to support any particular law would only stimulate our appetite to come up with more far-reaching and inclusive texts and reasons that would ground the texts and reasons we have already come up with, and so on ad infinitum. One way of achieving release from this turmoil of unending explanation and justification is to postulate the monotheistic God who is infinite as the ultimate source of all the laws that are binding upon us, even the most commonsensical.

What emerges from this account is that reason itself cannot be rationally grounded. Once one subscribes to the protocols of reason, then the moves that one makes in argument, speech, and action are or have to be ordained and sanctioned by the protocols of reason. However, it is not irrational to opt out of the framework of reason and to choose some other set of orientating principles, such as astrology, as a guide for one's life. It is only if one is already operating within the system of interconnections known as "reason" that it becomes irrational for one to abruptly switch out of there and treat his next move which should be locally governed by the protocols of reason as a global platform from which to alter his mode of relating to the world. Unless one self-consciously decides to quit and to move on to one of these alternative frameworks, the normal expectation is that one is proceeding with the rational approach that he previously followed. To negate this supposition, the rational civil law of Judaism therefore presupposes a divine sanction to be validated. Unlike the Christian and secular natural law tradi-

39 Rashi on *Exodus* 21:4, published online: sefaria.org, https://www.sefaria.org/Exodus.21.1?lang=bi&with=Rashi&lang2=en (accessed on 21.10.2024).

tions, the invocation of God in relation to Jewish legal materials is symptomatic of the absence of rationality and does not constitute its embodiment.

The infinite receding of God which is part of what the term "God" itself signifies is also a major factor responsible for catapulting the term *brit* (which means covenant or contract) to a pivotal position in Jewish delineations of the principles of law and justice. There is a *brit* with Noah, with Abraham and with Moses and the Jewish people. With Noah and his descendants, God commits Himself to the promise that "I will establish my covenant with you; that all flesh shall not be cut off any more by the waters of the deluge; neither shall there anymore be a deluge to destroy the earth."[40] With Abraham in the *Brit Bein Habeatarim* (the covenant between God and Abraham that took place between the pieces of animals and birds that had been cut in half), "God made a covenant with Abram, saying, Unto thy seed have I given this land, from the river of Egypt unto the great river, the river Euphrates. The Kenite, and the Kennizite, and the Kadmonite. And the Hittite, and the Perizzite, and the Rephaim. And the Amorite, and the Canaanite, and the Girgashite, and the Jebusite."[41] On the last day of his life,[42] Moses has the Jews reenter the covenant between God, himself, and the Jewish people:

> Ye are placed this day all of you before the Lord your God; your heads of your tribes, your elders, and your bailiffs, with all the men of Israel. Your little ones, your wives, and thy stranger that is in thy camp, from the hewer of thy wood unto the drawer of thy water. That thou shouldest enter into covenant with the Lord thy God, and into His oath, which the Lord thy God maketh with thee this day. That He may raise thee today for a people unto Himself, and that He may be unto thee a God, as He has promised unto Thee, and as he hath sworn unto thy fathers, to Abraham, to Isaac, and to Jacob.[43]

For the infinite monotheistic God who is beyond human conceptual and therefore also direct emotional reach, covenant, mutual agreement, seems like the appropriate category for capturing the basis of relationship in a humanly intelligible way.[44] We cannot penetrate God's essence with our intellect. He is utterly beyond our ability to comprehend who He is or how He functions. It is only with the irrational side of our nature – our will – that even a metaphoric connection with Him can be established. A covenant represents a meeting, mutual accommodation, of wills – and does not require, or presuppose, a mutual disclosure of inner being.

**40** Genesis 9:11.

**41** Genesis 15, 18–21.

**42** This is Rashi's commentary on the passage that I am about to cite.

**43** Deuteronomy 29, 9–12.

**44** On this Cf. also Walzer, Michael, In God's Shadow, New Haven: Yale University Press, 2012, 7 ff.

There is a second feature of covenantal imagery that makes it uniquely appropriate for conceptualizing the God-human being relationship. In a covenant or contract, each party to the relationship seeks to emulate and inspire the other. There are reciprocal rights and duties linking the parties that ideally should serve as a goad to each of them to outdo the other in actualizing the terms of the covenant. For example, in the covenant from Deuteronomy that I cited, if the Jews remain loyal to God and do not stray after strange gods, and follow His commandments, then God promises them secure tenure and occupancy of the land and continuing sustenance and nourishment provided from the land. God has a right to demand compliance with the terms of the covenant from the Jewish people because at Sinai (the scene for the entry into the original covenant) they voluntarily accepted its terms by uttering the phrase "*Na'aseh ve-Nishmah*" – we will do and we will listen (comprehend).[45] God therefore has a right to place demands of obedience upon the Jewish people, and, if they conform to His requirements, he has an obligation to ensure that they remain stably on the land. Correspondingly, the Jews have the obligation to obey the terms of the covenant since they had the right at the outset (and have an ongoing right, as I will discuss in a moment) to exit from it. From the perspective of the primacy assigned in the theology of Judaism to the category of *brit*, what makes the structure of Divine authority governing the Jewish religious community just is the mutual consent expressed by God and the Jewish people in affirming each other's role in the relationship.

Reb Ḥaim Volozhiner (1749–1821), a leading Jewish theologian of early modernity, gives us an augmented insight into the primacy of the covenant metaphor in Judaism. According to Reb Ḥim, it is our actions here below – our study of Torah (the Written and Oral Law, and our devotion to *Mitsvot* (Divine commandments) – that empower the Divine apparatus to function. Reb Ḥaim Volozhiner cites two astounding proof-texts for his thesis that human beings complete and empower God. The first comes from Psalms 121, 5: "God is your shadow at your right hand." If God is our shadow, then we control His movements. Reb Ḥaim elaborates further by saying that "God attaches Himself to tilt and adjust the worlds in accordance with the movements and the tendencies of human actions here below."[46]

A second proof-text comes from Exodus when Moses asks God what name he should use when the Jewish people ask him the name of the God who spoke to him. God responds by telling him he should say "I am that I am [or I shall be what I

---

45 Exodus 24:7.

46 Volozhiner, Reb Ḥaim, *Sefer Nefesh HaḤaim im Bi'ur Yirat Ḥaim*, Israel: Bnei-Brak, 2007, Gate I, Chapter 7, 51–52.

shall be].”[47] In Reb Ḥaim Volozhiner’s reading, this implies that I am devoid of being (i.e., I lack a specific identity) until the actions of the Jewish people fill me with content.[48]

A third proof-text comes from Reb Ḥaim Volozhiner’s commentary on *'Avot,* called *Ruaḥ Ḥaim,* where he re-inflects Rebbie’s statement in the first Mishnah of the second chapter, *Dah Mah Le-Malah Mimekha,* “Know what is above you,” so that it should read with the insertion of a strategic comma, *Dah Mah LeMaalah, Mimekha,* “Know what is above, it comes from you.” The moves that are taken in the upper worlds reflect, correspond to, moves that human beings have undertaken or initiated in the lower worlds. In the heavenly spheres, everything derives from human beings. In the light of what Reb Ḥaim Volozhiner says in his commentary on the two previous Scriptural passages I have quoted, we might say that he is underscoring here how human beings are the motive force behind the whole functioning of the Divine apparatus. It is our belief in such an apparatus that gives it its validity, and it is our actions that set it in motion to correlate with the actions that we are engaged in in the world.[49]

From Reb Ḥaim Volozhiner’s vantage point, “covenant” looms as a central category for capturing the conceptual interchangeability between human action and Divine response. What we do in the world and the chain of responses it evokes and engenders can be captured under the rubric of two alternative vocabularies: human actions and their rippling effects and Divine distribution of rewards and punishments. Regarding “covenant,” the self-restraining effects of covenantal calculations (perceiving how our daily actions can promote domestic peace or undermine it) give the idea of covenant all the realistic force that it needs to be efficacious in our daily lives without presupposing the literal presence of God as a partner to those deliberations. The duplicative language of covenant needs to be deconstructed as a set of solitary calculations that motivate human behavior. This does not mean that God is not real – or that He does not exist. It only suggests that He needs to be perceived as the *Ein-Sof* (literally, Without End) who occupies a space beyond human discourse and imagination.[50] At this point in time, He is literally only a name.

It is worth noting that the Biblical covenant between God and the Jewish community that Moses transacts on the last day of his life stretches forward across all the generations. In the Biblical idiom, this covenant is being enacted “with him

47 Exodus 3:14.

48 Ibid., 52.

49 Volozhiner, Reb Ḥaim, *Ruaḥ Ḥaim Al Masekhet 'Avot*, Israel: Bnei-Brak, 2007, 26.

50 The *Ein-Sof* is one of Reb Ḥaim Volozhiner’s most recurring names for God.

that standeth here with us this day before the Lord our God, and also with him that is not here with us this day" [Rashi: "Even with generations still to come."][51] The Bible's imagery and argument at this point prefigures the Burkean compact, which consists of a cross-generational covenant straddling all the generations of a particular society's societal and political time. This is the way that Burke phrases it:

> It [society] is a partnership in all science; a partnership in all art; a partnership in every virtue, and in all perfection. As the ends of such partnership cannot be obtained in many generations, it becomes a partnership not only between those who are living, but between those who are living, those who are dead, and those who are to be born. Each contract of each state is but a clause in the great primeval contract of eternal society, linking the lower with the higher natures, connecting the visible and invisible world, according to a fixed compact sanctioned by the inviolable oath which holds all physical and all moral natures, each in their appointed place.[52]

Situating the Biblical and the Burkean covenants in the light of our discussion of the dynamics of the term "covenant," we might say that future generations can be included in the covenant because even for the present generation the covenant or contract that they enter and/or affirm is monadic, rather than dyadic. It partakes of the nature of an individually invoked thought experiment concerning the possibility of justifying political and religious obligation, and therefore does not require the literal God as a partner, or an actual live human being as a direct participant in the argument. The agreement encapsulated in the notion of *brit* is fundamentally an abstract argument whose stages anyone can go through, past, present, or future. The argument is hypothetical (not historical) in character, and is available for use by any person in the history of any monotheistic religion or political society.

What I am suggesting is that the Burkean position about the inclusivity of future, unborn generations into the covenantal argument are already implicit in the original terms of that argument as Biblically formulated. The text in Deuteronomy itself constitutes an explicit elaboration of what is already implicit in the Biblical understanding of covenant.

A complementary notion to *brit* is found in the ceremony of *hakhel* introduced at the end of the book of Deuteronomy. Human voluntarism and initiatives must be continually re-asserted to establish or restore (as the case might be) the conditions of political and social order. At the conclusion of the festival of Tabernacles every seventh (*Shemitah*) year:

---

51 Deuteronomy 29:14.

52 Burke, Edmund, *Reflections on the Revolution in France*, Chicago: Henry Regnery Company, 1955, 139–40.

> When all Israel is come to appear before the Lord thy God in the place which he shall choose, thou [referring in subsequent generations to the king] shalt read this law before all Israel in their hearing. Assemble [in Hebrew, *hakhel*] the people together, men, and women, and little ones, and thy stranger that is within thy gates, that they may hear, and that they may learn, and fear the Lord you God, and observe to do all the words of this law. And that their children, who have not known anything, may hear, and learn to fear the Lord your God, all the days that ye live on the ground whither you pass over the Jordan to possess it.[53]

If, as I have argued, *brit* to a large extent is a matter of intellectual insight, noticing how the curbing and disciplining of one's appetites (predicated upon a parallel curbing and disciplining of their appetites by the other parties to the covenant) is the source of the security and stability of political as well as religious communities, then it behooves members of religious communities to re-engage this insight again and again to renew and potentially increase their level of fervor and commitment and enthusiasm for the laws regulating the community.

In addition, the concept of *brit* as deployed in the Bible constitutes a theory of incomplete sovereignty that requires re-enactment on a sustained basis. If, formally speaking, the notion of *brit* evokes bilateralism – an agreement between God and the Jewish or human community (as the case may be, depending on the context of the *brit*) – and if, substantively speaking, it presupposes the attainment of insight by each individual human participant in the *brit* as to how the mutual mechanisms of self-restraint enshrined in the *brit* are the source of their happiness and prosperity – then, in order for God's sovereignty to be complete, all members of the community, over the generations of the *brit*, must be given the gift of self-control. Then, for God's sovereignty to be complete, all members of the community, throughout all generations of its life cycle, must be given the opportunity to enter the covenant to validate the covenant qua covenant. The renewal connoted by the ceremony of *hakhel* was at least partially institutionalized to facilitate this occurrence. It is not only individuals who have to be renewed in their commitment – but the covenant *itself* must be renewed by the ongoing emergence of new generations of members of the religious community.

There is another very striking but barely noticed way in which the Bible contributes to our understanding of justice. This is contained in the narrative surrounding Pinchas, who was a grandson of Aaron the High Priest, in Numbers 25, 1–15. Pinchas witnessed as Zimri the son of Salu paraded his Midianite lover, Cozbi the daughter of Zur, who was a Midianite princess, before Moses and the congregation of Israel, and he immediately rose up and killed both Zimri and Cozbi. As soon as he did this, the pestilence that God had visited upon the Jewish community

---

**53** Deuteronomy 31, 11–13.

for succumbing to illicit sexual encounters with Moabite and Midianite women, who used the sex as a platform for enticing Jewish males to worship their idols and which led to the death of twenty-four thousand members of the Jewish community, ceased. At this juncture, God tells Moses that,

> Pinchas the son of Elazar. the son of Aaron the priest, hath turned my wrath away from the children of Israel, while he was zealous with my jealousy in the midst of them, and I did not consume the children of Israel in my jealousy. Wherefore, say, Behold, I give unto him my covenant of peace. And he shall have it, and his children after him, even the covenant of a priesthood forever: because he was zealous for his God and made expiation for the children of Israel.[54]

Why does Pinchas's manifestation of outrage and jealousy for God merit for him a covenant of peace and an enduring Divine commitment that he and his descendants would be priests forever? What is the relationship between his aggressive, violent acts of killing Zimri and Cozbi and the promotion and nurturance of peace? One persuasive way of reading the Biblical text is that the structure and content of public morality must be differently drawn than the structure and content of private morality. In the private sphere, where the relationship between means and ends can more easily be straightforwardly managed by human beings than in the public sphere, the foundational principle of morality should be the Golden Rule as stated in the Book of Leviticus: "Love thy fellow human being as thyself."[55] If a person feels love, kindness, or generosity toward another human being, his actions can immediately display and communicate these emotions. However, in the affairs of states where the welfare of faceless multitudes is involved, generosity can be interpreted as weakness and goodness can be perceived as being deluded and misguided.

Also, in public settings, leaders play a representational role which morally necessarily overshadows their private moral sensibility. They must do what will promote the interests and welfare of their members and constituents, and not assign priority to their private moral scruples. Since force and violence have been endemic to the collective profile of nationhood almost from the origin of states, political leaders can expect that on occasion they will have to have recourse to them in discharging the responsibilities of their office. Taking all these factors into account, we can say that Pinchas is the Biblical discoverer of the domain and constitutive principle of public morality. This principle is intrinsic in character: Minimize the use of force and violence to the greatest extent possible compatible with

54 Numbers 25, 11–13.
55 Leviticus 19:18.

your role as a political leader. Wagering that with his minimalist violent action in killing Zimri and Cozbi the collective hypnosis driving the Jewish community to adultery and idol worship would cease, he spectacularly intervenes at a strategic moment to administer collective shock therapy to the community's members. Since in accordance with the Biblical account, 24,000 Jews had already been killed prior to his intervention, his strategic assertion against Zimri and Cozbi can be acknowledged as a strategically honed move to bring the violence to an end. With the sets of factors that I have catalogued as background, we can appreciate why the Bible classifies Pinchas as a redeemer, rather than as a destroyer, of the Jewish community.

The Bible also communicates to us its teaching on justice by the way it sequences texts, and not just by their content. In the Book of Exodus, we are presented with a repellent view of justice in the sense that the administrative judicial bureaucracy for handling questions of justice is outlined first before the actual content of justice as encapsulated in the Ten Commandments is disclosed.[56] Chapter 18 of the Book of Exodus is devoted to the comparatively mundane topic of appointing local and more remote magistrates in Jewish society.

Chapters 19 and 20 set the scene for and then include the actual promulgation of the Ten Commandments. It seems to me that the passages detailing the routinization of charisma in Chapter 18 precede the account of the most charismatically charged moment in Jewish tradition the revelation at Sinai – as a way of instructing us how to assimilate and respond to the Sinaitic events. The revelation needs to be mediated and channeled through a series of authority structures that dilute its content suitably to the exigencies of daily life. There is a beginning before the beginning in Jewish life which consists in a recognition of authority as a precondition for and facilitator of humanly accessible and usable religious truth.

## 4.3 Justice and Equality in the Hebrew Scriptures

Within the text of the Hebrew Scriptures themselves, certain unusual and arresting formulations concerning justice occur. One of the most striking is the determined assertion of the principle of equality in the Book of Leviticus. The verse reads: "The land shall not be sold absolutely: for the land is mine; for you are strangers and sojourners with me."[57] The context here are the laws pertaining to *shemitah* (the Sabbatical Year) and *yovel* (the Jubilee Year). The restoration of

56 Exodus, Chapters 18–20.
57 Leviticus 25:23

equality proceeds in two stages in every fifty-year cycle. Every seventh year during the Jewish people's occupancy of the land of Israel is designated as the *shemitah* Year (the Sabbatical Year). Private ownership of property is suspended during this year. The Bible in *Leviticus* says:

> In the seventh year shall be a Sabbath of strict rest unto the land, a Sabbath for the Eternal: thou shalt neither sow thy field nor prune thy vineyard. That which groweth of its own accord of thy harvest thou shalt not reap, neither gather the grapes of thy vine; for it is a year of strict rest unto the land. And the Sabbath of the land shall be food for you; for thee, and for thy servant, and for thy maid servant, and for thy hired servant, and for thy sojourner that sojourneth with thee.[58]

The priority of open entry into the land that was exclusively yours in the previous six years is extended even to animals: "And for thy beasts, and for the animals that are in thy land, shall all the increase thereof be food."[59]

In this passage, one also detects an environmental-ecological motif. The Bible rejects a sheerly exploitative relationship between human beings and their physical environments. The inhabitants of planet earth must view themselves as custodians – trustees – of the "physical plant" wherein they all reside. Letting the earth lie fallow for one year in every seven-year cycle allows the earth to replenish itself with vital nutrients and minerals without undue human interference governed by the motive of exploitation. One ethical dimension of the laws of the sabbatical year is that it extends principles of genuine otherness from human beings to inanimate nature. Not only do people have to be regarded as discrete, autonomous ends (not means to enhance our pleasure and satisfaction) – "Love thy fellow/sister human being as thyself"[60] (Relate to others in the same manner that you want to be related to) – but you must extend the principle of unbridgeable otherness to external nature as well. Consider nature, as well as other people, as entities that fall outside the pure ambit of the self, and its needs and uses.

The laws of the seventh year constitute an important manifestation of inter-generational justice. What we bequeath our successor-inhabitants of planet earth must be as rich in nutrients and other sustaining elements as the earth that we inherited from our ancestors. By not working the earth for one whole year, we endeavor to make this outcome possible for those that follow us. This exemplification of inter-generational justice is also by way of furtherance of the ideal of equality. The next generation has the same right to benefit from the land that

**58** Leviticus 25, 4–6.
**59** Leviticus 25:7.
**60** Leviticus 19:17.

we had. Through our negligence and lack of concern, we should not diminish its bounty for them. It is interesting to note that the imperatives of inter-generational justice operate in a dual direction: not only from fathers to sons, but from sons to fathers as well. With regard to the Jubilee (fiftieth) year, the Bible states: "In the year of this jubilee, ye shall return every man unto his possession."[61] Since the Bible had already stated three verses earlier with regard to the jubilee Year, "and ye shall return every man unto his possession,"[62] what is the force (what innovation resides) in repeating this injunction here? Rashi in his commentary on this verse (following the Tanaitic Midrash *Sifra*) says that this apparent redundancy in the verse comes to teach us that in the case of a father who sold his field, and his son came forward and redeemed it, that it is also to be returned to the father in the Jubilee Year. The future owes an obligation to the past (even sons to fathers) to restore to them their original condition of land ownership as it prevailed before they sold any of their property.[63]

In the Sabbatical Year, private ownership of land is suspended (the poor, the strangers, the disadvantaged can feed off my property without my being able to protest), but I re-assume private ownership of my land once the Sabbatical Year is over. When the Jubilee Year commences (which follows a cycle of seven Sabbatical Years), then the imperative of equality is deepened to require re-circulation of property back to its original owner. It is not enough to make my property "ownerless" for one year. In the Jubilee Year, I must relinquish my private property ownership altogether. As the next 50-year Jubilee-Year-cycle starts up, I am allowed to resume private property ownership, only to have it again revoked when the following, fiftieth, Jubilee Year rolls around.

The upshot of the Sabbatical and Jubilee Years laws that I have been summarizing is to keep property relations extremely fluid and un-concentrated. No monopolies of wealth or status can be enjoyed by any one person or family. One significant indirect result that is achieved by the Bible's structuring of social and economic life in this manner is that it yields a powerful disincentive for investing one's energies in the amassing of wealth and the promoting of one's social status. The results of such investments are too ephemeral and unstable to be satisfying. The Bible is very subtly creating a context in which focusing on one's intellectual, spiritual, and religious development could compellingly become a major focus in one's life.

---

**61** Leviticus 25:13.

**62** Leviticus 25:10.

**63** M. Rosenbaum/ A.M. Silbermann (eds.), *Pentateuch with Rashi's Commentary,* 1929–1934, published online: Sefaria.org, https://www.sefaria.org/Rashi_on_Leviticus?tab=contents (accessed on 17.10.2024).

## 4.4 Justice and the Institution of Slavery

The Bible in a variety of overt and subtle ways denigrates and condemns the institution of slavery. Slavery is not regarded as a natural state. The original context in which the Bible formulates the laws of slavery relates to a Jew who has committed an act of theft and lacks the resources to make restitution to the owner: "if he have nothing, then he shall be sold for his theft" [i. e., will he be enabled to come up with the money to compensate the owner for his theft].[64] Presumably, after he pays his debt to the owner of the object that he stole, his self-respect and integrity are restored and he can resume his normal standing in the community. Slavery is not a legitimate "status category." The Biblical verse states: "For unto me the children of Israel are servants; they are my servants whom I brought forth out of the land of Egypt: I am the Lord your God."[65]

The Talmud in its gloss on this verse states: "For unto me the children of Israel are servants, they are my servants, and not servants of servants."[66] The Jew who temporarily has a Jewish slave in his household is not thereby elevated into the position of master. His predominant identity is/should be that what unites him with the slave is of much greater magnitude than what separates him from the slave. The temporary owner of the slave and his ward must both see themselves as servants of God. This should work to inscribe and reinforce upon the consciousness of both owner and slave that their status vis-à-vis each other is nothing more than temporary, a function of the concatenation of immediate circumstances that are unsavory for both slave-owner and slave – and does not reflect anything intrinsic about either party to the relationship. The infinite Biblical God confers an aura of overarching equality upon the master-slave relationship, dampening the arrogance of the one and mitigating the depression of the other.

The Talmud in its systematically working out the details of the master-slave relationship operationalizes some keyways in which the value of equality can still be nurtured and sustained within the context of the master-slave relationship:

> [The verse in Deuteronomy 15,16 states:] 'Because he is well with thee': he must be with [equal to] thee in food and drink, that thou shoulst not eat white bread and he black bread, thou drink old wine and he knew wine, thou sleep on a feather bed and he on straw. Hence it was said, Whoever buys a Hebrew slave is like buying a master for himself.[67]

---

**64** Exodus 22:2.
**65** Leviticus 25:55.
**66** The Babylonian Talmud, *Kiddushin*, 22b.
**67** The Babylonian Talmud, *Kiddushin* 22a, trans. Freedman, H., London: Soncino Press, 1977.

The Talmud goes on to add that during the six years of the standard period of servitude, the master is required to support the slave's wife and children since he is the prime person responsible for taking their chief breadwinner temporarily out of circulation. These rabbinic requirements form a seamless web with the Bible's own requirements about how a master must treat his slave: "And when thou lettest him go free from thee [after six years of service], thou shalt not let him go empty. Thou shalt furnish him liberally out of thy flock and out of thy threshing floor, and out of thy wine-press: of that wherewith the Eternal thy God hath blessed thee thou shalt give unto him."[68] The reversibility of the roles between master and slave is being dramatized for the occupants of those roles even while the original master-slave relationship is still being maintained.

## 5 Dialogical Encounters with the Other Two Monotheistic Religions

St. Paul in *Letter to the Romans* (which in many respects constitutes the foundational text of Christianity) levels a strongly worded attack against Judaism as misconceiving the nature of faith. At Romans 9, 30–33, St. Paul formulates the credo of the new monotheistic religion that he is working to found:

> What then shall we say? That Gentiles, who did not pursue righteousness have achieved it, that is, righteousness that comes from faith; but that Israel, who pursued the law of righteousness, did not attain to that law? Why not? Because they did it not by faith, but as if it could be done by works. They stumbled over the stone that causes stumbling, as it is written: Behold, I am laying a stone in Zion, that will make people stumble and a rock that will make them fall, and whoever believes in him shall not be put to shame.[69]

St. Paul in this passage (as well as in several others that one could cite) becomes the great architect and advocate of Christianity as the monotheistic religion that substitutes justification by faith for justification by works. Judaism in its preoccupation with elaborating upon and fulfilling the precepts of the law makes it look as if the individual believer can satisfactorily justify himself both in his own eyes and in the eyes of God by conforming to the requirements of the law. The innovation of

68 Deuteronomy 15, 13–14.

69 A literal translation of the last part of the sentence from the Hebrew of Isaiah 28:16 would read as follows: "He that believeth shall not make haste." The words "in him" are nowhere to be found in the Hebrew original – but are an interpolation either by St. Paul or by some redactor of his work.

Christianity consists in substituting justification by faith for justification by works.[70]

It is important to note, however, that this substitution accomplishes nothing – and leaves Christianity exposed to the same sort of critique that St. Paul levels against Judaism. Stated tersely, the theological problem attendant to justification by works is not "works." It is "justification." Because I have complied with Divine commandments – done enough "works" – I am entitled to Divine favor and acceptance. However, by substituting "faith" for "works," very little has changed in the structure and dynamics of the argument. The only factor that has altered is the entity that I rely on to secure Divine favor and affirmation. From St. Paul's newly innovated Christian perspective, that factor becomes "faith" rather than "works." But if I can come up with a humanly intelligible and coherent argument why "faith" should net for me Divine favor, I feel that I have appropriately rationally justified myself in the eyes of God – and that He now owes me the goods (rewards) promised by the religion. The argument supporting justification by faith is not hard to come by. It resides close to the surface of St. Paul's text. If I don't repose confidence in the theological efficacy of my own actions (even if those actions consist in attempts to comply with Divine edicts and pronouncements) but acknowledge in advance the numerous ways from ambiguity and self-interestedness of motives to incomplete grasp of the Divine ends to be attained through compliance with Divine law in which my actions might boomerang and fail, and therefore shift the basis of my overall allegiance and daily devotion to God from works to faith, then I am justified. I achieve a greater level of coherence in my own eyes and become a more coherently worshipping member of a Divine faith community by designing and theorizing my religious approaches from the perspective of "faith" rather than "works." In response to this one could say that based on St. Paul's premises, as long as I remain engaged in a justificatory project, shifting the basis of justification from "works" to "faith" doesn't accomplish anything. Either way I am attempting to breach the overwhelming distance that separates human beings from God by conceiving of my pattern of religious behavior (whether predicated on the primacy of the principle of "faith" or of "works") as being uniquely appropriate for serving and relating to Him.

The point that we need to become aware of is that if Christianity can be let off the hook at this juncture, so can Judaism. To validate "justification by faith" from a monotheistic perspective one would have to say that the point of "justification by faith" is not to transparently clarify for us that we are fully acceptable in God's

70 On this, cf. Botwinick, Aryeh, "The Dialectic of Monotheism: St. Paul's "Letter to the Romans"," *telos* 143 (2008), 113–32.

eyes but to help convince us that within a human frame of understanding we are organizing our religious lives in a maximally coherent way. "Justification by faith" merely assures us that we are measuring up in our own eyes – and tells us nothing about how we shape up on the Divine horizon. The gap between us and God can still be affirmed as conceptually unbridgeable.

The same kind of analysis is directly relevant for the idea of "justification by works." Our compliance with and fidelity to Divine commandments is a function of our wanting to improve the caliber of our own lives – our earthly existences – which we believe are exalted to a higher, more purified plane by our efforts to conform to (what we take to be) Divine requirements. Our structuring of our lives to meet what we take to be Divine demands is entirely compatible with our acknowledging that our actions have no impact upon and are not needed by God, and that His way of registering them remains entirely inscrutable to us, so that the terms Reward and Punishment in relation to God have no sustainable sense and no discernible reference in a human setting. "Justification by works," just like the concept of "justification by faith" can only be enunciated, defined, and defended with the human parameters of self and communal structuring in mind, and an unconditional relinquishing of any claims to Divine connection and acceptance.

St. Paul's genius consists in universalizing monotheism by making the organizing principle of monotheistic religion love – rather than law. Law particularizes and establishes boundaries and barriers. Love universalizes and erodes boundaries and barriers (between people, nations, and cultures). In this context, it is important to recognize that in his political quietism and passivity, St. Paul simply displaces law out of a·religious domain onto a secular one – endorsing the civil status quo. He doesn't get rid of law on the human scene. He merely rezones it to another locale within the traditional mapping of the human:

> Therefore, whoever resists authority opposes what God has appointed, and those who oppose it will bring judgment upon themselves. For rulers are not a cause of fear to good conduct, but to evil. Do you wish to have no fear of authority? Then do what is good and you will receive approval from it, for it is a servant of God for your good. But if you do evil, be afraid, for it does not bear the sword without purpose; it is the servant of God to inflict wrath on the evildoer. Therefore, it is necessary to be subject not only because of the wrath but also because of conscience.[71]

Judaism, in contrast to this programmatic formulation by St. Paul, by focusing upon law and making the elaboration of law and compliance with it central to its monotheistic project, could place in circulation values and standards that can

71 Romans 13, 2–5.

serve as a critique of existing political, economic, and social arrangements. For example, as we have seen, the laws of the sabbatical and the jubilee years within Judaism (Leviticus, Chapter 25) coincide after seven sabbatical years have passed. The law which then requires that the land lay fallow for three years after the six years of regular cultivation enshrines values such as respect for the environment and equalization and redistribution of property that can serve as the basis for critique of existing civil and positive law. St. Paul's passionate universalism leads to a dismantling and discrediting of this invaluable critical resource for raising the standards of justice of a political society.

Islam, by contrast, in rejecting the divinity of Jesus, emerges as much closer to Judaism with its stress on law as governing the multiple facets of people's lives. The major object of belief is the fully transcendent, infinite monotheistic God that Islam shares with Judaism. The God that the Muslims worship replicates in most key respects the God that the Jews affirm – the God of Abraham, Isaac, and Jacob. Sūra 112 of the Qur'ān could be recited with fervor by Jews: "In the Name of God, the Merciful, the Compassionate Say: 'He is God, One, God, the Everlasting Refuge, who has not begotten, and has not been begotten, and equal to Him is not any one.'" The austerely, radically one monotheistic God is beyond human comprehension and therefore also beyond the range of intelligible human statement. God constitutes the ultimately defiant human metaphor which on theological grounds can never be un-packed.

A central theme of the second sūra of the Qur'ān (called "The Cow", which because of the numerous, characteristic themes and topics that it covers is known as "the Qur'ān in miniature) is something we might call (following the literary theorist Harold Bloom[72]) the belatedness of Qur'ānic Revelation. Here is the way the Qur'ān describes its own location in the chain of monotheistic Revelation: Say you: "We believe in God, and in that which has been sent down on us and sent down on Abraham, Ishmael, Isaac and Jacob, and the Tribes, and that which was given to Moses and Jesus and the Prophets, of their Lord; we make no division between any of them, and to Him we surrender."[73]

The Qur'ān thus depicts one long continual chain of monotheistic Revelation that starts with Abraham and culminates with itself. What is the theological weight of the monotheism to which Islam lays claim to as being its latest exemplar and propounded? I believe that a central clue for addressing this question is contained in the pas-

72 Bloom, Harold, *The Anxiety of Influence*, New York: Oxford University Press, 1973; *A Map of Misreading*, New York: Oxford University Press, 1975; *Kabbalah and Criticism*, New York: Seabury Press, 1975; *Poetry and Repression*, New Haven: Yale University Press, 1976.
73 *The Koran Interpreted*, trans. Arberry, A. J., New York: Simon and Schuster, 1996, 2:130, 45. All references to the Qur'ān in this paper will be to this edition.

sage I have just cited. Belatedness is not just an explicit theme of the Qur'ān – as the text records the failure of the previous monotheistic Revelations to transform the world and the consequent belated need for Islam to fill the breach created by these failures. The historical belatedness of Islam can be read as a metaphor for the belatedness endemic to monotheistic doctrine generally. Monotheism captures the sense in which the metaphysical condition of the human community is sealed in eternal belatedness. The rational quest that triggers the postulation of the One Supreme God is the search for the ultimate reason or cause for the phenomena that we encounter in experience. On the surface, the monotheistic God seems like the ideal candidate to bring the explanatory quest to a halt because his total dissimilarity from things human disenchants any effort to pierce beyond Him in accounting for the human world. But by the same token that God is the ultimate explanatory datum, He also ends up explaining nothing at all. His ultimacy is achieved by His Total Difference (in a way that prevents us from even making sense of what the term "Difference" signifies when applied to Him) from things human – but that very factor debars Him from explaining anything in the human scene. Once God is conceived as having His Being beyond the threshold of total difference, all the verbs and adjectives that function in our explanatory vocabularies can only be applied to Him metaphorically. In a literal sense, He cannot figure in our explanations at all. In this crucial sense, therefore, the theological vocabulary of monotheistic religion is belated in that it can only be invoked after the fact of incoherence – after the project that it is supposed to verbally condense and represent has already failed in the breakdown of the dynamics of language that is supposed to reflect or enact it. Or – more precisely stated – our attempts to reduce our grappling with ultimate explanation to language (as if it were possible to conceive of them as taking place outside of language) is already the occasion for our belatedness. The supreme irony is that to be a monotheist in one's search for ultimate origins is already to be belated – to be graphically dramatizing the extent to which origins elude us.

## 6 The Perception of Justice Within Jewish Mysticism

Mysticism introduces the possibility of re-literalization of the Divine-human encounter, without in any way directly diminishing the inaccessibility of God. In fact, what motivates and licenses the re-literalization, is the infinite distance of God which allows us in our finite universe to utilize any vocabulary we deem fit (including one that is tilted toward literalism) to talk about God. This suggests that the status of justice as a humanly fashioned and adjusted ideal remains unchanged from earlier Biblical-Rabbinic discussions of the concept to later mystical ones. I can best tell this story through a brief recounting of the career of Reb Ḥaim Volozhiner (1749–1821).[74]

Reb Ḥaim is writing in response to the challenge posed by the rise of Ḥassidism. Ḥassidism emerged in the 18th Century partially in response to the despair engendered by the failed messianic movement of Sabbatai Tsevi, which in turn flourished at its inception because of the wholesale way it addressed Jewish oppression and poverty in large segments of Eastern Europe in the 17th Century. Many Jews experienced a sense of desperation after the collapse of the Sabbatean movement and Ḥassidism founded by the Baal Shem Tov sought to fill the breach. Jacob Taubes has wisely taught us about the need for establishing a unified history of monotheistic religion, rather than fashioning a sharp dividing line between Judaism, or Judaism and Islam, on the one hand, and Christianity, on the other.[75] Taubes emphasized that a common dynamic of collective monotheistic belief and group self-questioning overlap all three Western monotheistic religions. When the practice of monotheistic faith in all three religions results in protracted poverty, sustained or episodic oppression, and disappointment at the failure of the expected arrival of the messiah or redeemer, monotheistic religion assumes a radical inward turn where the primary focus of the religion falls on the interior emotional life of the believer rather than upon his actions and interactions within the world. St. Paul's salvation by faith rather than by works rather than representing an unparalleled and unduplicated moment in monotheism becomes paradigmatic for Taubes of successor-moments in the history of monotheistic religion where disappointment and despair experienced as a result of the failure of the messiah to appear or re-appear become transmuted into a re-awakening of the inner life of human beings as the appropriate arena for the conduct and organization of the religious life.[76]

The inward turn in both Ḥassidism and Reb Ḥaim Volozhiner's teachings is a response to a failed messiah – or to his enduring deferral. Reb Ḥaim Volozhiner is writing approximately one century after the failed Sabbatean movement. In a failed Messianic climate, Ḥassidism offers the solace of intense attachment to a Rabbi – a charismatic religious leader who presents his own order of usually less intellectualistic priorities among Jewish religious precepts to his followers, and becomes a conduit through which God's special blessings can be bestowed

74 Cf. Botwinick, Aryeh, "Torah Lishmah: The Linkage between Monotheism and Skepticism in the Thought of Reb Chaim Volozhiner," *Judaica Petropolitana* 12 (2019), 31–52.

75 Cf. Taubes, Jacob, *Occidental Eschatology*, Stanford: Stanford University Press, 2009; Gold, Joshua Robert, "Jacob Taubes: 'Apocalypse from Below,'" *Telos* 134, Spring 2006, 140–56.

76 Taubes, *Occidental Eschatology*, 59 ff.

upon privileged members of the Jewish community, such as those who belong to the Ḥassidic sect in question. The word Chasid means "pious" — and Chasidism emphasizes the importance of the cultivation of piety through engaging in adequate preparations, nurturing the right set of intentions, and developing the appropriate accompanying emotional states before engaging in *mitsvot* (performing divine commandments), rather than the engagement in the *mitsvot* themselves. These are some of the features of their religious life that Reb Ḥaim Volozhiner criticizes them for. Ḥassidism serves to regroup Jewish communal life around an intermediate savior, who if he does not represent total redemption himself can at least contribute toward hastening its arrival and soothe communal anxieties in the interim by the intensity of Jewish identification and mutual local communal involvements which he personifies. Reb Ḥaim Volozhiner in *Nefesh HaḤaim* offers a re-configured analogue to the consolations of Chassidism. Instead of intensification of horizontal community (with fellow Ḥassidim, and another live human being, the Rabbi, at the apex of authority) which Ḥassidism represents, Reb Ḥaim Volozhiner highlights vertical community in the creation of an internal partnership with God in the continuing creation and improvement of the world. God is in search of us because His creation and providential governance of the world is radically incomplete. In *Sha'ar Alef* (Gate 1), Chapter 16 of the *Nefesh HaḤaim*, Reb Ḥaim speaks about "God's connection through His own free will to the worlds below Him and His concealing Himself in them in order to sustain them in life. And this is the general principle that lies at the root of our service of God and of all of the Mitsvot. And this alone is our whole conception."[77]

What Reb Ḥaim has just done with this formulation is to insert the unknown and unknowable God into the fabric of the world itself. In effect Reb Ḥaim Volozhiner is showing us how the notion of *Hashgaḥa* (Divine providence) is the necessary dialectical counterpoint and corrective to the idea of God being the creator of the world. With the transcendent, infinite God being the creator of the world, there is no point of contact between us and Him. So as a theological postulate or axiom, we insert God into the world (hidden within it as its source of nourishment and revitalization – in short as the Providential supervisor and guardian of the world) to at least be able to assert the presence of God within human precincts.

The problem of course remains that the God who is in the world is the same infinite God who created the world, so that the challenge of establishing contact with Him remains the same no matter where we situate or envision Him — whether outside the world or inside it. The idea of *Hashgaḥa* — Divine providence — is

77 Volozhiner, Reb Ḥaim, *Nefesh HaḤaim*, ed. Yissochor Dov Rubin, Bnei-Brak, Israel, 1989, 55.

just a rhetorical flourish to enable us on the surface to feel close to God — but His distance remains unbridgeable no matter where we pinpoint His presence to be.

What Reb Ḥaim Volozhiner has in effect dramatized for us is the futility of proliferating metaphors of presence when all they do is highlight overwhelming distance. The only satisfactory approach to God is to build upon the resources of our starting point of inquiry. Rationally reconstructed, the human starting point that culminates in God is the search for ultimate explanation. The dyadic and relational nature of the idea of God (that He emerges in response to a series of human questions, and is not just brutely there from the start) must never be lost sight of. All the major theological concepts from providence to reward and punishment must be interpreted in this light. We discern God's greater or lesser providential oversight over us commensurate to the extent that we cleave to Him. The actions that we engage in with whatever configuration of motives, inner drives, and calculations are their own most significant rewards and punishments. Infinity is itself a metaphor. One of the things that it is a metaphor of are human striving for enlarged understanding, communion, and redemption.

The whole career of God in the world as recounted in Holy Scripture and the commentaries of the Rabbis must be traced back to the human movements and exertions that resulted in and continue to confer meaning upon the panoply of divine metaphors. Behind this – just like the God of providential overseeing has God the creator in the background – there is God. But being faithful to the mandate of faith, we can never speak of Him or claim knowledge of the mainsprings of His behavior or His providential design for the universe. He can only be mystically acknowledged and affirmed in silence. If we start to speak, we sully Him with our words and convert Him into another human artifact. This God above, behind, or beyond God can only be alluded to by the concept of the *Ein Sof.*

Reb Ḥaim Volozhiner transforms negative theology into mysticism on two levels. The rational irresolvability of negative theology means that the on the level of the daily structuring and organizing of Judaism, it is logically permissible for us to reverse course on the fundamental premise of negative theology (God's conceptual inaccessibility and unknowability) and to portray Him as being in search of us, who, through our conformity to His will and especially by devoting ourselves to the study of Torah, empower Him enact His role as God. The intimacy of contact that this conception facilitates between the individual believer and God evokes the pole of ecstasy and embeddedness that is characteristic of mysticism.

Mysticism also conjures-up unfathomable and unbreachable silence, connoting the breakdown of logic and language. It is this aspect of mysticism that confers upon Reb Ḥaim Volozhiner's argument whatever degree of coherence it has. Reb Ḥaim can only introduce the premise of God's overwhelming presence because it is backed-up by a recognition of how the God beyond God represents total difference. He is completely un-statable and un-thinkable by us. God's un-translatable and irreducible difference allows us to rhetorically configure Him as the most urgent of immediate presences to sustain the possibility of an ongoing relationship with Him that confers identity and vibrant meaning upon the religious life.

According to Reb Ḥaim Volozhiner, the great chain of being[78] moves in two directions — from above to below as well as from below to above. It is the latter chain that empowers the former chain. A kind of reversal of the great chain of being emerges from Reb Ḥaim Volozhiner's description of how the soul of man gives life to all the worlds that are above it.[79] The bottom controls the top – rather than the top controlling the bottom. The secret lore of Divinity is democracy. It is the actions of human beings that control the content and direction of Divine mandates and behavior.

Reb Ḥaim cites as a proof-text for this conception the verse in Genesis which says that, "And the eternal God formed the man of the dust of the earth and breathed into his nostrils the breath of life: and the man became a living soul."[80] The "the" in the last clause of the sentence is a translation of the Hebrew article *hey*, which means "the". In accordance with the first half of the sentence, however, the preposition should have been a *bet*, signifying "in". Once God breathed life into Adam's nostrils, then He fashioned in him a living soul. In the second clause of the verse, why does the Torah use the article *hey* rather than the preposition *bet?* Reb Ḥaim infers from this substitution that "man" in the second clause of the verse is not the object of God's actions (His infusing him with life), but is rather an independent subject who imbues all the worlds (upper as well as lower) with life. Man becomes a living soul, infusing life in the upper celestial regions.

In Reb Ḥaim Volozhiner's hands, linear hierarchy gets re-plotted and re-envisioned as a circle. On each level of the Divine and angelic hierarchy moving down toward human beings, the world or level that is above the one that we are focusing upon becomes the soul of the world or level that lies below it: "And the soul of each one [of these worlds or levels] is the world that is above it."[81] This is true until we get to the lowest level which consists of human beings which then becomes the *Nefesh HaḤaim* (the soul of life) of the highest level of all, thus enabling the downward hierarchical motion from the upper to the lower levels to function in its characteristic downward-moving way. This is the circle that empowers the

78 The classic work on the theme of the great chain of being is Lovejoy, Arthur O., *The Great Chain of Being: A Study of the History of an Idea*, Cambridge: Harvard University Press, 1936.
79 Volozhiner, *Nefesh HaChaim*, Shaar Aleph [Gate1], Chapters 4, 5, and 6.
80 Genesis 2:7.
81 Volozhiner, *Nefesh HaḤaim*, Sha'ar Alef [Gate 1], Chapter 5.

linear descending hierarchy. It is only because the lower (or lowest, post-divine and post-angelic level) feeds into the highest that the upper level can be appropriately designated as upper and have its vitalizing and fructifying powers move downward. It is only because the highest and the lowest levels (God and man) bear a circular relation vis a vis each other that the Divine apparatus and man can be viewed as manifesting a hierarchical relationship. Linearity and hierarchy are a mask — epiphenomenal – in relation to circularity. The imagery, content, and the outcome of the Divine-human encounter is determined by the actions of human beings. It is our actions here below — our study of Torah (the Written and Oral Law, and our devotion to *mitsvot* (Divine commandments) – that empower the Divine apparatus to function. The human role in the fashioning and administration of justice is clinched beyond retrieval by Jewish mysticism.

## 7 The Current State of the Concept in Judaism and Its Relevance for Future Development

In a contemporary international political setting in which terrorist and religious fundamentalists dominate the news, the normative Jewish understanding of justice that I have developed in this chapter points in the direction of weak messianism.[82] In many respects, the original weak messianist is Maimonides.[83] Maimonides theorizes the messianic age as being integral to human history, rather than being post-historical.[84] According to Maimonides, King Messiah is born, lives, and dies – and is succeeded by a post-messianic historical age. Given the premises of negative theology which Maimonides systematizes, the messianic age is a voluntaristic construction on the part of the community of believers. None of the terms that either the Bible or the community of believers ascribe to God can be literally construed because God is utterly transcendent and infinite, so that none of the key words in the Biblical or general human vocabulary concerning God can be literally applied to Him. God therefore does not speak the way human beings speak, so that

82 This is a term that Walter Benjamin coined in relation to Marxism. I am here extending its use. Cf. Benjamin, Walter/Arendt, Hannah (eds.), *Illuminations: Essays and Reflections*, New York: Schocken, 1969, 254.

83 For a discussion of Maimonides and his relationship to Hobbes who was also a weak messianist, Cf. my books, *Skepticism, Belief, and the Modern: Maimonides to Nietzsche*, 1997; *Michael Oakeshott's Skepticis*, 2011, Chapter 3.

84 Maimonides, *The Code of Maimonides (Misneh Torah): Book Fourteen: The Book of Judges*, trans. Abraham M. Hershman, New Haven, CT: Yale University Press, 1949, Treatise Five: Kings and Wars, Chapters 11 and 12, 238–42.

the whole idea of messianic redemption must be humanly organized and applied. The margin for error in designating a particular historical moment or epoch as messianic is as large as in all other political decisions.

Maimonides in his *Code* cites the case of Bar-Kokhba who led a rebellion against the Romans and who was touted as the messiah by Rabbi Akiva and was then later unmasked as a fraud by Rabbi Akiva among others because of the failure of his rebellion against the Romans. The messianic age can only be retrospectively charted and known. Prospectively, this notion is as fraught with ambiguity and uncertainty as all other human judgments and decisions. From Maimonides' perspective, the Messianic Age is doubly weak: It is potentially now rather than in the future and can only be fixed and known after one is already in it and not in advance.

The Jewish concept of justice that I have focused upon in this paper nearly always restores us back to the *tsedeḳ* before the *tsedeḳ* — the justice before the justice — the myriad factors that we must consider to pursue justice. Justice like most other human project must be classified as a pursuit — an undertaking embarked upon in a climate of uncertainty, where action is called for and knowledge remains fluid and scarce. In a sheerly realistic vein, one always must consider that the justice of the means chosen to deal with a particular issue might be the only legacy and tangible trace and result of our involvement.

## 8 An Outline of the Practical Application of the Concept

The classical image of justice in Judaism follows through on the vision of God I have been elaborating upon out of Biblical and rabbinic texts. Both normatively and descriptively, justice remains blind. Given the joint implications of monotheism and skepticism, it is not able to establish a secure hierarchy of the goals or values to be achieved by a system of justice – and it is not able to affirm in any case that its construal and constellation of facts is objectively right or appropriate. How is the judge who is the administrator and interpreter of justice to proceed? Maimonides gives us a classic portrait of the role and identity of the judge in Judaism which is all a piece with his discussion of God.

Maimonides' ideal-typological portrait of the *dayan* — the judge — in *Hilkhot Sanhedrin* — Laws Pertaining to Judicial Tribunals — in many respects represents a fitting and appropriate sequel to his discussion of God in the first four chapters of the Laws concerning the Foundations of the Torah. The *dayan*, we might say, represents for Maimonides the paradigmatic Jew who through a combination of his cultivation of knowledge of the Written and the Oral Law, analytical sophistication, and moral and philosophical sensibility becomes a principal embodiment of those characteristics that constitute a worthy complement to the description of God at the beginning of the *Code*. In his projection of the character and personality prerequisites, psychological attributes, and procedural norms affecting the behavior of judges, we catch a glimpse of Maimonides' vision of an ideally constituted human being.[85] How can we delineate the sites of transition between Maimonides' conceptualization of God and his theorizing of optimal human nature?

Perhaps the most significant and illuminating connecting link between the understanding of God and the description of man in Maimonides will be established by the recognition that all the things that God isn't from the perspective of negative theology cannot be literally withheld from Him without undermining or contradicting negative theology itself. Knowing what God literally isn't is already to know something terribly important about God which the postulates of negative theology debar us from knowing. So, saying that God is not all-powerful or all-knowing or all-merciful in the ways that human beings manifest any of these faculties or attributes or virtues does not mean that we can now securely say that God does not manifest any of these virtues in a humanly cognizable sense. Our vocabulary of divestiture is as metaphoric as our vocabulary of investiture. For the same reasons — and to the same extent — that we cannot know what God is, we cannot know what He isn't. From a Rabbinic perspective (extended by Maimonides) guided by the organizing imperative of *VeHalakhta BeDrakhav* (we need to follow in the ways of God; we need to extrapolate from the moves we make in relation to God and re-inscribe them in relation to ourselves), how do/should the austere limitations emerging from our theoretical encounter with God be translated in relation to our projects to comprehend ourselves?

The translation of negative theology into a human setting involves an appreciation of how what Maimonides calls "*Lev Ha'adam*" (human understanding) generally is bedeviled by the same limitations that haunt and undermine our attempt to know God. Just as for Maimonides knowledge of God needs to be interpreted negatively hermeneutically — it signifies not knowing that there isn't God, which is in no way equivalent to knowing that there is God in the full-blooded sense — so, too regarding to human knowledge more generally, our knowledge statements need to be construed negatively hermeneutically. Since our claims to certain knowledge founder on issues of underdetermination of words by things — the constitutive role of "*Lev Ha'adam*" (human understanding; human imposi-

85 Maimonides, *Sefer Shoftim*, Hilchot Sanhedrin, 3:10; Maimonides, *The Code of Maimonides: Book Fourteen: The Book of Judges*, 10 ff.

tion of names and categories) in the formation and development of human knowledge means that the shadow of underdetermination haunts and affects all of our knowledge statements and claims from the most factual to the most theoretical — then the most enduring and defensible of our claims are those that acknowledge that by and large most of the time we can't rule possibilities out. The more grandiose and encompassing a possibility, the less likely will it be vulnerable to effective, final refutation. Even when we are dealing with more intermediate levels of experience where rejection of possibilities occurs with greater frequency, the basis for disqualification of a category or a theory is more often grounded in pragmatic considerations than in a cognitive dismantling of the category or theory in question. What we take with us from our encounter with negative theology and need to apply to more narrowly human domains is the equal unsustainability of unqualified rejection and absolute affirmation. "Walking in the ways of God" means walking in the ways of deep, metaphysical uncertainty. The space of the category of "space" is as uncertain as the content that fills it.

It is this image that shapes Maimonides' projection of the judge from start to finish. The judge in the *Laws of Judicial Tribunals* emerges as a radically individuated self-capable of moving about (plotting his moves) with equanimity and aplomb in a realm of unrelieved uncertainty. The metaphysically unbreachable God is invoked as the Author and Final Legitimator of a Law of unfathomable ambiguity. Both the relevant facts of a case — and the appropriate legal categories to apply to them — are to a certain extent a function of human resourcefulness and inventiveness. A judge is someone who knows how to navigate imponderables, without losing his poise and his balance. In this sense, he becomes the ordinary Jew (the ordinary human being) writ large, holding up a mirror to the rest of us of how life becomes possible in the face of unconquerable metaphysical insecurities.

In his *Introduction to the Mishnah*, Maimonides posits that the texts that contain the oral law of Judaism (primarily the Mishnah and the Talmud) are addressed to the judge, rather than to the average members of the Jewish community.[86] The identity of the Talmudic text fully matches and corresponds to the personality-type within the Jewish community who is charged with interpreting and applying Jewish law. Because the texts of the oral law are fluid, intensely dialectical, and multi-layered, they constitute the ideal subject matter for the radically individuated judge re-forming (and reformulating) the texts from which he derives and synthesizes the judgments that are relevant for the cases at hand. The material

86 Maimonides, Moses, *Hakdamot LePerush HaMishnah* [Introductions to the Commentary on the Mishnah], ed. Mordechai Dov Rabinowitz, Jerusalem: Mosad HaRav Kook, 1961, 51.

in the Talmud is addressed to the judge because it is so interpretively malleable. The underdetermination of words by things in the case of the Divine vocabulary where you have a million words "chasing" the elusive and irretrievable Biblical God is matched by the underdetermination of meaning by text in the case of Talmudic argument. Moving gracefully and with aplomb in parallel universes of infinite distance and uncertainty becomes a hallmark of the judge's personality.

Who is qualified to serve as a judge in Judaism? A prime prerequisite is that he be someone who very keenly and palpably does not want the job. In the language of Maimonides:

> It was the habit of the early Sages to shun appointment to the position of judge. They exerted their utmost endeavors to avoid sitting in judgment unless they were convinced that there were no others so fit for the office as they, and that were they to persist in their refusal, the cause of justice would suffer. Even then they would not act in the capacity of judges until the people and the elders brought pressure upon them to do so.[87]

In this passage (which has innumerable precursor and cognate texts in Rabbinic literature), an ethical and an epistemological motif merge. Humility is clearly a prerequisite for being a fair and disinterested judge since it suggests the capacity to bend over backwards to empathize with people in all kinds of heterogeneous and unequal positions. Humility also has an epistemological sanction. Charitableness in judgment is a kind of behavioral corollary that follows from limited access to certain knowledge and truth. The original site for the display of charitableness is the resistance to sit in judgment on a fellow human being altogether. Situating oneself to be in a position of rendering judgment concerning someone else already represents a violation of that trust and bond that links human beings together that is a function of our common recognition of our rational limitations. The first hurdle the judge has to overcome in order to validate his role as judge is to account for how he came to occupy the position in the first place. Regarding this crucial constitutive question concerning authentic judgeship, Maimonides (and his Rabbinic precursors) and Plato are at one. They all say that the only justification for exercising a role of legal and political leadership is that if one did not undertake it, he would be condemned to be ruled and judged by his inferiors (i. e., people more arrogant than himself). Assuming a role of political and legal leadership is only defensible as the choice of the lesser evil – and never as an unqualified good worth pursuing and exercising.

87 Maimonides, *Sefer Shoftim*, Hilkhot Sanhedrin, 3:10; Maimonides, *The Code of Maimonides: Book Fourteen: The Book of Judges*, 1949, 12.

Maimonides' audacity and iconoclasm in envisioning the reestablishment of *Semicha*, ordination of rabbis (literally, "laying on of hands"), long after the line of descent of ordination stretching from Moses to later rabbis had lapsed also seems to me explicable against the background of Maimonides' discussion of *Divine Science* in the first two chapters of the Code. Why is the re-establishment of *Semicha* theologically and legally significant? In his youthful *Commentary on the Mishnah*, Maimonides spells out the large-scale theological import of the re-institution of *Semikhah*:

> And I believe that the Sanhedrin [the highest court in Israel, consisting of seventy-one judges] will return before the appearance of the Messiah and this will be one of the signs [heralding and facilitating his advent] in accordance with the verse which says, 'And I will restore your judges as at the first, and thy counselors as at the beginning; afterward thou shalt be called the city of righteousness, the faithful city.'[88] (Isaiah 1:26).[89] First, I will restore your judges as at the first and your counselors as at the beginning and [only] afterward will you be called the city of righteousness. And this without doubt will be when God will prepare the hearts of men and they will increase their good deeds and their desire for God and His Torah will grow and their righteousness will expand before the coming of the Messiah as is explicated in the verses of the Bible.[90]

Maimonides, whose vision of the Messianic age is voluntaristic in the extreme (with military, diplomatic, and political success being prime prerequisites for the identification of the true Messiah[91]), expands his voluntarism to encompass the preparatory phases leading up to the emergence of King Messiah. If the prophetic verse in Isaiah suggests that the restoration of judges will lead to the re-designation of Jerusalem as the "faithful city," then it is up to enterprising religious and political leaders to re-legitimate and re-convene the Sanhedrin as a stepping-stone toward launching a Messianic movement with any prospect of success.

Two other factors motivating Maimonides to favor the reintroduction of the *Semicha* are the opportunities it affords for levying and collecting fines (which within the confines of Jewish law only become judicially actionable and payable in a court consisting of ordained rabbis), and for the regularized procedures it makes available for legitimating and transmitting Rabbinic authority from one

---

**88** Isaiah 1:26.

**89** *Isaiah*, trans. I. W. Slotki, London: Soncino Press, 1949, 8.

**90** *Mishnah with Maimonides' Commentary*, trans. Joseph Kafiah, Jerusalem: Mossad Harav Kook, 1965, 102.

**91** Cf. the discussion in Botwinick, Aryeh, "Maimonides' Messianic Age," *Judaism* 33,4 (1984), 418–25; and in Botwinick, *Skepticism, Belief, and the Modern*, 166–70.

generation to the next. This is the way Maimonides formulates his case in *The Laws Pertaining to Judicial Tribunals*, Chapter 4, Paragraph 11:

> It seems to me that if all the wise men [scholars] in the land of Israel were to agree to appoint judges and to ordain them, the ordination would be valid, empowering the ordained to adjudicate cases involving fines and to ordain others. If what we have said is true, the question arises: Why were the Rabbis disturbed over the matter of ordination, apprehending the abolition of the laws involving fines? Because Israel is scattered and agreement on the part of all is impossible. If, however, there were one ordained by a man who had himself been ordained, no unanimity would be necessary. He would have the right to adjudicate cases involving fines because he would be an ordained judge. But this matter requires careful reflection.[92]

There are two variations in the constraints imposed upon the reestablishment of the *Semikhah* as between Maimonides' earlier *Commentary on the Mishnah* and his later *Code.* In the earlier work, Maimonides mentions students as well as scholars as being part of the consensus in Israel that selects the one person to serve as *Rosh Yeshivah* (the head of the academy) – who thereby can consider himself as *Nismakh* (ordained) – and is empowered to confer *Semikhah* on others. In the *Code*, Maimonides mentions only scholars but not (their) students as being necessary for the initial consensus to re-institute the *Semikhah.* A second difference between the two works on this matter is that in the *Code*, Maimonides introduces a certain modicum of caution. He says: "This matter requires careful reflection."

In any event, in both textual sources Maimonides seems to envision with greater or lesser equanimity the equivalence — the interchangeability — of a top-down system of authority with a bottom-up system of authority. As a matter of historical contingency (as recorded in the texts of the Torah and of the Rabbis), decision-making authority within Judaism was transmitted from God to Moses to Joshua and from thence to a whole sequence of prophetic and Rabbinic leaders. At some point in time (again as a matter of historical contingency), the chain of transmission becomes murky and un-certifiable. Maimonides innovatively intervenes at some point in the history of this disruption by saying if a top-down system worked to institute and sustain authority relations within Judaism, there is no reason why a bottom-up system should not be equally effective and legitimate to reestablish it. There are several factors that can be reconstructed as converging to support this argument. Given the premises of negative theology as outlined in the first two chapters of the *Code*, one could say that "bottom-up" is a translation of "top-down." Since to be referring to God as "speaking," "authorizing," and "legitimating" is only to be invoking a string of metaphors (we have no literal sense of what it means for the Singularly One, the Utterly Transcendent Being, to be

92 Maimonides, *The Book of Judges*, trans. Hershman, 15.

doing any of these things), we need to translate God-talk into an idiom that is comprehensible to us. What seems natural — and is in any case wholly inevitable, since even in the literalist Biblical account God is always acting through human agents — is to imagine members of the human community as acting and authorizing others to act to bring about outcomes that they take to be conforming to the will of God. God's speaking in the Biblical text must be construed negatively hermeneutically. God is asserted as speaking in the Biblical text only to block a certain claim that He doesn't speak, that His will cannot be effectuated at all — but not because He can be taken to speak in a literal, conventional human sense.

From the perspective of the negative theological principles enunciated at the beginning of the *Code*, spatial metaphors going in either direction are equally meaningless regarding God. "Top-down" is as much devoid of sense as "bottom-up." Instant reversibility becomes a natural response to irredeemable metaphor. If neither "up" nor "down" in relation to God are literally traceable or nameable, then we can configure ourselves in our authority-relations as proceeding in either direction: As moving from what our prophets and religious leaders (who are human agents) take to be the word of God to their communities of constituents — or from the will of the constituents to a scheme of ordering mechanisms (such as *Semikhah*) instituted at their behest.

There might be a tacit Biblical model lurking in the background to Maimonides' reversal of the scheme of Rabbinic authority relations in the case of *Semikhah.* In the *Book of Numbers*, the Torah speaks about the procedures to be followed in investing the Levites (out of which the priestly caste was designated) with their special order of sanctity within the community. The Torah very poignantly speaks about the Levites laying "their hands upon the heads of the bulls" (Numbers 8, 12) as part of the regular ritual of priestly sacrifice. Two sentences earlier, the Torah commands: "And thou shalt bring the Levites before the Eternal; and the children of Israel shall lay their hands upon the Levites." The idea of the exclusivity of a top-down system for ordering and legitimating relationships within the Jewish community is thus mocked and subverted in the text of the Torah itself. The Torah seems to be insinuating to us that since the spatial models invoked in relation to God cannot be literally embraced, movements of authority within Judaism can (and should) proceed from all directions at once. The priests must authorize and legitimate the sacrifices of the ordinary Israelite members of the community. But, by the same token, the broader Israelite community must invest, through a comparable laying-on of hands, the priests with their special authority and sanctity. This instantaneous reversibility and displacement of authority relations can be viewed as a Biblical precursor-text to the authority reversals envisioned by Maimonides.

The daily morning liturgy affords us another proof-text concerning the commingling of top-down and bottom-up schematizations of authority within Judaism. In the *Yotser Ohr* ("Who Forms Light") unit of prayer that precedes the *'Amidah* (the climax of each Jewish prayer service, where the Jew stands in lonely "confrontation" before God uttering God's praises and stating his own needs), we find the following formulation concerning the ministering angels: *Ve-Kulam Meḳablim Aleihem 'Ol Malkhut Shamayim Zeh MiZeh VeNotnim Reshut Zeh LaZeh LeHaḳdish LeYotsram BeNaḥat Ruaḥ BeŚafah Berurah UBeNeimah.* ("Then they all accept upon themselves the yoke of heavenly sovereignty from one another, and grant permission to one another to sanctify the One Who formed them, with tranquility, with clear articulation, and with sweetness."[93]) *Kabbalat 'Ol Malkhut Shamayim* — accepting the yoke of heavenly sovereignty – suggests a top-down movement of authority from God to the various categories of *Malakhim* and *Meshartim* — "angels" and "heavenly servants." This top-down transmission of authority is audaciously disrupted by the verse which suggests that the movement from "above" to "below" is mediated by the angels who accept the yoke of heavenly authority *from each other.* The phrase *VeNotnim Reshut Zeh LeZeh,* ("and grant permission to one another"), in contrast to the first part of the sentence, conjures-up a bottom-up image of authority relations. The angels and heavenly servants, after reaching a consensus amongst themselves concerning the need to sanctify their Creator authorize and sanction each other's doing so. The gap between God and even the angels is so unimaginably overwhelming[94] that the appropriate image for capturing their relationship to God is through acts of consent. The angels need to agree that despite the ostensibly unbridgeable metaphysical distance separating them from God, verbal acts of sanctification of Him are still appropriate. The conflation of the genre of deference with the genre of consent from the order of the daily liturgy that I have summarized provides Maimonides with another precursor-text for assigning equal validity to a bottom-up re-institution of the *Sanhedrin* in relation to a top-down reestablishment of it.

The conditional, instrumentalized uses to which the categories of "above" and "below" are put by Maimonides are further attested by the following legal formulation: "If a man who is not qualified to discharge judicial duties, either because of lack of adequate knowledge or because of unseemly conduct, has been clothed by the exilarch with authority to act as judge, in disregard of the would-be incumbent's unfitness, or has obtained authorization from the court, the latter having

93 Scherman, N., *Complete Artscroll Siddur,* 2003, 87.

94 Maimonides states in *The Laws* concerning the foundations of the Torah 2:8 that "none of [the heavenly hosts] know God as he knows Himself."

been ignorant of his unfitness, the authority vested in him is of no avail. It is as though one would dedicate to the altar a blemished animal; in which case no sacredness attaches to it."[95] Maimonides in this passage implicitly suggests how the categories of "above" and "below" must be deployed in such a way as to create an expanded free zone for pragmatic factors to operate and have their impact registered. If it turns out that a judge who has been appointed from above by the political leader of the Jewish community in exile called the exilarch — or by a court — is deficient in his knowledge of the law, or his behavior is morally or ethically questionable, then the appointment from above is automatically revoked and canceled by the actual behavior displayed by the judge in the discharge of his vocation. The initial decrees and investitures issuing from the original "above" (namely, God) being untranslatable in literal terms from the perspective of negative theology sets the stage for metaphoric, instrumentalized readings of all later human investitures of authority from a source located in an upper perch in an official hierarchical chain of command. If the appointed judge lacks substantive or personal qualifications, his authorization "is of no avail." Given the metaphoric status of the "above" and the "below" anchored in negative theology, there is always room for pragmatic testing of results, and there is always available a conceptual smoke screen behind which members and groups within the broader community can engage in making ongoing adjustments between judicial appointments and judicial reality.

In *The Laws Pertaining to Judicial Tribunals 8:3,* Maimonides codifies the following rule: "The judge who has formed no opinion [who says he doesn't know] does not have to give a reason for his inability to arrive at a decision, whereas the judge who declares for acquittal or for condemnation is bound to state the ground on which his opinion is based."[96] Maimonides' ruling is based upon a passage in the Babylonian Talmudic Tractate *Sanhedrin* 17a, where the language is even stronger. The Talmud does not leave it as a discretionary matter for the undecided judge to present his reason for his indecision, but states emphatically that "if he gives a reason, we do not listen to him." The medieval Talmudic commentator Rashi elaborates upon this dictum by saying that the reasons that he adduces buttress the case for guilt and for innocence and attempt to explicate his indecision. Even though Maimonides states the law weaker than the Talmud itself does (Maimonides speaks of the undecided judge not having to give a reason; whereas the Talmud states that we do not listen to him), Maimonides concurs with the Talmudic formulation. In Chapter 9, Paragraph 2 of *The Laws Pertaining*

95 Maimonides, *Hilkhot Sanhedrin,* 4:15; *The Code of Maimonides,* "The Book of Judges," 16.
96 *The Code of Maimonides,* "The Book of Judges," 28.

*to Judicial Tribunals*, Maimonides states that "The one who is undecided [literally, "does not know"] is as though he were nonexistent because he cannot afterward argue for conviction."[97] In other words, we do not listen to him because he is in no better position than a judge who emphatically voted to declare the defendant innocent in a capital case whom the Talmud prohibits from changing his verdict to "guilty." So, too, a judge who declares initially that he is undecided cannot alter his vote to "guilty." What is unusual in Maimonides is that given the fact that he states the law concerning the undecided judge in two separate textual locations, he seems to have teased out from the Talmudic text at *Sanhedrin* 17a two laws – and not just one. The first has to do with the undecided judge not having "to give a reason for his inability to arrive at a decision" — and the second law declares that the undecided judge "cannot afterward argue for conviction" (i. e., we do not listen to him). How do we make sense of the first law — and what is its larger significance?

Here, again, I believe that the larger ambiance provided by Maimonides' discussion of belief in God in the first two chapters of his *Code* gives us a context in terms of which to make sense of a peculiar and apparently unmotivated text. Just as in the case of God the not-knowing attendant to negative theology cannot be translated as knowing that negative theology's collapse of literal descriptions of God into metaphors means that the literal descriptions of His attributes are untrue — not-knowing has to be sustained as a not- knowing, even if the grounds or the protocols governing the not-knowing are acceptable and cogent — so, too, the undecided judge's not-knowing needs to be understood as possibly a reflexively encompassing not-knowing, that allows to stand as indeterminate (as itself open to question) even the original declaration by the judge that he does not know which verdict to render. One of the things that the judge does not know is whether it is justifiable and appropriate for him not to know. Therefore, Maimonides declares that "The judge who has formed no opinion [who says he doesn't know which verdict to render] does not have to give a reason for his inability to arrive at a decision" because his not-knowing might be validly logically situated as interrogating itself, so that all the reasons pro and con for guilt and for innocence — as well as for indecisiveness — cancel each other out, and there is no reason to be stated. A holistic, all-encompassing not-knowing in the case of a judge considering the fate of a defendant accused of murder leaves one exactly situated in the position of the negative theological believer vis-à-vis God, unable to utter a word, on the brink of silence.

97 Ibid.

Maimonides' formulation in *The Laws Pertaining to Judicial Tribunals* about the judge who says he doesn't know also casts an indirect light on the status of the negative theological believer discussed at the beginning of the Code. Regarding the judge, Maimonides says: "He who says he doesn't know is as though he were nonexistent." Maimonides can be read as indirectly glossing the status of the negative theological believer. Not-knowing is the most reverential of all gestures. The person who doesn't know is as if he were nonexistent. He restores the world back to God the way it was before creation – where there was only God and no world and no human beings.

Maimonides codifies into law what he takes to be a Biblical imperative that the judge be what one can only call a radically individuated human being — able to cultivate, read, and communicate with his own mind:

> Any judge in a capital case, whose vote – either for acquittal or for conviction – voices not his own carefully considered opinion but that of a colleague, transgresses a negative command. Concerning him Scripture says: Neither shalt thou bear witness in a cause to turn aside (Exodus 23:2). It has been learned by tradition that this injunction means, 'Do not say when the poll [of judges] is taken, it is good enough if I follow So-and-so; but give expression to your own opinion.'[98]

By way of institutionally fostering this radical individuality, Maimonides adds: "It has been learned by tradition that in capital charges we do not begin with the opinion of the most prominent judge – lest the others not considering themselves competent to differ with him accept his opinion. It is mandatory that everyone should voice his own view."[99] The theological backdrop to the radical individuality that Maimonides delineates as a key personality prerequisite for a judge is the God mapped in the first two chapters of the Code. The utterly transcendent God who cannot be conceptually accessed by human beings except by a limitless piling-up of metaphors both models a sublime aloofness and creates an infinite space for human beings to discover, manifest, and fill-in with content their own freedom. Moreover, since this radical autonomy, aloofness, and freedom cannot be literally ascribed to God from a negative theological perspective – the disowning of attributes and their larger metaphysical and moral implications, just like a literally faithful transcription of attributes, also cannot be literally ascribed to God (the disowning are discredited alongside their literal counterparts – and for the same reasons) – then the principle of *VeHalakhta BeDrakhav* (of walking in the ways of God) bids us to turn this whole vocabulary (both the literal attributes – and their negative

98 Maimonides, *Hilkhot Sanhedrin*, 10:1; *The Code of Maimonides*, "The Book of Judges," 29.
99 Maimonides, *Hilkhot Sanhedrin*, 10:6; *The Code of Maimonides*, "The Book of Judges," 30.

theological disowning) inward in relation to ourselves. We need to be skeptical of our own skepticism – and skeptical still of our skepticism of our own skepticism. There is no turning back to a secure vantage point – and, as we move forward, we can anticipate no secure places to drop anchor. The judge as the paradigmatic Jew – the one who sits in judgment over his fellow Jews – must be more exemplary in his cultivation and exercise of freedom (of his virtually total intellectual unmooring) than the rest of the community.

There is an arresting symmetry between the conception of liberal individuality that animates Maimonides' ideal-typological portrait of the judge and his portrait of the defendant in cases of capital and corporeal punishment. Regarding the warning that a defendant must have received prior to his commission of a prohibited act to be considered legally culpable for it, Maimonides says the following:

> Whether the accused be a scholar or an ignorant man, forewarning is a prerequisite, as the purpose of warning is to make it possible to distinguish between the unwitting and the presumptuous transgressor, for there is the possibility that the accused committed the offense unwittingly. How is he warned? He is told: 'Abstain, or Refrain, from doing it, for this is a transgression carrying with it a death penalty,' or, 'the penalty of flagellation.' If he abstains, he is exonerated. So too if he remains silent, or nods his head, he is exonerated. Even if he says, 'I know it,' he is not culpable, unless he surrenders himself to death, [more literally translated: opens himself up to death] saying, 'I know full well (the nature of the offense and the penalty it involves), nevertheless I will commit it.'[More literally translated: For the sake of receiving this penalty, I want to engage in the action.] If such be the case, he is put to death.[100]

The Biblical source for this extraordinary ruling comes from *Deuteronomy* (17:6) *Al Pi Shnayim 'Edim 'Oh Shelosha 'Edim Yumat Hamet.* In literal translation: "At the mouth of two witnesses or three witnesses shall the dead person be put to death." Rashi in summarizing the normative Rabbinic reading of this verse says that it implies that the defendant is already dead before he comes to court, having condemned himself to death by his own mouth (i. e., by his own utterance accepting the death penalty as a price for committing the action that he wants to commit).[101]

The extraordinary freedom and sense of individuality that the judge cultivates also must characterize (to the extent possible) the person he is sentencing. A warning addressed to the defendant by witnesses that does not elicit from him an explicit acknowledgement that he is willing to endure the death penalty for what he is about to do destroys (according to the requirements of Jewish law) the pos-

**100** Maimonides, *Hilkhot Sanhedrin*, 12:2; *The Code of Maimonides*, "The Book of Judges," 34. I have provided the literal translations in brackets.

**101** Maimonides, Moses, *Mishneh Torah*, "Sefer Shoftim," commentary by Shmuel Tanchum Rubinstein, Jerusalem: Mossad HaravKook, 1962, Footnote 9, 58.

sibility of imposing the death penalty upon him. Only if through an explicit act of verbalization does the defendant embraces death is he vulnerable to the death penalty. On anything short of this, he goes free. It is the very courting of death, as it were, that makes the defendant an appropriate subject of the death penalty. The willingness to accept the death penalty for the murder one is about to commit must be on a par with suicide.

The theological motif expressed here dovetails with that found at the beginning of the fifth chapter of *The Laws Concerning the Foundations of the Torah*, where Maimonides says the following:

> Should an idolater arise and coerce an Israelite to violate any one of the commandments mentioned in the Torah [except those pertaining to the prohibitions against idolatry, forbidden sexual relations, and murder] under the threat that otherwise he would put him to death, the Israelite is to commit the transgression rather than suffer death; for concerning the commandments it is said, 'which, if a man do them, he shall live by them' (Leviticus, 18:5): 'Live by them, and not die by them.' And if he suffered death rather than commit a transgression, this is considered *Mitḥayev BeNafsho* [He has to give a reckoning on the Day of Judgment for his wanton and irresponsible destruction of his own life].[102]

In both the case of someone who coerces a Jew to transgress one of the commandments of the Torah under penalty of death – and a defendant accused of murder – Maimonides, following his Rabbinic predecessors, goes out of his way to radically circumscribe the occasions in which the embrace or infliction of death would be considered morally and legally acceptable. If someone is being threatened with death if he does not violate one of the laws of the Torah (exclusive of idolatry, forbidden sexual relations, and murder), according to Maimonides he is positively prohibited from courting martyrdom and dying for the sake of sanctifying God's name.[103] In the hierarchy of monotheistic values, life (with the three exceptions duly noted) looms as the supreme value, even above glorifying God's name. Regarding a defendant accused of murder, Maimonides again drastically restricts (in accordance with Rabbinic argument and precedent) the occasions upon which the death penalty can be inflicted. Unless the defendant had responded to the warning issued to him by witnesses by saying that he is fully aware of the

**102** Maimonides, *Laws Concerning the Foundations of the Torah*, 5:1; *The Book of Knowledge*, trans. Hyamson, 40a – with emendations on my part.

**103** This is in opposition to the medieval Tosafists whose view is recorded in the Babylonian Talmudic tractate of *Avodah Zarah* 27b (the *Tosafot* beginning with the words, *Yakhol Afilu*) who hold that in coerced transgressions below the order of magnitude of idolatry, prohibited sexual relations, and murder one is given the option of transgressing without being killed – but one is not *required* to do so.

death penalty being attached to the action that he is about to commit and with full awareness that he will be receiving this penalty does he want to engage in the prohibited action, then – and only then – can a Jewish legal tribunal sentence him to death. Snuffing out another person's life is not a sufficient basis in Jewish law for imposing the death penalty. There must be something approximating to a voluntary renunciation of his own life on the part of the murderer accompanying the act of murder for the murderer to be punishable by death in Jewish law. Presumably, the life of the person that for irretrievable. Imposing the death penalty upon his murderer will not bring the deceased back to life. The dominant justification for judicially taking the life of the murderer is as the Rabbis and Maimonides project it because he has already taken his own life by acknowledging in advance of his act of murder that he is willing to pay the price of death for his destructive act.[104]

The overwhelming priority that Maimonides assigns to the value of life betrays subterranean linkages to his theorizing of *Ma'ase Merkavah* (metaphysics) and *Ma'ase Bereshit* (physics and cosmology) in the first four chapters of the *Code*. One can almost discern in Maimonides a reversal of the Platonic dictum that philosophy constitutes a preparation for dying. Instead of philosophy by its very abstraction from the physical and the concrete being viewed as a preparatory phase to dying, Maimonides insinuates how philosophy's confrontation with and cultivation of the irresolvable elements of human life (manifested in its analyses of God and of physical nature) —which can neither be negated nor transcended during the sustained moments of philosophical reflection – catapult us back into the process and prospects of human life. The urge to move beyond the fleeting impulses of human life represented by philosophy becomes just one more built-in fulcrum for restoring us to the urgencies and rhythms of daily life. Life endows and inspires us with resources and motivations to transcend its own limitations to facilitate our living most equitably within those limitations. In the end, one can project a straight line of continuity linking Maimonides' theology and metaphysics to key elements in his philosophy of law.

It would appear from our discussion of the Maimonidean judge that the unresolved logical and epistemological dilemmas bedeviling skepticism have given rise to the transformation of skepticism from a theory of knowledge into an ethics. Skepticism itself can serve as an inhibiting factor toward giving expression to some of the worst ethical vices such as anger. From the perspective of the same, one could say that the root cause of anger is an inability to live with and tolerate

**104** Deterrence begins to figure significantly as a motif in the calculations of Jewish law largely when a certain type of transgression has become rampant. When there is widespread flouting of one of the norms of Jewish law (say the prohibition against murder), then the factors I have outlined in the text might be relegated to a secondary status.

theoretical insufficiency. We are angry because we want to pierce limits and fortify and expand our sense of mastery. In this sense, anger and pride are correlative vices. Haughtiness and pride are a function of our claiming as our own (in terms of intelligence – and other kinds of resource) that which lies beyond our grasp — and anger results when one despairs of the prospect of remedying the deficiencies in his intellectual and other resources. Pride is a gleefully-and-externally-directed denial of limits — and anger is a despondently-and-inwardly-directed chafing against limits. Pride that is not able to muster the panache to deny that which defies and inhibits it becomes anger. Anger is self-lacerated pride — which takes out upon the self and others its inability to set up a confidence game to indiscriminately deceive itself and others.

From this perspective, cultivating the metaphysical terrain of the Same — learning to be at home in a skeptical mode of discourse and analysis — is not just a prolegomenon to ethics, but is itself ethics. One way to at least partially accommodate the dilemma that if skepticism truly resists certainty, then it needs to shed the mantle of being just one more theory of knowledge (because as a critique of the possibility of knowledge it becomes one more spurious variety of that which it rejects) is to envision skepticism as a form of ethical doing. In conformity with his own premises, the skeptic does not claim to know that there is no truth — but only perpetually dramatizes for himself and others what the condition of not knowing with certainty is about. This dramatization — this form of doing — the series of persistent enactments that we abridge under the rubric of skepticism very importantly includes an acclimation to limits and a delineation of a life of limits as part of the content of what its own skeptical quest is about. In this way, we can begin to theorize ethics as a vision of human life generated from the perspective of the Same — and its status as First Philosophy is sealed by the same fate that dooms us to be swirling endlessly within the ambit of skepticism.

## 9 Conclusion

In conclusion, this article has sought to explore the nuanced understanding of justice within Judaism and its interplay with Christian and Islamic thought. By examining key scriptural and rabbinic sources, the concept of justice was shown to be deeply embedded in Jewish tradition, shaped by a continuous tension between divine command and human responsibility.

In Judaism, the Biblical phrase "Justice, justice shalt thou pursue," (Deut 16:20) conveys one of the most central aspects of the concept of justice. The repetition of the term "justice" underlines that the process of achieving justice is as crucial as the outcome itself. The path to achieving justice cannot be compromised; the means must be as righteous as the ends. Jewish ethics do not rest on a static, perfect understanding of justice. Instead, justice is seen as a dynamic and continuous process. This ongoing process involves constantly adjusting and realigning actions and policies to ensure that justice is served. It acknowledges the imperfections and complexities of human efforts to achieve justice, emphasizing the importance of striving and effort.

The classical image of justice in Judaism follows through on the vision of God that was extrapolated from the Rabbinic sources. The *Tower of Babel* narrative symbolizes that direct access to God is foreclosed. This indicates that pluralistic routes grounded in the disparate languages and linguistic cultures of humankind are the only way to approach God. The skepticism about any substantive conception of God remains pivotal for the understanding of justice: following Rabbi Akiva, that one cannot infer the possible from the impossible, human justice must operate within the limits of human understanding, where divine will remains inaccessible. Therefore, both normatively and descriptively, justice remains blind. A secure hierarchy of the goals or values to be achieved by a system of justice cannot be established within the boundaries of monotheism and skepticism. Monotheism is also not able to affirm in any case that its construal and constellation of facts is objectively right or appropriate.

For the practical application of the concept of justice and "walking in the ways of God" – as Jewish tradition teaches – this means walking in a space of deep uncertainty, as God is invoked as the Author and Final Legitimator of a Law of unfathomable ambiguity. It is the task of humans specialized in law to use all their resources and inventiveness to navigate imponderables, without losing their poise and balance. The utterly transcendent God, who is conceptually inaccessible to human beings, models a sublime aloofness, but at the same time this creates an infinite space for human beings to discover and manifest their own freedom. So, walking in the ways of God really means to turn our attention to ourselves and to be skeptical of our own skepticism. Learning to be at home in a skeptical mode of discourse and analysis — is not just a prolegomenon to ethics, but is itself ethics.

# Bibliography


al-Jīlānī, Shaikh ʿAbd al-Qādir, *The Sublime Revelation: A Collection of Sixty-Two Discourses*, trans. Muhtar Holland, Houston: Al-Baz Publishing, 1992.

al-Jīlānī, Shaikh ʿAbd al-Qādir, *The Removal of Cares: A Collection of Forty-Five Discourses*, trans. Muhtar Holland, Ft. Lauderdale: Al-Baz Publishing, 1997.

Benjamin, Walter/Arendt, Hannah (eds.), *Illuminations: Essays and Reflections*, New York: Schocken, 1969.

Bloom, Harold, *The Anxiety of Influence*, New York: Oxford University Press, 1973.

Bloom, Harold, *A Map of Misreading*, New York: Oxford University Press, 1975.

Bloom, Harold, *Kabbalah and Criticism*, New York: Seabury Press, 1975.

Bloom, Harold, *Poetry and Repression*, New Haven: Yale University Press, 1976.

Botwinick, Aryeh, "Maimonides' Messianic Age," *Judaism* 33,4 (1984), 418 – 25

Botwinick, Aryeh, *Skepticism, Belief, and the Modern: Maimonides to Nietzsche*, Ithaca: Cornell University Press, 1997.

Botwinick, Aryeh, "The Dialectic of Monotheism: St. Paul's "Letter to the Romans"," *telos* 143 (2008), 113 – 32.

Botwinick, Aryeh, *Michael Oakeshott's Skepticism*, Ukraine: Princeton University Press, 2010.

Botwinick, Aryeh, "Torah Lishmah: The Linkage between Monotheism and Skepticism in the Thought of Reb Chaim Volozhiner," *Judaica Petropolitana* 12 (2019), 31 – 52.

Botwinick, Aryeh, "Machiavelli's Theorizing of Power Juxtaposed to the Negative Theological Conceptualization of God: Implications for Mideast Peace," *Journal of Ecumenical Studies* 57.1 (2022), 40 – 57.

Braune, W., "ʿAbd al-Ḳādir al-Dj̲īlānī," in EI$^2$, published online: /referenceworks.brill.com/display/entries/EIEO/SIM-0095.xml?rskey=1p3LB4&result=10 (accessed on 18.10.2024).

Burke, Edmund, *Reflections on the Revolution in France*, Chicago: Henry Regnery Company, 1955.

Epstein, Yekhiel Mikhel, *Arukh Ha-Shulḥan*, New York: Jonathan Publishing Compay, 1961.

Fuller, Timothy (ed.), *The Voice of Liberal Learning: Michael Oakeshott on Education*, New Haven: Yale University Press, 1989.

Franco, Paul/Marsh, Leslie (eds.), *A Companion to Michael Oakeshott*, USA: Penn State University Press, 2015, 8; 134 – 38.

*Genesis*, trans. M. Rosenbaum/A. M. Silbermann, Jerusalem, 1972.

Gold, Joshua Robert, "Jacob Taubes: 'Apocalypse from Below,'" *Telos* 134 (2006), 140 – 56.

Goodman, Lenn E., "Is Maimonides a Moral Relativist?" in: Curtis Hutt/Halla Kim/Berel Lerner, *Jewish Religious and Philosophical Ethics*, London: Routledge, 2017, 87 – 106.

Hampshire, Stuart, "A New Way of Seeing," *New York Review of Books* (1995), 48 – 53.

Harvey, Zev, "The Israelite Kingdom of God according to Hobbes," *Iyyun* 30 (1981), 27 – 38.

*Hebrew-English Edition of the Babylonian Talmud: Sanhedrin*, trans. Jacob Shachter/H. Freedman, London: Soncino Press, 1987.

*Isaiah*, trans. I. W. Slotki, London: Soncino Press, 1949.

Koller, Aaron J., *Unbinding Isaac*, Lincoln, Nebraska: University of Nebraska Press, 2020.

Lovejoy, Arthur O., *The Great Chain of Being: A Study of the History of an Idea*, Cambridge: Harvard University Press, 1936.

Maimonides, *The Code of Maimonides (Misneh Torah):* Book Fourteen: The Book of Judges, trans. Abraham M. Hershman, New Haven, CT: Yale University Press, 1949.

Maimonides, Moses, *Hakdamot LePerush HaMishnah* [Introductions to the Commentary on the Mishnah], ed. Mordechai Dov Rabinowitz, Jerusalem: Mosad HaRav Kook, 1961.
Maimonides, Moses, *Mishneh Torah*, "Sefer Shoftim," commentary by Shmuel Tanchum Rubinstein, Jerusalem: Mossad HaravKook, 1962.
Maimonides, Moses, *The Guide of the Perplexed*, trans. Shlomo Pines, vol. 3, Chicago: University of Chicago Press, 1963, III:15:461.
*Mishnah with Maimonides' Commentary*, trans. Joseph Kafiah, Jerusalem: Mossad Harav Kook, 1965.
M. Rosenbaum/ A.M. Silbermann (eds.), *Pentateuch with Rashi's Commentary*, 1929–1934, published online: Sefaria.org, https://www.sefaria.org/Rashi_on_Leviticus?tab=contents (accessed on 17.10.2024).
Oakeshott, Michael, *On Human Conduct*, Kiribati: Clarendon Press, 1975.
Oakeshott, Michael, *Rationalism in Politics and Other Essays*, Indianapolis: Liberty Press, 1991.
Oakeshott, Michael, *On history and other essays*, Indianapolis: Liberty Fund, 1999.
Scherman, N., *Complete Artscroll Siddur*, 2003.
Schorr, Gedalia Halevi, *Ohr Gedalyahu*, vol. 2, Brooklyn, NY, 1984, 101–102.
Soloveitchik, Haym, "Rupture and Reconstruction: The Transformation of Contemporary Orthodoxy," *Tradition* 28,4 (1994), 64–130.
Taubes, Jacob, *Occidental Eschatology*, Stanford: Stanford University Press, 2009.
*The Koran Interpreted*, trans. Arberry, A. J., New York: Simon and Schuster, 1996
Volozhiner, Reb Ḥaim, *Nefesh HaḤaim*, ed. Yissochor Dov Rubin, Bnei-Brak, Israel, 1989.
Volozhiner, Reb Ḥaim, *Sefer Nefesh HaḤaim im Be'ur Yirat Ḥaim*, Israel: Bnei-Brak, 2007, Gate I, Chapter 7, 51–52.
Volozhiner, Reb Ḥaim, *Ruaḥ Ḥaim Al Masekhet 'Avot*, Israel: Bnei-Brak, 2007.
Walzer, Michael, *In God's Shadow*, New Haven: Yale University Press, 2012.
Weiss, Shira, *Ethical Ambiguity in the Hebrew Bible: Philosophical Analysis of Scriptural Narrative*, Cambridge: Cambridge University Press, 2018.
Tsevi Yehudah Berlin, Naftali, *Sefer Shemot (Book of Exodus). With the Commentary Ha'Amek Davar*, Jerusalem: El Hamekoroth, 1966.

## Suggestions For Further Reading

Cohen, Aryeh, *Justice in the City*, Boston, MA: Academic Studies Press, 2012.
Goodman, Lenn E., *On Justice. An Essay in Jewish Philosophy*, Littman Library of Jewish Civilization, Liverpool: Liverpool University Press, 2008.
Plen, Matt, *Judaism, Education and Social Justice. Towards a Jewish Critical Pedagogy*, London/New York/Dublin: Bloomsbury, 2022.
Sicker, Martin, *The Idea of Justice in Judaism*, USA: iUniverse, 2006.
Unterman, Jeremiah, *Justice for all: How the Jewish Bible Revolutionized Ethics*, Philadelphia: University of Nebraska Press, 2017.
Walzer, Michael, *Spheres of Justice: A Defense of Pluralism and Equality*, United Kingdom: Basic Books, 1983.

Elisabeth Gräb-Schmidt

# The Concept of Justice in Christianity

## 1 The Terminological, Theological and Philosophical Principles of the Concept of Justice in Christianity

As an aim justice characterizes a fundamental ambition of humanity: to live as humans, among humans. It describes humanity as being "open to the world" ("world-open").[1] As such beings, open to the world, humans are not only to be regarded as a part of nature and its processes – they also engage with them and shape them.

Thus, the concept of justice is fundamentally contextual even before we introduce its manifold iterations across different cultures. As there are differences in the notion of justice between classic Greek philosophy and those of modernity, the different religions reveal distinct and contextual references as well, while the shared commitment to the idea of justice points to the existence of a common ground. Cultural frameworks and their historical and conceptual specificities do not leave the idea of justice untouched, but neither do they fully change its nature as a relational concept referring to a shared order. Thus, the concept of justice not only describes a social system but the relationship of humanity to nature as well. A tenable definition of justice must take the rights of future generations as well as those of different regions of the world into account. A present-day treatment of the concept of justice requires a reevaluation of the traditional philosophical idea of reciprocity.

The understanding of what form a shared order should take varies depending on the historical and cultural context in which it is conceived. While in antiquity a (cosmologically guaranteed) eternal order was presupposed in a widely unquestioned metaphysical understanding of the world, modern thinkers no longer subscribed to the idea of an ontologically fixed order. Instead, the concept of a social order came to signify a functional construction geared toward equality and liberty – be it in the early modern fashion, guided by the idea of human reason, or in the modern variant that draws on the idea of human dignity.

Through this development, the issue of justice came to be contained in the question of human rights. It appears in debates on globalization, questions of eco-

1 Scheler, Max, *The Human Place in the Cosmos*, trans. Manfred Frings, Evanston IL: NUP, 2009, 28–33.

https://doi.org/10.1515/9783110561692-003

nomic and ecological justice, of overcoming poverty and hunger, and of the just allocation of resources and sustainability. In this sense, the two major Christian churches in Germany deliberately addressed present issues in a Christian manner by linking future, solidarity, and justice in their shared statement on justice in 1997.[2] Thereby, they follow the Christian maxim: "But seek first his kingdom and his righteousness, and all these things will be given to you as well" (Matt 6:33). Thus, all the important societal fields – politics, economics, social issues, and ecology – must be built upon the foundation of justice, be it explicitly or implicitly.

In this chapter, the historical development of the concept of justice will be treated as well as its current relevance (2). Its historical development will be traced from Greek (2.1) and biblical (2.2) antiquity to the Middle Ages (2.3). In the section that follows this treatment of its origin, the differentiation of the concept of justice into a range of understandings in the early modern period (3) will be considered and we will ask to what extent a continuous influence can be traced from the now-hidden roots of the idea of justice to the current discourse. We will show that in spite of their seemingly radical differences, current discourses on justice make references to problems and dimensions within the idea of justice that are strikingly similar to those that shaped the biblical concept of justice. This conceptual kinship is further developed by showing that as an ethical core concept justice can be understood to define the horizon of modernity itself. Thereafter, in a fourth section, another process of differentiation will be accounted for by exploring the differences and commonalities between the concepts of justice in various Christian denominations. Lutheran and Reformed Protestant as well as Roman Catholic and Orthodox perspectives will be analyzed. Not only can a focus on the biblical understanding of justice show us how these traditions engage with the text to create their own distinctive reading – this perspective can be widened to include Jewish and Islamic concepts of justice in a constructive dialogue (4) In the next section, the importance of the concept of justification will be traced from the theory of justification (*Rechtfertigungslehre*) to understandings of justice as a central category of modernity. A special focus will be placed on the understanding of justice as justification as it was developed in the reformation (5). Through the concepts of theodicy (5.1), human rights (5.2), and (religious) freedom (5.3) and their persisting relevance, we will shed light on the importance and undiminished influence of the theological concept of justice on the present-day discourse. In the next section,

2 "Wort des Rates der Evangelischen Kirche in Deutschland und der Bischofskonferenz zur wirtschaftlichen und sozialen Lage in Deutschland," in: Kirchenamt der Evangelischen Kirche in Deutschland (ed.), *Für eine Zukunft in Solidarität und Gerechtigkeit*, Hannover/Bonn: Self-published, 1997.

current debates on justice (6) in theology (6.1) and in social ethics and philosophy (6.2) will be shown to face some of the same issues that were presented in the previous sections on its historical development. Especially in the context of globalization (7), the early modern notion of freedom as an expression of justice (7.1), together with the theories of justification and the biblical understanding of justice (7.2), are essential for a redefinition of justice that is up to the challenges of the global age (7.3). This multifaceted account of the notion of justice will allow for the conclusion (8) that a clear influence of the theological notion of justice on modern discourses concerning this issue can be shown to exist.

# 2 The Development and Current Relevance of the Notion of Justice in Philosophical and Theological Traditions

## 2.1 The Tradition of Justice in Greek Antiquity

The concept of justice is relevant to any horizon of life and action. It is therefore regarded as a core concept within both philosophical and theological traditions. The concept of justice is of fundamental importance for the entire occidental ethical tradition. This holds not only for theology but for philosophy as well. Since actions are not possible without guiding principles, they are relevant to the understanding of human agency. Since Greek antiquity, the concept of justice has been a guiding principle in human thought. It pertains to the whole of being as well as the lives of individuals. The ontological qualification of being follows from an insight into the forms of order and the corresponding existence of the individual, in its place in the world.

The two great philosophers of classical times, Aristotle (384–322 BC) and Plato (d. 348 BC), regarded justice as a core element of philosophy that marked out the horizon of thought and action. The virtue of justice is the highest of the cardinal virtues, outranking prudence, courage, and temperance. In Plato, it serves to allocate the proper place and relation of each virtue among within the entirety of the virtues.[3] The virtue of justice serves this purpose not only in the order of societal interaction, but in the foundational order that underlies it – the order of the human capacity for action, the order of the soul. Justice is an integral virtue for the well-ordered state as a whole. This makes justice a founding principle for

3 Cf. Platon, *Pol.*, 443c–e.

the life of the individual and the order of the *polis:* The *polis* is imagined as a larger-than-life individual. Plato's concept of justice, therefore, refers to the ethics of the individual and the social sphere, respectively. Both realms of ethics need justice as a guiding principle to set out the goals of action, and to bring about not just any but the best possible order.

This motivates Plato's reference to the concept of *physis*, which he takes to be normative. Justice is the true nature (*physis*) of the soul. It is a good and must be desired for its own sake. Justice must be aspired to because only it corresponds to the true nature of the soul. This shows Plato's particular understanding of justice, in the way it serves to give to each their own. This does not primarily refer to goods but to tasks and actions.[4] Plato contrasts the concept of justice to that of honor, the aristocratic preservation of esteem, which does not account for justice.[5] A social community is only just if everyone's tasks correspond to their predominant gifts and capabilities.

This meaning of justice as giving to each their own has been preserved in the following times, in its Latinized abbreviature *suum cuique.* In this form, the Roman jurist Ulpian (170 – 228) declared it to be the foundation of ethical justice: "Justice is the constant and perpetual will of giving to each their own right."[6]

Thus defined, justice gains special importance since a necessary link to the freedom of action has been established. The set ethos of traditional order is thus taken up into the freedom of the individual.[7] Justice is tied to action. Yet Platonic freedom should not be confused with its modern understanding, which is tied to an autonomous subject. In antiquity, the individual and its freedom were integrated into the well-ordered life of the *polis.* In spite of this focus on the collective, there is another marked difference in the understanding of social ethics. To our present eyes, Plato's concept of justice seems to be less focused on social justice in the present sense. His focus is not on the just allocation of goods but on the harmony of the order of the forces within the soul. Yet this can also be understood to foreshadow present-day concepts of justice, especially the capability

4 Cf. Platon, *Pol.*, 433a–b.

5 Flaig, Egon, "Ehre gegen Gerechtigkeit: Adelsethos und Gemeinschaftsdenken in Hellas," in: Jan Assmann (ed.), *Gerechtigkeit: Richten und Retten in der abendländischen Tradition und ihren altorientalischen Ursprüngen*, Munich: Fink, 1998, 137.

6 Ulpianus, Domitius, *Liber primus regularum*, ed. T. Honoré, D I,1 – 10, Oxford: Oxford University Press, 1982.

7 Rohrmoser, Günter, "Platons politische Philosophie," *Studium Generale: Zeitschrift für interdisziplinäre Studien* 22 (1969), 1094 – 134, here: 1125–27.

approach, as developed by Amartya Sen[8] and Martha Nussbaum.[9] Furthermore, the Platonic tractates are relevant for understanding the functioning of our highly specialized and differentiated society. The notion of *suum cuique* (to each his due) can still be insightful especially when faced with possible oversteps in competency. Plato recognized this possibility in the agglomeration of activities, which he regarded as an intrusion of particular interests into politics and thus as a fundamental vice of Attic democracy.[10] Yet we must be critical as well: The Platonic adherence to the forces of the soul provides a guideline, but it is clear that in order to bring the real issues to the fore, justice must be more clearly rooted in social interaction.

This issue was taken up by Aristotle. He understands justice in reference to the interpersonal sphere of the interactions among citizens and between them and the *polis.*[11] He further distinguishes the idea of justice into various types of justice by identifying different forms of relationality.[12] He distinguishes between justice in a general (*universalis* and *legalis*) and a particular (*particularis*) sense. The latter is further divided into an allocating (*iustitia distributiva*) and a balancing (*iustitia commutativa*) mode of justice. The latter pair represents the moment of equality at the heart of justice, which comes to bear on both forms of justice.[13] The distinction between commutative and distribute justice secured Aristotle's concept lasting relevance. To this day, it has been essential to the development of distinctions between different aspects of justice. Aristotle focused his theory on the problem of how individuals could enjoy justice. This is represented by the notion of *epikeia*[14] (reasonability), a reflection of the individual appropriation of justice.

Over time, Aristotelean ideas have been developed into more clearly defined notions. Justice serves as a guiding principle of human life that is expressed in the duty of the individual to contribute to societal life as well as the societal obligation to make individual participation possible in an active and productive manner. Aristotle's questions about Plato's conception of justice remain fruitful: How can one judge the fair distribution of resources when individuals share certain characteristics but also exhibit significant differences? The Platonic principle,

---

**8** Sen, Amartya, "Capability and Well-Being," in: Amartya Sen/Martha Nussbaum (eds), *The Quality of Life*, Oxford: Clarendon Press, 1993, 30–53.

**9** Nussbaum, Martha, "Human Capabilities, Female Human Beings," in: Martha Nussbaum/Jonathan Glover (eds.), *Women, Culture, and Development: A Study of Human Capabilities*, Oxford: Clarendon Press, 1995, 6–104.

**10** Gadamer, Hans-Georg, "Platons Denken in Utopien," *Gymnasium* 90 (1983) 434–55, here: 459.

**11** Holzleithner, Elisabeth, *Gerechtigkeit*, Vienna: Facultas, 2009, 22.

**12** Aristotle, Nicomachean Ethics, ed. C.D.C. Reeve, V, 3–8 1129b–1133n, Indianapolis [u. a.]: Hackett, 2014.

**13** Cf. Aristotle, *NE* V, 7, 1132a, 20–25.

**14** Cf. Aristotle, *NE* V, 14, 1137b–1017.

which implies equality as well as difference, remains: The measure of justice lies in the question of how equality can be defined under the premise of difference, to each their due, not to each the same. Difference can be measured by either individual contribution or need. This distinction shows that no mere intuitive judgment can be the measure of justice. Furthermore, it becomes evident that the issue of justice is affected by various interests, goals, and value-systems. This leads to more questions: How can we set some standards in this seeming jungle of diverging interests which could serve as universally binding criteria for justice? Is the attainment of such standards even possible, or can a given definition of justice never be anything more than the product of political power struggles?

Its intrinsic complexity and the question of universal standards that might deliver binding criteria for justice were paradigmatically articulated in the ideas of justice set out in antiquity and are still relevant today. The principle, which is regarded as a common denominator, the Platonic *suum cuique*, is taken up by Aristotle. However, he developed the concept further by providing reflections regarding the conditions of its implementation. In early modernity, this led to the differentiation of the concepts of rights into the categories of civil liberties and the rights to political and social participation, in which the different forms of *iustitia correctiva, iustitia commutativa* and *iustitia contributiva* are mirrored.

Justice presupposes an order which allows for clearly defined interrelations between individuals and their respective relationships to society as a whole. Because of its relational nature, no definition of justice can circumvent the issue of how justice in itself – as such an ordering principle, or as *summum bonum* – can be defined. In this very possibility of defining a *summum bonum*, a horizon regarding the highest good, the concept of justice developed in the biblical tradition surpasses the classical, virtue-based theory of justice.

## 2.2 The Biblical-Theological Tradition of the Concept of Justice

What are the features of the theological concept of justice, the roots of which can still be seen in our ideas of justice?

The concept of justice is central not only to Judaism but to Christian faith as well. In the Old Testament as well as the New Testament, justice touches upon the innermost core of faith. Wherever faith is challenged, we encounter the issue of justice, be it in the skeptical challenge of theodicy in Job (42:1 ff), as a central category of theology in Paul (Rom 8:28 f and Rom 9—11), or in Jesus himself (Mark 15:34 and Matt. 27:46). It is referenced primarily with regard to the coming salvation. Justice points forward to the future of the kingdom of God. Thus, justice is essentially an eschatological concept. As such, it contains the dimension of judgement by which God creates justice (Ps 82). God's very being is deeply informed by justice in that his very being is defined *as* justice.[15]

Just as in philosophical antiquity, a universal concept of justice can be found in the Bible and the biblical tradition also places the concept of justice at its center. In spite of this similarity, the biblical standpoint always kept its distance towards a virtue-based concept of justice as well as to a symmetrical relation of balance. On the contrary: Justice by law was the very concept by which Paul exposed humanity's incapability for virtue (Rom 7); and prophets like Amos and Hosea emphasized not balance, order, and symmetry, but the asymmetry of justice. It is God who brings justice and to restore what is right in the face of human disobedience and unjust actions (Amos 5; Hos 2).

The Hebrew concept of "*tsedaḳa*" – in analogy to the Egyptian "*ma'at*"[16] – especially in its use in the prophets, but in the tradition of wisdom and the psalms as well, expresses the all-encompassing work of God. In these contexts, justice and mercy are combined in the concept of God as a just judge. This expansion of the concept of justice surpasses the notion that had been developed in philosophical antiquity in which justice is limited to the actions furthering community. A version of the communicative aspect of Aristotelian justice can be found in the Old Testament. This is especially the case when the term is used to refer to justice and rectitude as Godly attributes. Nevertheless, even in these instances, the combination of justice and mercy, renders justice understood as God's justice as something entirely distinct that moves beyond its definition in philosophical antiquity. In the interpretation of justice as mercy, this aspect refers to the actions furthering community (Ps 72:4.12–14; Gen 38:26). Even when faced with human disloyalty, God is merciful (Amos 5:18–20; Hab 23). God's justice is merciful. It perseveres, despite the unjust actions of humanity, despite their sin (Isa 52:13–53:12), because it is God who upholds the relationship of justice (Amos 5:18–20; Mic 3:12; Hos 11). The remarkable difference to the Greek tradition, therefore, lies in a fundamental asymmetry that allows the biblical account to transcend the concept of justice as proportionality.[17]

However, when it comes to the perspective of social justice there is a commonality in the biblical and the Aristotelean account. The guiding principle of the latter notion of justice is also as an important principle in Deuteronomic and prophetic

15 Janowski, Bernd, "Die rettende Gerechtigkeit: Zum Gerechtigkeitsdiskurs in den Psalmen," in: Bernhard Greiner et al. (eds.), *Recht und Literatur: Interdisziplinäre Bezüge*, 239–55, here: 249, Heidelberg: Winter, 2010.

16 Assmann, Jan, *Ma'at: Gerechtigkeit und Unsterblichkeit im Alten Ägypten*, Munich: Fink, $^{2}$1995.

17 Janowski, Bernd, "Die Tat kehrt zum Täter zurück: Offene Fragen im Umreis des 'Tun-Ergehen-Zusammenhangs'," *ZThK* 91 (1994), 247–71.

literature about justice in social relations. But in the asymmetric relation of God's justice with respect to human behavior, justice and equality are not fully aligned, because the underlying relationship is not transactional. As mercy, it is a gift as well as a reciprocal relationship since this gift transposes the individual into God's sphere of power. Justice results from the relationship to God,[18] who is characterized by and identified with mercy.

The concepts above also hold for the New Testament. By establishing a relation between justice and the salvation brought about by Jesus Christ, justice is equally placed in God's sphere of power. What had been represented by the idea of the covenant in the Old Testament, is taken up and confirmed once and for all in the incarnation of Christ in the New Testament.

In Paul, the issue of justice is presented in a Christological sense as a renewal of the covenant in the blood of Christ. In Jesus' parables as recounted in *Matthew*, the perceived injustice of this world is turned into a parable for God's kingdom. Justice also transposes the individual into God's sphere of power, in as much as it is understood in relation to salvation in Christ. Paul's reception of the Christological tradition is thus focused, just as much as the tradition itself is, on the issue of God's justice as it relates to humanity and the world. Their relationship consists in the liberating nature of justice. Justice becomes a liberating force for just actions, finding its expression in love (Gal 5,14; Rom 13,8–10). Paul sets out the foundational ideas for the specific understanding of Christian freedom that rests in a critical relationship with the law as a norm that is to become its characteristic hallmark. Primarily, however, it shines a spotlight on the nature of justice as a virtue: On the one hand, the reference of justice to freedom highlights the human capacity for action. On the other hand, this very human freedom is itself limited by the state of the social order and their position in the world, and thus the role that virtue can play is challenged. Freedom is granted through the gift of justice, which, in turn, does not cancel out the idea of justice as a virtue but exposes the problems therein. Before they can realize their potential, humans must be made capable of virtuous actions.

The nature of justice as a virtue remains juxtaposed to the biblical roots of the concept of justice, in spite of the role of the classic cardinal virtues and the additional virtues of faith, love, and hope in Christianity. For we are faced with the question of the relationship between justice as a gift, as a positive accomplishment, and as a virtue in the sense of an active creation of justice. The biblical concept of

---

**18** Koch, Klaus, *Sdq im Alten Testament: Eine traditionsgeschichtliche Untersuchung*, Heidelberg: University Publikation, 1953; Schmid, *Gerechtigkeit als Weltordnung: Hintergrund und Geschichte des alttestamentlichen Gerechtigkeitsbegriffs*.

justice sharpens our awareness of the limitations human efforts to bring about justice in conceiving of justice not as something to be attained through human efforts alone, but as founded in God's justice. A justice towards which we can open ourselves, while we are unable to produce or even preserve it. In biblical terms, justice is therefore a relational concept, which places action squarely on the side of God in the underlying asymmetry. God has promised to uphold the relationship of justice. This is the main import of the covenant between God and humanity. Both the notion of the covenant and that of the relationship bear the same relational characteristic: God is acting and giving within a deeply asymmetrical relationship. This asymmetry is most visible in the biblical notion of justice as mercy. This is what an account of justice that is overly focused on human virtue, even one put forth in Christian terms, threatens to cloud. The notion of justice as mercy that is manifest in God's justice appearing in advance, has, however, already become obscured with the translation of *tsedaḳa* to δικαιοσύνη (*dikaiosýne*). The Hebrew term *tsedaḳa* contains the notion of ἐλεημοσύνη (*eleēmosynē*), of mercy. The Greek term δικαιοσύνη (*dikaiosýne*) only stands for one aspect of the Hebrew concept of justice. *Tsedaḳa*, however, contains a "tense unity of justice and mercy."[19] In effect, it also contains the Aristotelean distinction of distributive and commutative justice, yet in a manner far surpassing the Greek understanding of both aspects. The Greek model assigns benefits according to capability and contribution. It is focused on proportionality. The guideline of "to each their due" is informed by the principle of everyone's lawful entitlements. The biblical model, however, qualifies this notion of mere proportionality according to the asymmetry of justice. It holds on to a fundamental difference, which cannot be evened out, without giving up on the idea of justice. This concept is not compatible with Greek thought. Such an asymmetrical understanding of justice cannot be easily transposed onto the Aristotelean concept of justice, which is built upon reciprocity and equality. A notion that has been a guiding principle in definitions of justice from the Middle Ages to the present and was especially relevant in the early modern period. Admittedly, Aristotle must presuppose an inequality which is to be equalized and there is an asymmetry in the Platonic idea of "to each their due". However, these moments of asymmetry only relate to the capabilities and qualities of humans, which are expressed through virtue. (This also affects the virtue of faith as it was defined by Thomas Aquinas.)

Justice in the biblical sense rests on an obliging act of God independent of human action, which can be understood as a gift despite its also including the terms of God's *mishpat* – retribution and punishment by which a just situation

19 Janowski, "Die rettende Gerechtigkeit," 255 [translation by the author].

is established. Mercy and love represent this overflowing act of God's justice, which results in the notion of solidarity. An understanding of social justice that is informed by the justice of God must thus adhere to a notion of difference that moves beyond reciprocal compensation. Even before the introduction of the image of the suffering righteous (Isa 53), it is contained within the covenant of loyalty between God and his people that remains unchanged by their disloyalty, and finally in the death of Christ as the epitome of the suffering righteous. Hence, the biblical concept of justice is of foundational as well as eschatological importance, but in neither respect does it rest upon proportionality and equality. Instead, asymmetry and difference are the hallmarks of God's justice. From an eschatological perspective, this merciful justice of God accounts for the intricate variations and unjust occurrences in human existence.

When we turn to the biblical concept of justice, we must therefore grasp a broader notion than that of the Aristotelean account, which is guided by the idea of allocations along the lines of distributive and commutative justice in the interpersonal realm. Since it fundamentally includes the relationship of God to humanity contained in the concept of the covenant, we must broaden the relational understanding of justice. The biblical account breaks with the idea of proportionality and reciprocity in favor of God's commitment to communion with his creation, not as a mutual treaty but as a one-sided commitment to loyalty.

Thus the notion of God's justice contains his self-definition as love. Even the expression of God's justice takes on the form of love. For it is primarily expressed in his liberating acts, in his turning towards the poor and disenfranchised. God frees Israel from servitude and exile in Egypt. It is the poor and the outcasts who will receive justice and who require our solidarity. It is a new kind of justice as apostrophized in the benedictions (Matt 5). The concept of justice is, therefore, all-encompassing. It can even be said to contain a cosmic dimension.

This cosmic dimension is equally present in the concepts of justice and love. Sometimes, Christianity even tends to even interchange justice with love. But the allocation of justice and love must be strictly adhered to. The Christian faith is grounded in the belief in God's justice, and this conviction is meant to guide the intention and purpose of life and action. In this account, God's "saving justice",[20] which is not identical with judgement but contains it, becomes the central focus. This aspect of the tradition of God as a judge in the Old Testament, giving "to each their due" – reward or punishment —, should not be overlooked. Such an oversight can be found in the work of Marcion (85–160) who attempted to completely separate the punishing God of the Old from a loving God in the New Testa-

---

**20** Cf. the title of Janowskis article: "Die rettende Gerechtigkeit".

ment.[21] When the realization of judgment is neglected in favor of an emphasis on God's love, as tendency especially prevalent in the early modern period, inconsistencies arise. For without justice, love is in peril of becoming powerless. The world cannot forgo justice – a truth reflected in the casualties of history. Justice always implies a horizon of order, meant to set things right for those who have been wronged.[22]

The biblical understanding of justice and the different veins of theological interpretation that stem from it have been taken up in different ways in the historical development of theology. The social and cultural contexts of the specific traditions played a decisive role in these respective modifications.

## 2.3 The Development of a Religious Tradition of Justice in the Middle Ages and in the Early Modern Period

In antiquity as well as the Middle Ages, conceptions of justice were founded on and legitimized by making reference to a cosmological order or to natural law. Cosmological and ontological arguments are of importance to the development of theological doctrines on the properties of God. In these lines of argument, God's justice becomes the standard by which perception and, therefore, truth and reality are measured. It is through our knowledge of justice and God's other attributes that we come to know God and his relationship to the world. Through the preservation of his creation, God makes his properties visible. These qualities grant an insight into his otherwise unknowable nature.[23]

In the Medieval tradition, we encounter the issue of justice as a virtue once again. Thomas Aquinas (d. 1274) draws on two aspects of the Greek definition of justice: He treats justice as a virtue and as the measure of the goodness of a societal order. Yet the way he makes use of these concepts transcends the original Greek way of thought. Aquinas achieves this by adding the three theological virtues, faith, love, and hope, to the four traditional cardinal virtues of justice, courage, prudence, and temperance. Aquinas also takes up aspects of the Aristotelean theory justice by aligning the three basic modes of justice – law, exchange, and alloca-

---

**21** Cf. Janowski, "Die rettende Gerechtigkeit," 239–40.

**22** Zenger, Erich, *Ein Gott der Rache? Feindpsalmen verstehen*, Freiburg im Breisgau: Herder, 2003, 131.

**23** Ockham, William of, "Super 4 libros sententiarum. In sententiarum," *Opera Plurima* 3/4, l. 1, d. 3, q .2, Farnborough, Hants: Gregg Press, 1962.

tion – with the three fundamental relations and structures of the community.[24] Yet the theological orientation of reason already influences the way justice is perceived. Inner-worldly justice is tied to God's being and justice, and hence structures the relationship of the individual to their human neighbors and to God. Faith, therefore, becomes a crucial factor in the enjoyment of justice on the side of humanity. He broadens the concept of justice to include faith, the answer required by God's justice. Aquinas thus remains within the biblical tradition that regards justice not as a human deed but as a gift from God, yet he emphasizes our corresponding voluntary freedom to respond to this Godly justice. In this manner, Aquinas assigns a systematically justified place to justice as a virtue, that is as an ethical category. Human agency is compelled into action by the notion of virtue, while the asymmetrical nature of the human relationship to God, whom we can only meet through faith, is accounted for in equal measure. For this reason, the addition of the theological virtues to the traditional catalogue is essential to this account. In the added virtues, Aquinas transformation of the classical theory of virtue is expressed. For the virtues can no longer be regarded as the fully realizable aspiration of humanity towards perfection, as they were seen in Greek thought. While the traditional virtues retained their importance in Christianity, their meaning underwent a necessary transformation. Only through faith, taking up God's grace, humans are made capable of following the other cardinal virtues, or rather, of acquiring them and thus turning towards good. Human beings, therefore, are dependent upon God's grace to render them capable of believing. Thus, they can become virtuous through faith, capable of acting in love and living in hope, ready to serve the just order of communion.[25]

Before the rediscovery of the Aristotelean theory of justice as virtue in Aquinas, other strands had developed in Medieval theology, which were essential to this development in the theory of justice. Like Aquinas, the Old Church defined justice through the framework of virtue and was thus able to tie it directly to human agency. Other strands of Christian thought in the Middle Ages focus on the theological idea of the incarnation of God as an expression of God's justice through salvation. In a highly elaborated and exemplary fashion, this is found in Anselm of Canterbury's (d. 1109) *Cur deus homo*[26], where justice is the reason for God's becoming human and the focal point of God's redemption.

---

24 Aquinas, Thomas, *The Summa Theologiae of Saint Thomas Aquinas: Latin-English Edition, Secunda Secundae*, Q. 57–140, here: II/II, q. 58, NovAntiqua, 2013.

25 Huber, Wolfgang, *Gerechtigkeit und Recht: Grundlinien christlicher Rechtsethik*, Gütersloh: Gütersloher Verlagshaus, 2006.

26 Anselm of Canterbury, *Cur Deus homo: Why God became man*, trans. Edward Prout, London: Religious Tract Society, 1886.

Classical theology, from Augustine (354–430) through Anselm to Aquinas, holds that salvation occurs through God's grace. It is therefore not earned by human merit, a mode through which we might otherwise seek to persist in the face of God. Martin Luther (1483–1546) aligns himself with this tradition as he underscores that we are made capable of acting just by God's grace alone. While humans are required to actively strive for goodness, they cannot become just by any means other than God's grace. The desire to achieve salvation through merit is founded on an understanding of justice as justification. In this understanding that is shaped by a forensic interpretation of justice, humanity is thought to be indebted to God. The repayment of this debt thus becomes the guiding principle of human action and human agency advances to the foreground, in spite of the fact that its realization is dependant upon God's provision of his justifying act for us. When justification is based on forensic thought in this manner, God's justice threatens to be absorbed by a notion of justice as one of collecting debts and doling out punishments, which would push the notion of mercy – the transformative complement to justice in the biblical tradition – far into the background. This forensic notion of justice as it was developed by Cicero (106–43 BC), is already taken up in Augustine: Justice is brought into being by just action (*iustum facere*). Although Augustine adds a soteriological foundation, the strictly forensic interpretation is preserved. Anselm softens its hold by relating it primarily to the notion of order and less to the actions of the individual, yet it remains at the heart of the Christian tradition.

The new system of academic sciences, which was developed in the 12$^{th}$ century and represented a kind of scientific enlightenment *avant la lettre*, had some influence on the understanding of justice as presented by John of Salisbury (1115–1180). While he remained committed to the biblical tradition insofar as his understanding of the idea of the law mainly contains the moral principles as exposed in the Bible[27], in his *Policraticus*[28] he anticipates secular understandings of justice in that he develops a somewhat "autonomous" principle of justice and thus moves beyond an exclusively biblical justification. In this, he even develops a qualified acceptance of tyrannicide[29] that he grounds in the claim that when a ruler is not guided by moral principles, the legitimacy of his rule can be called into question. Since worldly authority is bestowed by God, the ruler must rule justly and in adherence

27 Cf. e.g. *Policraticus* IV, 4.

28 The *Policraticus* has been edited in various versions, yet no full translation or current full edition exist. References are given with Book and Chapter to facilitate comparison across editions. The most comprehensive translation is: John of Salisbury, *Policraticus: Of the Frivolities of Courtiers and the Footprints of Philosophers*, ed. and trans. Cary J. Nederman, Cambridge: CUP, 1990.

29 *Policr.* VIII, 20.

to the law (*iustitiae et iuris famulus est*).[30] The tyrant, however, suppresses justice and subsumes the law under his will. Thus, justice can legitimize tyrannicide: If the tyrant spurns the law, the just need to rebel against him. The tyrant is guilty of high treason[31] and of a violation of the cosmic order, and tyranny is his public crime. It is everyone's duty to oppose the tyrant since it would go against the community's interests to do otherwise. In this train of thought, we can discover early signs of a theory of government based on desacralized natural law as early as John of Salisbury. This tendency is also expressed in his adherence to Roman concepts of government, which forego the sacralization found in Greek concepts. Instead, Salisbury argues that society should emulate nature, since he considers it to be the best guide through life.[32]

## 3 The Concept of Justice in Luther's Theology of the Reformation

Although Augustine had already provided a soteriological foundation to the forensic theory of justification, and as much as he had drawn a focus on the grace-giving acts of God, his concept does not anticipate that of Martin Luther. Luther keeps to the forensic reading of the act of justification, yet he radically rejects any notion of merit through just actions. This insight follows from Luther's new understanding of God's justice (*iustitia dei*). Going beyond the forensic tradition, Luther essentially rediscovered the definition of justice found in the Old Testament. God's justice is to be understood as an expression of the self-determination of God as mercy. In this light, Luther discovered how his study of theology had misled him to accept a fallacious reading of God's justice. According to Luther, there is no special capacity that angles us to have God's grace bestowed upon us or allows us access to it. Neither our actions, our love, nor our will to be good can decide whether we will stand the test of God's judgement. His grace cannot be understood as a means that enables us to become good people. There can be no simple transformation of classical virtues into Christian virtues, which Aquinas had proposed as a viable manner in which we could make ourselves virtuous and capable of fulfilling the deeds of love required by God. God cannot create justice through us, but must grant it independently of us. He *is* and *remains* justice, and his reign of justice cannot be

30 *Policr.* III, 15 (= Keats-Rohan [Ed.], *CCCM 118*, 230).
31 Koch, Bettina, "Johannes von Salesbury und die Nazari-Ismaeliten unter Terrorismusverdacht," *Zeitschrift für Rechtsphilosophie* (2013), 18–38, here: 24.
32 *Policr.* VI, 21.

taken from or given back to him by us. It encompasses even our very being as subjects.

In this understanding of justice as a gift from God, under the doctrine of justification we are seen as just. The doctrine entails that God has declared us just, irrespective of whether or not we are just in the sense that we actively strive for justice. God's grace is therefore – this was Luther's insight into the justice of God – far greater than the gift of a variety of individual virtues could ever amount to be. In his eyes we are just, good, and beautiful. The truth of the phrase: "I have loved you with an everlasting love" (Jer 31,3) becomes visible in God's acts of justice. According to Luther, this can only be understood to mean that no gap, however small, is allowed to arise between God and his creation. Nothing is permitted that would obstruct divine closeness or diminish the esteem owed to God.

This notion is at once the characteristic hallmark and a delicate spot in the doctrine of justification in Reformation theology. A recurring critique claims that the concept of justification exposes Luther's position to the danger of lapsing into a mere ethics of disposition (*Gesinnungsethik*). When all focus is placed on God's grace, one may be rendered blind to the import of humanä actions. Without an awareness of actions and their consequences, one may fail to hold oneself accountable. "The Christian does rightly and leaves the results with the Lord,"[33] as Max Weber succinctly put his criticism, which is directed towards such a moral interpretation of the theory of justification. His critical reception correctly identifies the underlying understanding of God's justice. It taught us to separate the law from the Gospel and thus leaves the law opposed to the Gospel in a problematic fashion. The resulting – not only immoral but often also anti-Judaist – disposition, which has been exhibited by Protestant ethics in the aftermath of the Reformation, fundamentally overlooks the fact that Luther did not intend this opposition of law and Gospel to be understood as a separation. Rather, both are presented as two sides of the same coin.[34] Law and Gospel coincide. They represent different perspectives on the same situations and issues and thus belong together. The claim of justification is that we can only grasp the law through the Gospel. If we do not do so, the law alone convicts us of our sin by showing us that we cannot fulfil its requirements. Thus, Luther holds: Through works in adherence with the law, we cannot be justified. Those works express our moral motivation through actions aimed at performing in a good and meritorious fashion. The reference to the Gospel does not negate our morality. It only opposes the notion that we can become

33 Weber, Max, *Politics as a Vocation*, repr. from Soc. Essays, New York: OUP, 1946, 41.

34 Korsch, Dietrich, *Glaubensgewissheit und Selbstbewusstsein: Vier systematische Variationen über Gesetz und Evangelium*, Tübingen: Mohr, 1989.

good or just by the means of our own achievement; justice is and remains an attribute that belongs to God alone. For Luther, faith enables us to distinguish between the law, that which is justly required of us, and the Gospel, which grants us what we are promised and given unjustly, or rather: undeservedly. Luther follows Paul in his understanding of the law as a representation of God's just order.[35] According to Rom 7, the law is true, holy, and good. Luther can subscribe to this attribution through his understanding of order. The law is by no means obsolete, but we cannot perceive the truth contained in the law by our own limited means. We must be made capable of it – through the Gospel. Only through the Gospel, only through God's liberating power that affects us, can we perceive the law, i. e. that which is required of us in each situation, and become capable of acting in accordance with it. God's liberation is bestowed as a gift.

The central challenge of freedom, as modern theories of liberty have shown, has always been that freedom tends to overburden us as much as the law does. For freedom, in its nature, is infinite and indeterminate, while it lies in our nature that we are finite and definite. To live in a state of freedom is thus just as overburdening for humanity as perceiving God's justice. We realize this through the insight that God allows us into his justice, into its meaning for humans in their finite and definite existence. True freedom lies in the acceptance of our finitude through the insight that it is not as a constraint but rather the quality that integrates us into God's infinite enactment of justice. This is achieved by the incarnation of Jesus Christ and the freedom bestowed upon us and brought about by Christ's redemption of our sins. This liberation and redemption serve no other purpose than to allow us to perceive and accept our finitude. The incarnation of God establishes a faith that enables us to serve the just cause in and with Christ. This is the deep conviction underlying Luther's theory of justification. The central difficulty that faces the human quest for justice lies in the inability of our judgement to guarantee that our actions will help us to achieve our goals. Thus, the human commitment to goodness is a matter of having trust in God's justice, which is given to us through faith and allows us to act in a manner trusting that God will fulfil his plan and guide our ways. Supplemented by the requisite trust, Luther might assent to Leibniz's theory that this is the "best possible world". If it is God's world, then it is the best possible world, and God's justice is that which serves his creation and therefore us, for it was created for our sakes.

35 Luther wrote on the topic of law and gospel on many occasions, Cf. for example: Luther, Martin, *Kirchenpostille*, WA 10/1,155–161.206 f., Weimar: Hermann Böhlaus Nachfolger, 1910/1925; *Kleiner Galaterkommentar* (1519), WA 2, 466–530, Weimar: Hermann Böhlaus Nachfolger, 1884; *Dritte Disputation gegen die Antinomer*, WA 39/1,354—356.519 ff. Weimar: Hermann Böhlaus Nachfolger, 1926; but also, in the *Tischreden*, e.g. WA Tischr. 11, 1234.

What does this mean for justice in the sense of justification? Justification finds a trust in God's justice that is based on the insight into his justice that god allows us through his enactment of grace. This is achieved through the liberating effect granted by this insight, which is gained through the ability to trust him and to act in a manner motivated by this trust in his justice. This is how Luther's advice – *peccate fortiter* – to the disheartened Melanchthon (1497–1560) is to be understood: It is not meant as a frivolity but as the earnestly given advice that, "God is in government and governs all so perfectly." For theodicy, this means that we can happily leave such worries to God. Trust is all-encompassing. Even when encountering the calamities of the world, it transcends them – though only in a shadowed fashion – through the truth contained in God's creation; its beauty, which is, at times, hidden; God's goodness, which allows us to be convinced of his faithfulness. Only when we consider the world as God's space of justice, as his just order, can we glimpse and attain justice. This is expressed by the two concepts tied together by justice despite their tension: law and mercy. Both refer to a horizon, which is not only a necessary presupposition for our actions but for our self-perception as well. This self-perception is tied to justice as a requirement since it requires an insight into our guilt.

Herein lies the big deficit of early modern and modern concepts of justice: Their inherent neglect of an existential dimension of human existence – guilt. Admittedly, guilt is not fully ignored. Treaties, a central element of modern political thought, contain the notion that one party has legal and moral obligations to the other party. Yet this understanding of guilt is limited to the sense of conditional obligation in the form of dues. Yet it is not considered in its absolute sense, in which guilt is seen as a *debitum* that is a preestablished aspect of our existence. In this sense, guilt places claims on our actions even before we take on concrete obligations. This conceptualization of an overarching *debitum* that is brought about by the inherent finiteness and imperfection of human existence does not negate the crucial conceptual connection between accountability and human agency. Instead, it aptly situates this relationship within the context of the human condition. Only when we consider this fact can we appropriately speak about our obligations and accountabilities.

We do not effect our entrance into life nor (ideally) our death. Our life is at once something given to us and something that we owe. One must relate at once to one's own suchness (*Sosein*) and to be able to act in a manner that is in alignment with the given circumstances. This is not only true biologically, in the sense of the necessary adaptation to an ecological niche, nor is it solely a moral obligation. Instead, there is a sense of destiny. For humans are at once beings able to form a relationship with themselves, and they owe this self, which they form, not to themselves but to destiny. No human life is ever without such a destiny.

Every life comes to mind under this destiny in its longing, but even before that in its guilt and regret. This *debitum* defines humanity not only in its postlapsarian but also in its supralapsarian state. Already manifest in the createdness of humanity, it predates sin. The idea of the *debitum* expresses that we begin life by owing it to someone or something. This indebtedness is acknowledged through thankfulness. The possible omissions of such gratitude makes this debt visible in a striking manner. These omissions are always present below the surface of visible human action due to the nature of the *conditio humana* as one being destined to become and to follow a destiny. We *are* not – we *become*. Our life proceeds as a continuous formation, infused with a duty according to destiny. We are exposed to this duty, against which we are obliged to prevail, yet we continuously fail to meet its standards. Albert Camus' "Sisyphus"[36] expresses this failure to meet a seemingly unfounded duty. Yet this failure does not change the fact that we are called to the duty of following our destiny.

# 4 Theological Expressions of the Classical and Biblical Concepts of Justice in their Historical Development, Especially Regarding Inner-Christian, Interconfessional and Interreligious Distinctions

The concept of justice is not only present in various Christian theologies but is a constant found in many religions. This is especially true for the foundational concept that underlies religious concepts of justice: The justice of God. Even within the Christian tradition, there are not only remarkable differences between Western and Eastern Orthodox theologies but also within the different Protestant confessions. These distinctions are the result of the different receptions of the biblical and Greek as well as Roman traditions, which influenced the respective understandings of the idea of justice. It has already been noted[37] that the Greek understanding of justice was limited in comparison with the full meaning of the Hebrew concept. What is "just" in the Greek sense is guided by cosmology and ontology. It reflects the notion of an order, which brings about an impartiality towards the individual and a balanced distribution effected by the principle "to each their due".

**36** Camus, Albert, *The Myth of Sisyphus: And Other Essays*, New York: Vintage Books, 1961.
37 Ibid., 10.

The salient concept in this account is the goddess of justice, figuratively represented through the image of a blindfolded woman. She judges not according to an individual's esteem but in the service of a higher order that accounts for just allocations under differing individual circumstances. The idea of God's justice with its emphasis on a notion of justice carried by mercy, as it is predominantly conceived in the prophetic tradition in the Old Testament, is alien to this cosmological and ontological concept of justice.

The marginalization of the aspect of mercy in Western theology is further enhanced by the intrusion of the Latin understanding of justice, which is purely focused on a forensic reading. This understanding took on its defining shape in the concept of "*iustitia*" that was adopted by occidental Christianity. In philosophy and in Western theology the notion of justice and the justification of humanity is described in these forensic categories, not only in Medieval theology, but in the various kinds of protestant theology as well.

The direction of the biblical understanding of justice, which is guided by the horizon of mercy, holds true not only for the Lutheran but for the Reformed protestant denomination as well. In Reformed Christianity, Karl Barth (1886–1968), continuing in the vein of Calvin (1509–1564), prominently emphasized sanctification in order to underscore the fact that justification is more than a mere declaration that might leave the individual unchanged. Calvin described justification and sanctification, i.e. regeneration, as the double grace of God. Therefore, the sanctification in accord with justification is to be regarded as a calling.[38] God's justice shall be brought into the world. In consequence, Karl Barth defines justice[39] not only as a soteriological fact but also as the focal point of Christian life in the world – it denotes the existential struggle of all Christians.[40] Yet as much as Lutheran and Reformed Christians were divided in their understanding of sanctification – as concurring with or as a consequence of justification – they both understand justification in Christological and soteriological terms as a change taking place in the subject. Thus, both lines of thought bring an element of the forensic tradition to bear on the act of salvation. Through this transformation of the subject, the believers are regarded as just even though they perceive themselves as sinners. This radically new interpretation of justification as an imputative justice has been docu-

---

**38** Barth, Karl, *The Christian Life: Church Dogmatics IV,4. Lecture Fragments*, 1, §58, 4, e.g. 147, Grand Rapids, Mich.: Eerdmans Pub. Co., 1981.

**39** The translation of *Gerechtigkeit* (justice) as "righteousness" (German: *Rechtschaffenheit*) is a somewhat poor choice, as it might shift the focus onto the individual Christian and thus invite a misinterpretation along the lines of *Gesinnungsethik*.

**40** Cf. Barth, Karl, *CD IV, 4*, §78, esp. 1. and 4.

mented in the *Formula of Concord*[41] (54–57) and it is the joint foundation of faith for the Reformed and Lutheran churches. It is the truth of the gospel that God declares the sinner as just through the self-sacrifice of Christ.

While the forensic way of thinking about justification has thus proved essential for the concept of justice defined in the Reformation, Eastern theology regards this as an erroneous, or – put less bluntly – as a one-sided interpretation of God's justice. Even the term "God's justice" is controversial, since it is God himself who represents justice. God's justice is but a tautology. In Orthodox terms, one cannot talk about justice without talking about God and his creation. Thus, salvation is not understood as justification but as "deification" (*homoiousios theou*). We are transposed into God's area of power in order to more closely emulate God.[42] Against this backdrop it is quite remarkable that Orthodox theology does not require a dispute between the biblical and the Greek notions of justice, since the forensic tradition, provoked by Cicero's definition of "*iustitia*", had been fundamentally engaged by this dispute.

Orthodox theology teaches that the justice of God does not only have a juridical dimension but also a transformative one. It is determined by the concept of theosis. The term "theosis" is not found in the Bible. However, in the Gospel of John 10:34 it says: "I said, 'You are gods.'" Through theosis, humans partake in a mystical union with God and thus share in God's divine nature. In this context, justice has a specific Christological significance. Christ can fulfil his mission and return to the Father through his sacrifice on the cross and his resurrection.[43] The fulfilment of Christ's mission is referred to as the justice of Christ.[44] The deification of humans is achieved through a participation in divine grace and the ensuing communion with it through "imitation" or "participation."[45] This deification is

**41** BSLK 767–1100.

**42** Staniloae, Dumitru, *The Experience of God: Orthodox Dogmatic Theology*, vol. 2, *The World: Creation and Deification*, ed. and trans. Ioan Ionita, Brookline, Mass.: Holy Cross Orthodox Press, 2000, 205–15.

**43** Ionita, Viorel, "Rechtfertigung und Vergöttlichung des Menschen nach dem Apostel Johannes," in: Klaus Schwarz (ed.), *Rechtfertigung und Verherrlichung (Theosis) des Menschen durch Jesus Christus. Fifth bilateral theological dialogue between the Romanian Orthodox Church and the Evangelical Church in Germany from 18 to 27 May 1988 in Kirchberg Monastery*, ed. Klaus Schwarz, Missionshandlung Hermannsburg, 1995, 86.

**44** Ibid, 86.

**45** Ibid, 91. Orthodox theology emphasizes the cooperation between God and man in the healing process. Righteousness is not achieved through human endeavor alone, but through cooperation with divine grace. Man is called upon to actively participate in his own sanctification.

never the mystical merging of the soul into God but rather a participation in the communion with God in connection with the incarnate Son.[46]

The social dimension of justice is also considered in Orthodox theology. In the early and Byzantine periods, the Orthodox Church strongly advocated for social justice, as seen in the teachings of John Chrysostom (d. 407) and Basil the Great (330–379). The latter vehemently condemned any Christian withdrawal from worldly affairs and deemed any eschatology promoting escapism as heretical and dangerous.[47]

In the present discourse, the social dimension of justice continues to be emphasized.[48]

> The pursuit of social justice and civil equity – provision for the poor and shelter for the homeless, protection for the weak, welcome for the displaced, and assistance for the disabled – is not merely an ethos the Church recommends for the sake of a comfortable conscience, but is a necessary means of salvation, the indispensable path to union with God in Christ; and to fail in these responsibilities is to invite condemnation before the judgment seat of God (*Matthew* 25:41–45).[49]

In summary, it can be said that the understanding of justice in Orthodox theology is strongly influenced by the idea that God's justice is not only punitive but, above all, characterized by sanctification and love. In this context, humans are called to actively contribute to their own sanctification and to be in a loving relationship with God.

At any rate, justice becomes a guideline not first and foremost in the form of political and ethical thought in antiquity but primarily for theological thought. This holds not only for Christianity but for Judaism and for Islam as well.

In Judaism, justice is not only a measure of the exceptional figures of the Tora, like Cain, Abraham, and Job, but it can also be regarded as the very essence of the

---

**46** Kretschmar, Georg, "Rechtfertigung und Vergottung," in: Klaus Schwarz (ed.), *Rechtfertigung und Verherrlichung (Theosis) des Menschen durch Jesus Christus. Fifth bilateral theological dialogue between the Romanian Orthodox Church and the Evangelical Church in Germany from 18 to 27 May 1988 in Kirchberg Monastery*, ed. Klaus Schwarz, Missionshandlung Hermannsburg, 1995, 161.

**47** Rev. Dr. John Chryssavgis, "Toward A Social Ethos of the Orthodox Church, A New Document of the Ecumenical Patriarchate," published online: Greek Orthodox Archdiocese Blog, 29 May 2020, https://blogs.goarch.org/blog/-/blogs/toward-a-social-ethos-of-the-orthodox-church-a-new-document-of-the-ecumenical-patriarchate (accessed on 05.01.2024).

**48** Hart, David Bentley/Chryssavgis, John (eds.), *For the Life of the World: Toward a Social Ethos of the Orthodox Church*, Brookline (Mass.): Holy Cross Orthodox Press, 2020. https://www.goarch.org/social-ethos?fbclid=IwAR2RSPrgYRhPfAgT9p2iIQkd9wqtOYJ74Gtjnpmyq9xYdxshwqr6U1FJFiY (accessed on 05.01.2024.)

**49** Cf. Ibid. §33

Tora's message to humanity. This can be seen in Hab 2:4, a verse which the Rabbinic literature regards as representative for the expression of God's will in the Tora: "The Just shall live by his faith." Justice is the presence of *Shechina* through the life of the just on earth. Abraham serves as the paradigm for what it means to be a just person, since he unites the highest forms of fear of God and love in an exemplary fashion. The same has been shown to apply to the concept of justice. A loving trust, enabling one to serve in awe of the just judgement of God, is visible in his relentless trust. Job, on the other hand, emphasizes the importance of adhering to the just order as well as the fear and awe towards God in the face of the opacity of his order. Cain, on the contrary, represents a purely human manner of existence that is devoid of God's justice, which rebels against God and his just order and grace out of mistrust. While Job's rebellion leads to a confession, Cain's leads to fratricide.

For the biblical understanding of justice, it is apparent that justice can only present itself as justice when it considers the weak. Thus, it is an expression of God's justice that *tsedaḳa* is often equated with the giving of alms. The Jewish tradition even identified those aspects with the names of God, JHWH and *Elohim*. While JHWH was meant to refer to mercy and grace, *Elohim* was to stand for jurisdiction, the aspect of enforcement in God's mercy. The just, for whom creation was created, is the image of this dual reference of God's justice manifest in law and mercy. Where these two aspects are brought into play together and mutually interpreted though one another, the perfection of the just is realized. Rabbinic interpretations of the Talmud, as well as later forms of Medieval and patristic literature keep true to this interpretation of God's justice.

In the Old Testament, the relation between the horizontal and vertical dimensions of justice are crucial to its definition. Without a stable relationship between both aspects, no future is imaginable, since justice is relevant to the interpretation of life's meaning and how it should be led. It is connected to the notion of a cosmological dimension from primeval times until eternity, as an all-encompassing order of life. In Rabbinic Judaism, the Tora is regarded as an essential space for the discourse on the issues of justice for Israel. For Jewish thought, it is obvious that an individual's actions should be guided by God's justice so as to mirror it in one's own life through one's actions. Creation is an expression of God's mercy. It is even thought to encompass justice, since justice is the immanent relationship between God and his creation. The concept of a unity of justice and mercy in God is the central guideline.[50] The goal is *shalom*, uniting humanity, animal life, cosmos and God (cf. Isa 11:1–9).[51]

---

50 Janowski, "Die rettende Gerechtigkeit," (see note 15) 239–55.

In the Islamic understanding of justice, special emphasis is laid on social justice, and the Qurʾān explicitly highlights the duty to support of the weak, i.e. by giving alms (*zakāt*, for example Q 2:43; 9:60). A special emphasis is placed on the just actions of human beings. They should be "consistent with the ideal of the right measure and moderation."[52] In this context, the obligatory nature of rightful action is highlighted. A responsibility of which humanity is reminded by God (Q 60:90; 4:58; 6:152; 49:9). There is an obligation to act in a just manner towards others, especially towards parents, relatives, the poor, the weak, and the orphaned (Q 2:83). These issues of right and just human actions are further elaborated in the prophetic tradition (*sunna*).[53] It should not be overlooked that this insistence upon justice as a core value of Islam is more than a mere feature of current Islamic discourse. While notions on social and political justice are rooted in the Islamic tradition, they have become more explicitly addressed in early modern and current discourses.[54] In essence, we can identify a similarity between the Jewish and the Islamic understanding of divine law, with a mutual focus upon the agency of the individual.

Justice is a common thread to which all theologies and religions have something to contribute. It also spans across cultures. Not only in Western traditions – Greco-Roman antiquity, Judaism, Christianity and Islam – but Asian cultures as well, it is a philosophical and religious concept that has had a decisive influence on core outlooks and social structures. In Confucianism, for example, justice is defined as "the right state in the framework of the five natural social relations and inseparably linked to goodness"[55], while Hinduism focuses on an order appropriate to the doctrine of *Karma*. Buddhism, in turn, emphasizes the notion of order. Justice refers to being in accord with the eight ways to *Nirvana*, the measure of which is empathy.[56] Throughout this chapter, we have seen that there is a certain constant to be found in the religions interpreting justice along the lines of humanity relating itself and its social interactions to a higher order. The role of the individual is accentuated differently, as the example the combination of the notion of virtue with the idea of justice in Greek antiquity shows. In Confucianism, this pattern is visible in the composition furthering order, in Buddhism it is contained in

51 Ibid.

52 Krämer, Gudrun, "Justice and righteousness: VIII. Islam," in: Hans Dieter Betz et al. (eds.), *Religion in Past and Present*, vol. 7, Leiden: Brill, 2010, 115–16.

53 Cf. Ibid.

54 Cf. Ciftci, Sabri, *Section 3* of the article in this volume.

55 Yong-Bock Kim, Art. "Justice and righteousness: VII. Missiology," in: Hans Dieter Betz et al. (eds.), *Religion in Past and Present*, vol. 7, Leiden: Brill, 2010, 114–15.

56 Cf. Ibid.

empathy, while other religions like Hinduism emphasize the worldly order as such.

To conclude, we can note that the Eastern religions assign a central role to justice that is similar to its central function in Judaism, Christianity, and Islam. It remains an essential guideline for theological thought through the ages, from antiquity through the Middle Ages and the early modern period up to the present day, transcending confessional and perhaps even interreligious boundaries. Within the Christian tradition, the different accentuations between the poles of law and mercy can be understood as a result of the different receptions of Greek and Roman theories of justice. The notion of order, as it defines the Greek tradition as well as the Christian understanding of God, was a main point of debate in the Middle Ages and took the form of a reflection of the nature of justice as a property of God.[57] Nonetheless, we also find the notion of a just order with regard to society, taking up the concept of *suum cuique* from Plato and Ulpian. These developments, however, tended to obscure the biblical notion of justice, in which the accompanying notion of mercy is not only presented as a corrective but as the content of God's enactment of justice. The insight that the biblical reflections on God's justice all relate his law, ire, and judgement to his all-encompassing mercy was repressed. This one-sided approach to justice was detrimental because it stood in the way of the insight that the very being of JHWH is expressed as mercy, and that it represents the goal of creation and makes God's acts comprehensible as acts of justice towards his creation. In this, the biblical understanding of justice had a soteriological dimension beyond and prior to its forensic interpretation. The possibly ground-breaking implications of this theological interpretation of justice for current discussions in politics and society will be demonstrated in the following section.

# 5 The Definition of the Concept of Justice in the Early Modern Period

## 5.1 The Issue of Theodicy and the Justification of God in the Early Modern Period

The characteristic of the viewpoint developed in the early modern period lies in the shifting of the frame of reference. In accordance with the fundamental criti-

---

57 Cf. Krämer, Art. "Justice and righteousness" 115.

cism of metaphysics, a new focus is placed on understanding justice in human terms and the requirements necessary for human action to realize justice. The interplay between justice, peace, and creation is questioned, especially as to how the *shalom* intended in creation comes to bear in the just orders and the just relations between institutions that are supposed to govern the relationship between order and the individual in society. This connection is also evident in the Old Testament, particularly in Deuteronomic literature, where the theme of social justice is already present. Theologically, the issue of theodicy takes the stage in the early modern period,[58] that is the question of how ire and mercy, the judgement and the grace of God can be related in such a way as to prevent the discussion (and God) from being caught up in a hopeless dualism. Thus, theodicy is an issue for all three monotheistic religions since such a dualism would challenge their monotheistic beliefs.

Leibniz, of course, was not the first to discuss the issue of God's justice. Anteceded in exemplary fashion by the book of Job in the Bible and by Lactantius in Roman Antiquity, the early modern discussion represents a threatening force that sets free a fundamental questioning of God. The reason that such a doubt could take hold is that in the wake of the early modern period, humanity came to understand itself to be free and thus entitled to challenge everything in its quest for knowledge. Accordingly, humans now seek to develop their own criteria for a just order, grounded in nothing but their own understanding of the relationship between reason and freedom. These criteria now claim – and this is the big problem of modernity— an ultimate justification in purely human terms. Thus, they cannot be content having to trust God's enactment of justice, in fear and obedience, and cannot surmount its seeming contradiction to the human faculties of judgement and estimation. The flood of literature seriously devoted to this issue in its theological and its philosophical dimensions has not ceded since Leibniz posed and answered the question in a sophisticated and – for some – definitive theoretical argument. The various modern transformations of the issue into an "anthropodicy" or "cosmodicy" show that this issue cannot simply be set aside. After Nietzsche's (1844–1900) declaration of the death of God,[59] according to which humanity or nature are placed exclusively "in front of the court of philosophy,"[60] it

---

**58** Cf. Ibid.

**59** Cf. Nietzsche, Friedrich, "Die fröhliche Wissenschaft," in: Giorgio Colli/Mazzino Montinari (eds.), *Nietzsche Werke: Kritische Gesamtausgabe*, vol. 2, 11–335, Berlin/New York: De Gruyter, 1967, 159 (§ 125).

**60** Kant, Immanuel, "Über das Misslingen aller philosophischen Versuche in der Theodizee," in: Immanuel Kant, *Schriften zur Anthropologie, Geschichtsphilosophie, Politik und Pädagogik*, 103–24, here: 114 [=AA VIII, 263], Darmstadt: Wissenschaftliche Buchgesellschaft, 1964.

has become an endless enterprise. All those attempts which, in the fitting words of Elie Wiesel (1928–2016)[61], do not cease to accuse God and to demand an answer to the glaring injustice in the world, can only end up resorting to a recusal of a humanity on the grounds of its incapacity of answering the question of God's justice.

In spite of this consistent relevance of theodicy, the issue gained additional urgency through the singularly harrowing scenarios of horror, incomprehensible even in the face of eternity, of the mechanically executed and ideologically "legitimized" genocide that is represented by the holocaust. For it calls into question not merely the moral actions of the involved individuals or a single people but the morality of humanity itself. "This ought not to have happened,"[62] this exclamation voiced by Hannah Arendt (1906–1975) when faced with the inconceivable news of what happened in the concentration camps, is more than a futile ex post gesture, shuddering in the face of an unfathomable truth, rather it is a judgement on the *conditio humana*. What it means to be human is no longer temporal but has become divided into a before and after. Arendt's statement thus accounts for the qualitative change in what had previously been known as human nature and its connection to humankind's humanity in a normative sense in the occidental Greek, Jewish, and Christian culture – and not only in these contexts but around the world.

Theodicy after Auschwitz, as a program, must state the question of God's justice fundamentally anew, and it is questionable if it can be content with traditional answers, which themselves could never quite be regarded as proper answers to the question of God's justice. These might still be resorted to in some cases because there simply were no answers to be found beyond the theoretical analysis put forth by Leibniz. The issue of justice – of which theodicy is one aspect – cannot be solved by any account that fully meets the challenge contained in existence. This impossibility was apparent even before the 20th century. The problem was equally unsolvable when Leibniz asked the question after the earthquake of Lisbon. Even in the biblical account centered on Job, he decisively clung to the notion of God linking actions to just consequences and refused to become exasperated with God and his justice, but he never received a concrete answer to the question of the justness of his misfortune.

Theodicy must be framed within the horizon of the mercy and grace of God. Because God created the world for the benefit of humanity, he will preserve it. This is the insight at the heart of God's incarnation. It is the expression of the will of the

61 Wiesel, Elie, *Night*, New York: Hill & Wang, 1960.
62 Arendt, Hannah, *Essays in Understanding 1930–1954, Formation, Exile, and Totalitarianism*, ed. Jerome Kohn, New York: Schocken, 1994, 14.

creator through his just actions of mercy. Seen in this light, the piercing questions of humanity and the urge to denounce Job's situation are owed to our human perspective. They are owed to the finitude of our intellect and our freedom.

Martin Luther, in turn, also tied the issue of justice to the question of theodicy. He saw a clear connection between the issue of God's justice and the question of his relation to the world and to humanity. In his own life, he himself had experienced and understood justice anew. This insight challenged the forensic narrowing of justice to an issue of reward and punishment, of just allocation and judgement, as it was established in Medieval theology. Additionally, it opened his eyes to how injustice and calamity in the world must be judged. And like Job, Luther understands that it is to be regarded in the light of God's good creation. This perspective preserves the trust in God's faithfulness. Thus, his new discovery of justice, in turn, led Luther back to the insight of the Old Testament that the justice of God is encompassed by his mercy. Even more radically put, that the content of this justice, and God's very being, is mercy. God's enactment of justice is his enactment of mercy – that is the core of the doctrine of justification. As it was later put by Karl Barth, it is God's self-definition to turn towards humanity and to take pity on them. This mercy is what his justice consists of.

We cannot understand the ways of God, which he takes up in his enactment of justice. Yet this does not reduce us to irresponsible entities who are merely the objects of outer forces. We are not free to adopt a *laisser-faire*-attitude simply because it is God himself who creates justice. Justification obliges humans by offering a clear distinction between that which is in their power and is thus their responsibility, and which is not. These are the fruits of faith that stem from the insight into the just actions of God. They allow us to share in God's justice.

## 5.2 The Issue of (Rational) Law and Freedom

Theodicy is not the only concept that became central in the early modern period. The rights of humanity gained equal relevance, since the concept of justice informed by natural law was supplanted by one based upon rational law.

Despite later efforts made by Roman Catholic scholars and other early modern legal philosophers to ground human rights in natural law, the development of human rights is mostly seen as the consequence of the transformation from natural law to rational law. The concept of justice according to rational law is guided by the notion of freedom. It accounts for the freedom of humanity – of every individual. In this new framework, justice presupposes a balance between the rights of the individual in relation to society as a whole and between the immediate claims of the individuals toward one another. To successfully establish these conditions is to secure justice in the sense of liberty and reason in the name of humanity.

This development towards a concept of justice in human terms can be understood as a rediscovery or self-discovery of humanity. Because justice now takes on a central role in the foundation of humanity's relationship to the world and its relationship with itself, justice and with it the law must be redefined to reflect the idea of being rooted in the exercise of human freedom. Justice is now tied to freedom in the societal context. For this reason, the order of the state and the law is tied to the need for a coordination of the freedom at the base of society through assent. Against the backdrop of free self-determination, human justice is now required to take on a contractual form. The social contract theories proposed by Thomas Hobbes (1588–1679), John Locke (1632–1704), Jean-Jacques Rousseau (1712–1778), Immanuel Kant (1724–1804), and John Rawls (1921–2002) are expressions of the theoretical realization of these notions.[63] They not only show that the previously accepted metaphysical assumptions that presupposed God and nature, have changed but that they have been abandoned.

This moves freedom to the center of our attention. Freedom gains fundamental importance: It grounds all possible claims in the qualities that are considered to be constituting elements of being human. This implies consequences for the concept of reason. Reason can no longer be the *logos* presiding over the *cosmos*, but reason appears as freedom in its self-defining power as autonomy. The consequences of this shift cannot be overlooked, as is especially obvious with respect to the concept of justice. It no longer represents a notion of the *summum bonum*, already guaranteeing an order in and of itself and thus able to serve as a fixed measure. The exposed state of freedom requires relating justice to freedom in a constitutive fashion.

The mutual intersection of freedom and justice leads to a further differentiation of the concept of justice itself. It now appears in the triad of liberty, equality, and solidarity. Not by accident, these are the goods through which humans assume to be able to let their humanity and dignity take shape. The French Revolution leads to a movement which can legitimize its revolutionary power on the basis of its claiming the ability to establish a lawful order on a new foundation. Claims are no longer made by making reference to an order of nature or an order of God but by pointing to a freedom that supports this order only as long as it assents to it.

---

**63** Cf. Locke, John, *The Second treatise of government: an essay concerning the true original, extent and end of civil government and a letter concerning toleration*, Oxford: Blackwell, 1956; Hobbes, Thomas, *Leviathan*, New York: Liberal Arts Press, 1958; Rousseau, Jean-Jacques, *The social contract*, trans. Maurice Cranston, London: Penguin Books, 1968; Kant, Immanuel, *The Metaphysics of Morals*, trans. Mary J. Gregor, Cambridge: Cambridge University Press, 1996.

In this sense, freedom gains an exceptional place once assigned to justice – it comes to embody a categorical horizon. All individual thought and action, as well as all societal right and order, must submit to it and adhere to its guidance.

As a result of this constellation, freedom is realized through a self-restriction in the name of the freedom of others. The binding force of this principle is thought to rest in the fact that everyone can assent to it. In the early modern period, there is an interplay between freedom and justice, where one explains the other and vice versa. Freedom requires justice to restrict itself so that it can be preserved. Self-restriction as a result of freedom is the hallmark of the early modern contractual interpretation of justice. The justice of a social order and of interpersonal circumstances is measured by the extent to which they enable the freedom of one to coexist with the freedom of another. Therefore, justice entails the reign of freedom for all humans without distinction. Justice itself is the measure of freedom and vice versa.

This is expressed clearly in all theories of a social contract. Kant can be seen to express this notion of the self-restriction of freedom most clearly, in as much as he defines the very concept of autonomy as self-restriction. Self-restriction is the pinnacle of self-determination and of humanity expressing its freedom:

> Right, therefore, comprehends the whole of the conditions under which the voluntary actions of any one Person can be harmonized in reality with the voluntary actions of every other Person, according to a universal Law of Freedom.[64]

### 5.2.1 Justice in Modernity: Further Distinctions, Pluralization, and the Concept of Human Rights

While the concept of order, in cosmology or natural law, could provide guidance in antiquity, the abandonment of assumption of an ontological whole in modernity has meant that many questions have become ever harder to address. Contrary to the presumption that justice can only become manifest in the interpersonal realm, as it was suggested by the emphasis on freedom in the early modern period, it must now be recognized that this line of thinking resorted to the notion of justice as a horizon. The contractual model is indeed nothing more than a human refiguring of order through representation, which is meant to take on the place of the order of cosmology or natural law. The contract is represented as a horizontally liquefied form of a previously vertical order, now focused on rational law. This col-

64 Kant, Immanuel, *The Philosophy of Law: An Exposition of the Fundamental Principles of Jurisprudence as the Science of Right*, trans. William Hastie, Edinburgh: T&T Clark, 1887, 45.

lapse in the vertical dimension – which is always present in forms of order – into the horizontal renders a legitimation of the ensuing order more difficult yet not impossible. The main change, however, is that the concept of justice is now focused upon that between the equal partners of the contractual model. Contracts are entered between equals or, at least, between those able to agree on the grounds of mutually benefiting from each other's interests. This bestows an emancipatory guise onto the early modern contractual understanding of the concept of justice. It is expressed in the concept of freedom. The concepts of justice can be regarded as being guided by liberalism or the relationship can be regarded in reverse with the early modern emphasis on the subject as a reasonable entity bringing liberalism about. Accordingly, hierarchies are rejected, and the very pathos of the revolutions, declaring liberty, equality, and solidarity to be the measure of justice, appears. The liquefaction of the classical notion of a horizon of cosmological order, as it was preserved in natural law, into the triad of equality, liberty, and solidarity, is a consistent implementation of the abolition of hierarchies and a recognition of the dignity of humanity.

These developments in the notion of freedom lead to translation of human rights in their various concretions into civic rights meant to guarantee political freedom, as well as rights to cultural participation and other claims. These are expressions of a modern understanding of justice based on the concrete freedom of the individual. Justice as the idea of societal cohabitation based on the freedoms of the individual becomes the political and ethical foundation of the democratic states in modernity. This shows that the state itself is not only led by a positivist understanding of the law, but that the law itself rests upon a moral foundation – the preservation of freedom. This touches upon fundamental issues of the law, especially with regard to its interplay with justice. Despite the importance of the authority of the law, especially the enforcement of the law, we must consider that Western concepts of the law, especially of constitutional law in democratic states, contain pre-legal principles. The notion of human rights thus introduces a two-stage understanding of the law: Existing frameworks of positive law and their pre-legal foundations are to be understood separately.

An untethering of the law from justice, as it can easily occur in the course of the development of positive law, must therefore be opposed. This concerns core aspects of early modern theories of justice, as is reflected in the institutions and processes of democracy and the separation of powers that seek to prevent an usurpation of the law through power.[65] Since the state is no longer solely committed to

65 Cf. Dreier, Ralf, Art. "Justice and Righteousness: V. Law," in: Hans Dieter Betz et al. (eds.), *Religion in Past and Present*, vol. 7, Leiden: Brill, 2010, 113–14; Kriele, Martin, *Recht und praktische Ver-*

the preservation of power but also to the preservation of freedom and its expression in the moral practice of the community and the individual, the notion of justice becomes an irreplaceable guiding force for the orientation of societal and political life in alignment with its understanding of the *humanum*. The common good is now seen to take form through the justice of various realms of society. Their rightful order must therefore – especially as it pertains to justice – continually be examined with regard to its capability to preserve freedom and a structural order guided by liberal law.

## 5.3 Challenges in Defining Justice in the (Early) Modern Period

This shift to the contractual model in the (early) modern period brings about an implicit change in the interpretation of justice itself. This shift can be considered a departure from the Biblical and Jewish understanding of law.

For the Greek as well as the Hebrew understanding of justice, a two-fold meaning is constitutive: first, the understanding of justice as an order, as it is present in the terminology of *dike* and of *tsadiḳ*. And second, justice as a moral concept of δικαιοσύνη (*dikaiosýne*), and even stronger in the Hebrew connotations of attention, as they are expressed in the aspect of mercy in *tsedaḳa*.

The early modern outlook attempts to preserve both aspects, yet they are no longer seen as two poles but rather combined in a tense relationship. This enhances the dynamic of the understanding of justice since it becomes harder to neglect one pole for the other. Yet the danger also arises that one might turn a blind eye to both aspects, namely when both are combined in a manner that contains no more than the rudiments of both. The search for a qualified concept of justice, therefore, must preserve both aspects of justice. The communal aspect of the shared order on the one hand, and the attention to the individual and the benefaction towards those in need, on the other hand.

Thus, the issue of the legitimization of justice in modernity arises with regard to the very aspect at the center of the biblical account, namely mercy. For the universal order cannot only be regarded as it relates to the free individuals capable of contributing to it but to those unable to directly contribute as well, be they marginalized, foreign, or poor. The notion of justice and liberty, conceived as a joint con-

*nunft*, Göttingen: Vandenhoeck und Ruprecht, 1979, Habermas, Jürgen, *Faktizität und Geltung: Beiträge zur Diskurstheorie des Rechts und des demokratischen Rechtsstaats*, Frankfurt am Main: Suhrkamp, 1992; Dreier, Ralf (ed.), *Gustav Radbruch – Rechtsphilosophie: Studienausgabe*, Heidelberg: Müller, 2003.

cept in early modern and modern societies, could arguably be realized to some degree within the national borders of a well-established order. The very limitations represented by national borders allow for some balance to be struck between freedom and law. These balancing acts become challenging, or even impossible, in constellations no longer defined by national borders, where justice is meant to be enacted on a globalized and international level. Modernity thus complicates the balancing of law and justice through the very distinction of the domains of the state and society that arose to address this challenge because these ideals are now not only relevant within but rather between states and on a global level. The resulting social and economic interactions not only complicate the issues of just and free forms of order, but they also threaten to torpedo any such order guided by justice and freedom. A libertarian international economic order threatens to become dissolved by the very principles of freedom underlying it that is commonly represented by the concept of the "invisible hand". This is not only a return to the proverbial law of the jungle and a widening of the gap between rich and poor on a global scale, but also an attack on the very core of the concept of justice, namely the provision of peace and prosperity. The capacity to secure peace is itself tied to a working economic order, yet freedom and justice for the individuals contributing to and engaged in it are of equal relevance to its promotion. If the rights guaranteeing political participation and the rightful entitlements of the individual are hollowed out by a reduction of justice to a merely formal notion of liberty, the result will void both justice and liberty. A decisive factor in modernity is the pluralization, not only of cultural lifestyles, but of fundamental attitudes as they are represented in religion or *Weltanschauung*. Any kind of argumentative exposition of justice and freedom, of human dignity and human rights, cannot ignore its task to express the very plurality of notions on what they should contain.

We are faced with the fundamental problem of early modern contractual concepts of justice. We must abandon the attempts undertaken in antiquity and the Middle Ages, as well as in the early modern period that aimed to identify a foundational principle. Early modern contract theories essentially presuppose a kind of freedom, according to which individuals come together in a rational fashion and enter into contracts in such a way as to minimize collisions between the freedom of one and that of another. Contractual theories thus regard order itself as posited. Formal obligations to God and others may be included in the social contract concept (as in Hobbes), but the foundation *etsi deus non daretur* puts these notions into positional perspective. Justice as adherence to the law coincides with the notions in the Hebrew Bible and in Greek antiquity, in the sense of a transposition of some laws of nature into natural law. Yet the very impossibility of naming a foundation of legitimization – because of the prohibitive costs of metaphysical foundations – bestows it with an irrevocably positive nature.

This exposition of the problems in (early) modern thought is not intended as a plea to return to premodern categories of order. It is simply aimed at calling our attention to the fact that even (or especially) modernity cannot forgo these categories of legitimization if it seeks to resist a hollowing-out of its understanding of the law. The presupposition is that freedom is indeed a focal point of the early modern notion of justice. This would imply that justice and freedom can serve to mutually interpret each other. Thus, justice can be accessed criteriologically. This would mean that circumstances can and should be questioned with regard to their alignment with the claims of justice since we are to answer for them in freedom. One could object to this as an exaltation of freedom, as it was regarded in the theological interpretation of the fall. This is a common objection to early modern freedom, yet it is incorrect. The core difference is that the early modern perspective questions authority but not the very nature of irrevocable freedom.

Freedom as self-determination has its place in Christianity. As freedom itself represents a horizon – in the very context of justice – it gains an aura of its own, thus surpassing merely technical definitions of liberty. Considering the incorporation of freedom into justice and justice into freedom, the phase quoted by Kant and direly pertinent in the $20^{th}$ century gains its weight: *fiat iustitia et pereat mundus*. The phrase expresses the goal of preserving freedom in justice. Despite the self-determination of humanity, human action should not merely strive for the preservation of one's own life or of life in and of itself – nor for its negation. The shared goal of freedom and justice must always lie in the very preservation of freedom. For, as Kant continues, without justice, life has no meaning.[66] Justice and freedom keep returning to their inherited framework, from which they received their authority, and which can now only find expression in this focal point of self-determination.

Only how can this be argued? It is precisely in this area that the modernity of Luther's theory of justification can prove its relevance beyond early modern and modern thought, offering a way forward in the face of their aporetical challenges. But are those challenges still present in current discourse, or how have they been transformed?

66 Cf. Kant, *The Metaphysics of Morals*, 114 [= AA VI,332].

# 6 Current Debates on Justice in the Discourse of Theology and Social Ethics

## 6.1 The Discourse in Theology

Current reflections on justice are motivated by social ethics and social politics but also by new perspectives in Western theology, leading to two strands of discourse, one guided by church theology and one focused on social ethics and politics. The motivation behind this focus on justice in theology stems from new research in the field of the New Testament focused on the *corpus paulinum* and on its understanding of justice and justification. It is discussed under the label of the so-called "New Perspective on Paul".[67] This research has been focused on a re-evaluation of Paul beyond Martin Luther's reading of Paul as the theologian of justification, which had remained essential for protestant theology. Contrary to the established reading, current research on the New Testament[68] produced a new evaluation of Paul's view on faith and justice. Luther's interpretation had been shaped by his reading of the *Epistle to the Romans.* This new perspective on Paul is aimed primarily employed to find a critique of the forensic reading of justification that guided Luther.[69] Justice in Paul is, as this reading claims, not focused on an equalization or the repayment of an individual debt, but it must be read as a term referring to the community as a whole. That which serves the community of Christians and can function as proof of the community's being in a communion with Christ is to be regarded as just. This understanding of community mirrors the Christian way of life and its understanding of justice.

Christian life is led in community, in *ecclesia* and in service.[70] Justice according to Paul is, therefore, presented as the dominion of God within the Christian community. It is the realm of God's justice in Jesus Christ. This realm is marked by its clear distinction from the world of everyday life. People find themselves in holy communion as a remembrance of Jesus Christ, the risen Lord. Baptism and Communion are the signs of community, which as such serve to separate

---

67 Schröter, Jens, "'The new perspective on Paul': Eine Anfrage an die lutherische Paulusdeutung?," *Lutherjahrbuch* 80 (2013), 142—58.

68 Sanders, Ed P., *Paul*, Oxford: Oxford University Press, 1991.

69 Ibid.

70 Cf. Wolter, Michael, "Das neutestamentliche Christentum und sein Gottesdienst," in: Elisabeth Gräb-Schmidt/Reiner Preul (eds.), *Marburger Jahrbuch Theologie XXX, Gottesdienst und Kirche,* Leipzig: EVA, 20.

the community from the world around it. Different modifications show the degrees to which this relationship of one sphere to another, of *ecclesia* to the world of everyday life, is one of mutual permeability. All the shapes this communion takes, however, contain a tension brought about by the contrast between the Christian community and the world, of service and everyday life. This tension defines everyone's life in different ways and is never fully resolved.

For the understanding of justice resulting from this reading it will therefore prove crucial how this tension can be dealt with as a way of life and how we can understand the justice of God in such a way as to be guided by its light. We need to address how Paul's understanding of justice as a justice of community, with its consequences for the individual on the level of faith as well as action, can become effective. Furthermore, we need to address how this reading of justice in community can be expressed in a way that does not abandon Luther's development of a soteriological reading of justice, of law and mercy in a forensic framework. We need to show how Luther's reading of justice can be related to and informed by the discovery of Paul's notion of justice as community and how we can translate the importance of community for justice into protestant theology.

Besides this strand of Christian theology emphasizing the role of the inner-Christian community and that of service in its definition of justice, an additional new strand line of thought has emerged. Liberation theology[71] is motivated by social injustices and thus focuses on issues of social politics and ethics. In accordance with the tensions described above, this qualifies everyday life as the stage where Christian justice must prevail. This is not meant to marginalize service in favor of mere everyday life. It merely demands an interchange between the freedom of the Gospel and the realization of its liberating effects on the world. Despite this pairing, the tension between service and everyday life is maintained here and understood to result from the eschatological nature of the kingdom of God. Yet the emphasis rests on the well-founded perspective of the faithful as the justified. As the adherents of Early Christianity had experienced God's justice in their shared existence, the communion of liberation theology sees itself called out to relate this experience of liberation and to represent it to the outside world.

Both lines are extremes of how Christian faith can be lived and preached, and its inherent tension is strained to its maximum. This results in open controversies that cannot be easily reconciled. With Karl Barth, one could argue that it is appropriate for justice as a polemical concept in the Christian struggle to refer to its so-

71 As an introductory survey of the topic, I refer to Gutierrez, Gustavo, "The Task and Content of Liberation Theology," in: Christopher Rowland (ed.), *The Cambridge Companion to Liberation Theology*, Cambridge: Cambridge University Press, 2007, 19–38.

teriological roots. For it is the event of Christ through which God's justice has been expressed to humanity once and for all. The incarnation of God can only indicate that this justice is not meant to remain on its own but rather to flow over and benefit others. This does not render philosophical definitions of justice obsolete. They retain their function, be it as an integral virtue or as a single virtue, rather they are specified and qualified. And, again, this occurs due to the transgression of justice as a merely reciprocal relationship, as has been shown with regard to the biblical and philosophical tradition: God creates a righteous order against any claim of rights by humanity. This is expressed in God's actions through the ages. God's acts in Christ even expose remnants of such a focus on purely human claims in otherwise thoroughly Christian viewpoints, sharpening the asymmetry in a Christological fashion. This sharpened asymmetrical reading shall now be taken into account in its current relevance for the discourse on justice as a concept of order.

When focusing on Christology, the following four aspects can be extrapolated from the Christian understanding of justice: 1. the notion of creation, 2. the notion of covenant, 3. the theology of the cross, and 4. the eschatological aspect.

Considering creation, justice is informed by the creation of humanity in the image of God and by the dignity expressed therein. According to the covenant, community and the ability to participate in it become a human right. In this sense, the concept of covenant pre-empts the notion of solidarity as an embeddedness of the individual in a community for the benefit of the whole as well as for the best possible flourishing of the individual. This attention to the individual also implies a general attention towards the weak and the worst-off because of the communion with God in the covenant. In the New Testament, this is expressed in Christ's attention to those in need, mirroring God's attention to his chosen people in the Old Testament. This definition of election as a sign of justice shows that it does not limit election to the big, strong, and beautiful, but rather the small, low, weak, and ugly.

This special attention given to the weak as an expression of the preservation of community through solidarity culminates in the cross and leads to a possible foundation of justice following from the theology of the cross, which itself lays the foundation for all solidarity. As such, it is the justification of all those incapables of helping themselves, of all those who are either not yet capable of or can no longer make a contribution to the community. The "outcasts" and "outlaws" of global society, together with any society's disenfranchised and those in need of help, become recognized as God's creations They are addressed by his attention in an aim towards a more expansive communion. "Whatever you did for one of the least of these brothers and sisters of mine, you did for me." (Matt 25:40) The cross separates those who are presumed to be strong and in the right from those who are seemingly weak, who are awarded what they are due by God and are taken up into his community. This leads to a reversion of hierarchies: "But many who are first will be last, and many who are last will be first." (Matt 19:30)

God's justice appears in this reversion of hierarchies aimed at the constitution of a well-ordered state of human community, founded in God's desire for communion with all of humanity. It has not yet appeared, but all of us partake in it through the hope for it. This eschatological foundation of justice does not point towards a utopian or transcendent justice, but it obliges humanity to anchor their eschatological existence in this hope and to live a life in aid of its realization.

We can summarize biblical thought about justice in both Testaments: The asymmetry in the notion of justice must be respected. Mercy encompasses justice and bestows it with an inner purpose. Humans are always at the receiving end of this relationship and indebted to God in a way that is infinite and cannot be equalized. This leads to even more fundamental challenges to the early modern development in the idea of justice, which had employed freedom as its basis and its goal.

## 6.2 The Discourse of Justice – Social Ethics and Philosophy

The early modern developments in the concept of justice point to a problem present in modern thought: The subject as a *fundamentum inconcussum* cannot deliver a legitimation of law in the sense of justice, and thus cannot serve to guarantee the possibility of freedom. The aporetical consequences that arise from the shift away from a framework of natural law and of ontological cosmology in favor of the subject and its freedom as a sole base for any legitimization can be seen in the lack of a clear foundation. Theories rooted in contractual or processual thought are pushed to their limits. Freedom must be given a foundation and such a foundational notion was arrived at in the idea of the process of consensus.

Even before the clear deficits in justice resulting from a lack of consideration given to the claims of others sharing our globe and those of future generations became apparent during the process of globalization, these problems were already visible. They had been foreshadowed in the very development of this understanding of justice, as the struggles for freedom and justice emerged through revolutions in civil and international rights. These problems can only be solved if justice is not only understood in a formal sense, referring to contractual or processual theory. Instead, its foundation must be developed from a definition rooted in the very idea of the *humanum* itself. This cannot be achieved by merely pointing to the subject as a criteria in itself in the way a libertarian might. Such a basis can only hold and serve as a legitimization if the subjects experience this definition as a material[72] insight into their nature. Their destiny as a *humanum* must be presented to them. Only such material knowledge can provide the individual with his destiny and guiding vision.

Throughout antiquity and the Middle Ages, the existence of such a material destiny as a teleological or theological definition of humanity was taken for granted. Because it could be developed from a metaphysical foundation, the idea of destiny was capable of providing a sound argument defining justice. In the wake of the early modern period's new modes of critique, this became both metaphysically and theologically untenable. The philosophical standards of criticism, as well as those of nihilism, positivism, and constructivism following in its tracks, prohibited any such attempt, at least in any direct fashion. The attempts to address the issue of ultimate foundations and their circularity were described repeatedly by Karl-Otto Apel as well as Jürgen Habermas.[73] They have clearly demonstrated the contradictory nature of any attempt to circumvent the problem of an ultimate foundation by employing pragmatistic, processual ways of legitimizing justice and freedom. The most remarkable attempts in this field are those seeking to establish a new foundation for practical philosophy that can address this problematic loss of the capacity to answer questions of legitimacy. This is attempted by a re-definition of justice as "fairness" by John Rawls[74], or by an emphasis on "spheres of justice" and communal values by Michael Walzer.[75]

All these attempts at a new foundation show that when freedom is employed as a foundational concept, it must be accompanied by justice as its corrective. This holds not only for material guidelines for actions but also for the definition of the individual's relationship to itself and the world. All action is interaction and, therefore, dependent on consideration for other individuals – this insight is threatened by an exclusive emphasis on freedom. Justice expresses a sensibility on which freedom depends as a transcendent enabling space. This horizon is needed for freedom to encompass an interest in mutual equality as an expression of universal freedom.

In the present, an age critical of metaphysics, and after the abolition of any question of ultimate foundations, these issues converge in the conditions of the *humanum:* How can we keep to an idea of freedom and justice that confronts humans with their very humanity, and thus defining the *humanum?* As we have just seen,

72 Material is meant in the sense of a concrete and individual destiny, with a definite content, which is only clearly accessible to the individual.

73 Habermas, *Faktizität und Geltung: Beiträge zur Diskurstheorie des Rechts und des demokratischen Rechtsstaats.*

74 Rawls, John, *A Theory of Justice,* Cambridge: Belknap Press of Harvard University, 1971.

75 Walzer, Michael, *Spheres of Justice,* Oxford: Robertson 1983.

this challenge cannot simply be glossed over by introducing a new philosophical concept with seemingly convincing arguments. That would amount to nothing more than a philosophical sleight of hand. Rather, the very roots of the issue must be identified in modernity itself and addressed directly. Current challenges to the concept of justice must now be considered in this light.

# 7 Justice as Freedom in the Global Age?

## 7.1 New Challenges Posed by Globalization and the Doubts Regarding the Foundations of the Early Modern Concept of Justice

Globalization sets out the task of designing just environments not only for societies across the globe but for future generations as well. This perspective is the result of a rather recent shift within ethics and in the understanding of justice. International economic relationships, global digitalization, and the ensuing fall of national barriers have led to individual states and cultures more broadly moving closer together, at least regarding spatial and temporal distances. Yet from this entanglement and interconnectedness created by the globalized economy a new challenge has arisen, namely that of regulating emerging global relationships. The hope of many liberal economists that an economy left to its own devices would result in self-regulation has not come to fruition. This error in judgement is evidenced not only by the immense ecological issues that have resulted from unbounded economic growth and drawn our attention to ecological concerns and the question of the efficacy of resource use. It is further evidenced by the fact that the supposedly self-regulating nature of economic transactions has proven itself to be an untenable thesis. The idea of an "invisible hand" as put forth by Adam Smith has not proved itself applicable to economic relationships on a global scale. Governed by the strongest players, which gain advantages in the economic sphere, these relationships are often of little or no benefit to their less powerful counterparts in the long run. The widening of the gap between rich and poor and the exclusion of a large portion of global society from partaking in the wealth thus created have shown this hope to be an illusion. Without a political governing body studying the current state of affairs and drawing the according economic conclusions, there can be no improvement of these inequitable relationships – we are faced with a challenge for the implementation of justice.

The interrelation of globalization and justice has, thus, become an especially relevant topic, creating a high demand for contributors from ethics and philosophy, ethics commissions, and economic forums. The search for binding guidelines rooted in early modern and modern concepts of ethics is underway, which could, ideally, be implemented into economic and political actions. Yet the aporetical challenges faced by such theories when applied to current affairs are strikingly apparent. This holds for all concepts of justice based on contracts and informed by an early modern understanding of the "subject". It is equally true for economic drafts suggesting that a social market economy can be served as a means by which a more just social order can be attained through state guidelines. In the first case, arguments are made based on a concept of equality which is not present in the world today and which will not exist for future generations. In the second case, we must acknowledge that the dismantling of national barriers within the global context complicates the introduction of economic regulations in the pursuit of true justice. The efforts of the World Economic Forum in Davos and the International Panel of Climate Change (IPCC) are evidence of these difficulties. Despite their proclaimed goals, they are producing more and more of the unjust consequences we have been witnessing for years. On the one hand, we are faced with the flows of refugees fleeing economic exclusion, political persecution, and the effects of climate change. These numbers will only increase in the coming years. On the other hand, we are faced with growing nationalism in the wealthy nations that are attempting to shield themselves against these developments and the ensuing dangers, thus seeking to conjure up an ideal community closed off from the rest of the world.

These developments in global society expose the aporetical foundations of early modern theories of a justice built upon contracts and reciprocity. Such theories cannot adequately account for those who have been excluded from the contract and thus from the order of reciprocal exchange who are left incapable of economic or political contribution. Current political and philosophical theories of justice attempt to further develop the contractual model of the early modern period by implementing a clear concept of justice into the constitutive freedom of the subject. John Rawls' attempt at such a renewed contractual theory of justice has become influential not only for later theories of justice but for practical philosophy as such. His theory of justice challenged a fundamental development within the philosophical grounding of ethics. He gave renewed attention to questions of normative validity and the binding force of norms that had been abandoned in the rise of analytical philosophy. This reappearance proves that ethical problems cannot be solved on a merely analytical and discursive level. The theories of Rawls,

Habermas, and (later) Höffe[76], can be understood as a response to these issues from the perspective of action. Yet all the theorists named above are themselves tied up in the modern inability to establish well-founded and binding norms without presupposing some foundation for them to draw on. While Rawls account draws on a combination of utilitarianism and Kantian principles, Habermas' search for a fully inclusive consensus further develops contractual theory by basing it in discourse.[77] Despite the difference in their sources, both ensuing standpoints are located within the bounds of rationalism. Rawls and Habermas share a common approach in the sense that both seek to stay the course of early modern philosophy. This limitation engenders strict, self-sufficient argumentation devoid of all metaphysical or religious borrowings.

The current shift in the perception of the state of society has given rise to a challenge Rawl's fundamental assumptions that ask how the basic forms of human conduct relate to his core principles of equality and difference.[78] Who can take on the role of moving every single agent to recognize their obligations? What can inspire them to adhere to those principles meant to pave the way for justice? Utilitarian calculations, expose the original deficit contained in the early modern paradigm: The abandonment of the issue of motivation and its relevance for the definition of freedom itself. For Kant, the freedom of the subject is the freedom of reason, which itself is not mere rationality but gains its very contours in an individual's respect for the moral law. This understanding locates reason within an irretrievable and unsurpassable horizon, within which all the assumptions necessary to assign humanity its destiny are contained. Utilitarianism cannot simply be added to this understanding of reason, since it precludes any consideration of utility by calling the consideration that can be given to the consequences of an action into question. This is not expressive of a disinterest in the issues of responsibility but rather reflective of an insight into the limited and definite nature of human freedom. This limit to the extent of what can be realized through human responsibility must be recognized if it is not to descend into despotism or totalitarianism.

The inadequacies faced by contractual theories built on equality and just exchange with respect to current issues have been most decisively criticized by proponents of communitarian concepts of justice, like those of Michael Walzer and

---

76 Höffe, Otfried, *Political Justice: Foundations for a Critical Philosophy of Law and the State*, Hoboken: Wiley, 2010.

77 Habermas, Jürgen, *Between Facts and Norms: Contributions to a Discourse Theory of Law and Democracy*, Cambridge MA: MIT Press, 1996, 26–41.

78 Cf. Rawls, *A Theory of Justice*.

Stanley Hauerwas.[79] The proponents of communitarianism have pointed to the fact that libertarian concepts not only disfavor the poor but also the community as a whole. They also neglect the institutional dimension that lies at the very heart of justice – its function in the establishment of order. Communitarianism has renewed our awareness for the central function held by the horizon that justice is placed in and has thus brought about a new appreciation for the traditional concepts of justice rooted in clear frameworks. In addition, contractual theory is criticized regarding the freedom of the individual. The exclusion of those individuals who cannot enter into any contract or those who don't have the means to contest existing contracts appears to void individuals the very freedom and dignity that theories of justice should defend. Beyond the mere equality of a justice understood as fairness, a communitarian concept of justice must provide access to the means of freedom to those unable to advocate for themselves. Those who cannot join into discourse because they have been marginalized to exist at the fringes of (global) society are thus given new attention.

Martha Nussbaum and Amartya Sen developed a philosophical framework to address questions of inclusion, participation, and capability.[80] They identify the search for a means to provide chances of participation to all people through access to contractual relationships as an essential issue of the present. This engendered a third generation of human rights, namely the rights of participation. They are aimed at providing access to education, equal starting conditions, and equal chances for self-development. The effort to further participation is focused on providing chances that are yet being denied to individuals and whole swathes of global society and will continue to be inaccessible to them if we do not actively take on the task of enabling them to partake in the societal sphere and the whole of global economics. The "Capability Approach"[81] proposed by Nussbaum and Sen thus highlights the neglected, painful issues that were already present in the conception of early modern contractual theories. Now we are faced with the effects of the narrow early modern paradigm on the concept of justice.

The narrowing not only in the understanding of justice but also of freedom resulted from the interplay between the theory of freedom and the role that subjectivity took on in delivering the very normative horizon that rendered action an object of pure subjective discretion. Contractual theories developed a notion of justice based solely on subjective freedom. Prior to this development, justice had always contained the just order of institutions and the aspect of interpersonal justice

**79** Cf. Walzer, *Spheres of Justice*; Hauerwas, Stanley, *After Christendom? How the Church is to Behave if Freedom, Justice, and a Christian Nation are Bad Ideas*, Nashville: Abingdon Press, 1991.
**80** Cf. Nussbaum, "Human Capabilities, Female Human Beings,"; Sen, "Capability and Well-Being,".
**81** Cf. Ibid.

as well as the relational aspect of relating institutions to individuals in a just manner. This is the organic center of the issue of justice, setting the tracks for all further developments of justice. Contractual theories of justice reflect the loss of horizon effected by this shift in an especially marked fashion. The reduction of justice to freedom as all but one of its established aspects leads to a dead end regarding the issues of its implementation and disregard the responsibility that we are faced with when dealing with justice, even and especially in terms of our freedom. Evidently, some aporias result from the neglect of the importance the grounding in a horizon has for the concept of justice. This lack of a horizon points to the fact that the very existence of excluded individuals forces the issue of justice to be addressed anew. There have always been marginalized individuals, but now we can see that their exclusion not only calls the just allocation or participation into question but the very nature of justice itself. Equality and exchange, as they appear in the Aristotelean model of justice, are not sufficient to realize justice as the "good." The inclusion of the excluded can only be conceptualized if justice itself is understood as an overarching horizon. It is also a prerequisite for any material definitions of justice as mercy, grace, and love along the lines of the Old and New Testament. In these traditions, the excluded do not only irritate societal order but dissolve the very concept of justice.

In this sense, Nussbaum's "justice as capability" with its emphasis on the conditions of entry for the excluded – in contrast to Rawls' theory – shows that justice must be more than a mere preservation of rules or a functioning order. It shows that justice must include a sense of belonging for each individual human being, especially for the excluded. Merely alleviating the economic and political burdens faced by the most disadvantaged – an approach Rawls attempts through a form of a "safety marker" – does not fully address this demand. Although Rawls's theory improves the material conditions of the marginalized, critics argue that it leaves those who cannot effectively participate socially or politically in a state of exclusion. In their view, these individuals are not fully recognized as free subjects within his framework.

Nussbaum, on the other hand, perceives this very challenge as a task for all theories of justice. A notion of justice that is tied to freedom in keeping with the early modern tradition must provide for a way to enjoy this freedom. A merely caritative attempt to provide care to the less fortunate is not sufficient – justice can only be implemented when they are enabled to participate in the design of the rules of the societal game, as well as the makeup of the game itself.

Theories like those of Nussbaum's mark a return to the concepts of justice developed in the Hebrew and Christian traditions that grounded justice in the preemptive acts of God towards humanity. God's mercy and acts of grace allow for humanity to participate in his justice, enabling them to participate in justice freely and responsibly. This raises the question of how foundation and motivation are conceived in Nussbaum's theory. According to biblical thought, both were visibly and truly located in God's continuous creation as the overarching order in God's justice as mercy. The modern viewpoint that rejects any resort to metaphysical or theological horizons is left with nothing but freedom. Freedom itself, as we have seen, can only be conceived as an effective motivating and obligating force through a tangible definition that relates it to the destiny of humanity.

## 7.2 Early Modern Theories of Freedom and their Consequences for Understanding Justice

Presently, we are faced with the need for a new starting point in the quest for a basis for justice. No recourse to a cosmological order, to natural law, or a model of contracts entered by individuals can deliver such a basis – we need a model accounting for difference and strangeness; a constitutive other to our own concepts, convictions, and needs. This new model must be intrinsically capable of plurality. It, therefore, must take up a different insight, which is also part of modernity and make it part of its foundation: Not only the universal can serve as a guide for knowledge. Knowledge can also, and in some cases only, be attained through the insight individuals gain by means of their particularity.

Kant's theory of liberty can be further developed along the lines of self-limitation, that is, that freedom must limit itself for the sake of justice. Kant's theory of freedom as self-limitation is not only motivated by tactical calculations. Rather, this self-limitation serves to define an idea of freedom that is grounded in the trace of justice preserved in freedom. The idea itself refers to the transcendent, to the three *transcendentalia.* In other words, freedom is only fully expressed (also in the sense of its early modern definition) if it can be projected onto the true, good, and beautiful. The truth is mirrored in the concept of ideal order, an idea accessible to free individuals. The good appears through freedom and this insight is accessible to all, thus resulting in valid freedom for all. The beautiful appears in the harmony brought about by self-limitation. This harmony is not that of the societies of antiquity, which allowed for slavery, and it is not that of the Middle Ages, which prescribed a sacred hierarchical order that divided society into the three estates. Both models established a common sphere at the cost of the individual. The harmony of beauty can occur in the way represented in the biblical view on justice as mercy, which is guided by the notion of requesting freedom for the individual.

The direction brought about by early modern and modern thought can be summarized very simply: Justice appears through freedom. Freedom appears as the innermost core of justice. It is the truth. "The truth will set you free" (John

8:32), this is the goal of creation in the spirit of *shalom.* For only freedom prevents the moments of resentment, which are an expression of lack of freedom in a pure form. Additionally, we can now identify exactly how freedom and justice are connected. Not only in early modern but in Christian and in Hebrew thought before it, freedom *to* adhere to the law became the material definition of justice. Freedom is in interplay with justice. Thus, Luther's discovery of God's justice must at once be understood as the discovery of the freedom of the Christian. Thus, Luther only arrives at his rediscovery of sin as a perversion of freedom and the relationship to God. Kierkegaard's (1813–1855) saying, "The good is freedom"[82] takes up this notion. What was lost in paradise is not freedom itself (for it is, in the words of Kafka (1883–1924)[83], indestructible). Only the knowledge of and the trust in freedom were lost. This lack of trust arose because the justice of God was not perceived. The conditions of justice as God's justice dictate that freedom and justice must go together. One cannot be truly realized without the other. For justice without freedom always leads to oppression and to a loss of harmony which itself cannot exist in opposition to but only in accordance with the freedom of the individual.

Thus, justice and freedom depend on each other and equally represent the true, good, and beautiful. This is the deep truth contained in Kant's concept of self-limiting freedom. Freedom truly exists insofar as it can be the good for all and can thus bring about harmony, which is the beautiful for the individual. Looking back from Kant, the development in early modernity should not be regarded as a deterioration, neither with regard to faith, rationality, nor justice. Instead, it should be regarded as a necessary step in the chain of the definitions of justice. It represents a development and a distinction already prefigured in creation, in God's justice, towards justice for the individual, meaning each individual human being as God has made them into his mirror-image. Humanity is, thus, endowed with dignity and freedom not by its independence or self-sufficiency, but by God's very justice.

This brings us back to the philosophical relevance of the theory of justification: In the light of the early modern notion of justice, we can now grasp its significance more fully.

---

82 Kierkegaard, Søren, *The Concept of Anxiety: A Simple Psychologically Orienting Deliberation on the Dogmatic Issue of Hereditary Sin,* ed. and trans. Reidar Thomte, Princton: Princton University Press, 1980, 111.

83 Schillemeit, Jost (ed.), *Franz Kafka – Schriften, Tagebücher, Briefe: Kritische Ausgabe, Nachgelassene Schriften und Fragmente II,* Frankfurt am Main: Fischer Verlag 1992, 129.

## 7.3 The Actuality of the Theory of Justification in the Perspective of (Early) Modern Definitions of Justice

One initial misconception must be avoided: We shall point to the theory of justice and justification in Reformation theology as a means to overcome the aporias in early modern theories of justice. However, this position does not entail a functionalist reduction of theology that leaves it to operate as nothing but a "God of the gaps", providing the foundations philosophy cannot deliver. Rather, reformation helps us to identify and address an issue we have already encountered: If the concept of justice is to be applicable to human actions, the normative commitments motivating them must be tied back to the contents that shape our experience. For justice to become enacted, we must be able to present justice as at once realizable and clearly defined. Only when it is framed in such a manner that can motivate and oblige us, by providing us with a horizon of certainty for our actions, can it become a viable motivating impetus. Material convictions enable the individual to secure statements of a fundamentally binding quality for the free subject as such and can thus guide provide guidance. The very content of justice is itself an expression of the intersection of justice and freedom. Through the infusion of content provided by justice, principles can be proved to be binding and thus the individual can exercise its freedom in a manner that is normatively legitimate. The content of the individual's faith in God's creation of justice through salvation provides such a guiding force since it expresses that legitimizing claim as a truth for the individual.

This becomes most strikingly apparent in the way that justice, truth, and freedom come to coincide in conviction. Conviction implies not only a formal but a materially defined freedom. In other words: Religious experience is a *shibboleth* of the preservation of justice. Without encounters with justice through experience, which divulge freedom as our own destiny through justice, justice cannot persevere. This was Luther's experience, and it is valid beyond confessional or religiously defined contexts. It is an anthropological definition that transcends the differences between cultures, based upon the notion that individuals attain convictions about their own origin, self, and world, as well as a sense of obligation towards their own destinies, through such experiences.

This tangible definition points us towards the consequences of this constellation of arguments as they relate to modernity. Their relevance lies in the withdrawn nature of the contingent encounters at the heart of justice. First, it emphasizes the material component of justice, through which the concrete individual becomes the focal point of legitimization. This is an innovation compared to the "universal" subject of modernity. The shift from the subject to the individual is, however, a concretion of the essence of the notion of the subject, that is of its irreplaceable judgement as a guarantee for a normativity able to oblige other subjects. The modes of legitimization that are required must now refer to material definitions, represented by the individual. But how can the individual demand its universal or common claim? The decisive factor can be gained from the theory of justification. It refers to passivity as a foundation for all of our activity, as emphasized by the notion of justice as a gift and includes an acknowledgement of freedom as a gift as well. It refers to an unattainable and presupposed horizon, yet it also states that this unattainability must respect the withdrawal of the object of any definition as soon as it is to be gained by the means of rational argument. This is also represented in the event of justification, which is based upon an encounter, an experience, an event. In its very nature as a contingency that we are confronted with passively, we find a structure of foundational thought capable of going beyond early modern positivity – which will always become entangled in the struggle for ultimate definitions – without giving up rationality. Even more so, it does not surrender a horizon and has to be limited to the argumentative level of positivity. This is the surplus of Luther's concept compared to that of the early modern period.

As an inevitable consequence, this will mean having to account for a kind of transcendence, the rational expression of which is expressed in the notion of contingency. Only transcendence can point to a material order and preserve a sense of meaning amidst the experience of contingency. It remained part of the theory in early modernity, as well as with Kant, that guidance could ultimately be informed by a notion of justice in the sense of higher justice, in the sense of justice as an idea of reason, or as a guarantee in the sense of God. In modernity, this higher purpose and higher obligation is preserved in the notion of solidarity. It was not by accident that it was taken up into the triad of the Enlightenment as a complement to freedom and equality. And yet it was also no accident that this concept found no expression in contractual theories, besides the recent attempts by Rawls to include it through a principle of difference. Yet it can no longer be ignored in the context of the new issues of inclusion in a globalized world.

The effect of experienced justification is twofold. On the one hand, it refers to the fact that convictions cannot be disposed of, since they are what immediately affects individuals. A foundation in religion or *Weltanschauung* is thus part of the *conditio humana.* The question of whether or not someone regards themselves as being affected by religion is thus about as relevant as the question of whether or not they regard themselves as free.[84] For to be free does not only imply being ca-

84 Dalferth, Ingolf, "Justification by Faith as Key to Understanding Human Existence," *The Japan Mission Journal* 71 (2017), 33–43.

pable of indefinite expansion, but rather it entails defining oneself according to criteria through actions and decisions. Such criteria can only be derived from states of affairs which appear convincing to us. This cannot be equated to fundamentalism or dogmatism and neither does it imply proclamations of universality or attempts at ultimate definitions. The point of access does not lie in the application of universal concepts but in experience, which is contingent and beyond disposition. Contingency refers to the level of experience on the plane of conceptual arguments, but it is not intended as a blind contingency. On the religious level, it refers to a material insight into justice – into that which is true and valid. This new layer appears as the layer of thoughts and actions; their performance also reveals their claim to guidance, or their descendance from an option of guidance. This very performance itself exposes a causal mechanism, resulting from such convictions as they demand respect through their material content. It is the effect of God's justice, showing in the performed free acts and thoughts.

Through this special constellation, which becomes apparent when considering the individual in the sphere of human freedom of conscience, a new structure of argument takes shape. It can preserve truth and universality without having to cozy up to or be knuckled under by any given universal thus avoiding the risk of normativity dissolving into an arbitrary mentality of "anything goes."[85] Freedom can only be regarded as such if it appears within the individual and its irreplaceably contingent insight into its own destiny. This configuration is expressed in religious convictions, allowing for an insight into the conscience as a place for the truth and clarity of one's own orientation in life that manifests itself in encounters with others.

The insight into the conditions of the genesis of perception demands for perception itself to be laid out in a processual fashion and for it to account for the individual self in exchange with others, in dialogic intercommunication. The concept of perception thus gains concretion. The individuals in their very individuality form the basis for arguments, and they demand plurality within and through themselves. For plurality is required as a result of the insight into fundamental equality as it suggests itself to the individual. In turn, it pushes towards allowing the genesis of the conditions of one's own insight for the benefit of all others, i. e. all other individuals. Plurality, thus, stems from the same roots as individuality. It

85 Cf. Feyerabend, Paul, *Wider den Methodenzwang*, Frankfurt am Main: Suhrkamp, 1976. Regarding the broader theme, an astonishing parallel to the kabalistic interpretation of the justice of God can be drawn, since it acknowledges action and interaction which not only symbolically represents God's justice in the real world, but can influence it as well. The idea that basically sees God as talking to himself, brings this tradition closer to Lutheran theology, albeit in other form of directness.

is just as necessary, since it corresponds to the possibility that individuals gather as many individuals as possible.

This concept of an insight that is to be provided for all, which opens up individual and thus plural perspectives for action, becomes visible in the modern understanding of justice, as it was expressed in human rights, especially in the right of the freedom of religion. As an especially meaningful example, this right to the freedom of religion reveals the foundation of freedom as one which cannot be regarded as a principle or a force inherent to universal reason. Freedom of religion shows that human rights are tied to the conscience of the individual in an irreplaceable fashion. As such, freedom of religion is the space within modernity where the foundation of freedom and justice can come into focus.

In this remarkable, secular detour on the understanding of fundamental law and through the moral foundations of freedom and justice as its preliminaries, we can discover an insight which had been reached before modern or even early modern times, in the theology of the Reformation. It is the challenge to an undisputed authority of reason as it was developed by philosophy at the outset of humanity. The unbroken relevancy of Martin Luther's reformatory insights lies in the fact that any knowledge of justice beyond faith must remain empty, since it lacks any kind of foundation. Without such a foundation, justice becomes untenable. Luther realized his life-long misconceptions about the nature of knowledge as he discovered the specific nature of justice. As a result, Luther held that a faith-based definition of justice must coincide with a criticism of reason. This insight guided his perspective on humanity in the *Disputatio de homine.*[86] In a sense, we encounter a criticism of reason *avant la lettre* in this work, which can point beyond it to the dialectic of modernity.

## 8 Conclusion: The Consequences of Theological Notions of Justice for Modernity and the Present

We can conclude: The early modern theories of justice placed freedom at their center to function as a basis for legitimization. Such legitimization cannot be attained in a purely empirical manner. Foundations require a categorical status. In a post-metaphysical world, such a status cannot be attained without recourse to a tran-

**86** Luther, Martin, *Disputatio de homine*, WA 39/1, 175–7, Weimar: Hermann Böhlaus Nachfolger, 1926.

scendent foundation capable of guiding all thought and action. Therefore, the question of the foundation of freedom remains essential. As a basis of legitimacy, such freedom must presuppose the broad understanding of reason that still held for Kant. He secured a quasi-metaphysical base for the binding force of reason through its definition, which preserved the ideas of freedom and justice as entities desired by reason. In this manner, the claim of universality could be made by reason itself. While set within clear limits with regard to theoretical knowledge, reason's capacity for judgement in the practical realm could legitimize human agency. God, freedom, and immortality represent the former *transcendentalia* of the good, true, and beautiful within Kant's concept of reason. All three are retained in a compact representation of the idea of justice. Even though he could only recognize its role in a heuristic sense, his notion of the awe that the moral law imposes on us allowed him to be certain that the maxim of justice could vouch for the existence of normativity – not only for those alive in his day but for all reasonable beings within the universal *cosmos*. Yet modernity challenged these certainties, not least by questioning reason itself as a base for validity. The dialectic of enlightenment, as well as the discovery of Freud that the "ego" is not "the master within its own house,"[87] demanded a re-evaluation of the place and state of reason, which meant taking its role as one power relative to other and its finitude seriously. This ties back to the role of justice as a horizon for ethics.

The issues of foundation, which modernity had attempted to address through contract theories, finally arrived at aporetical contradictions. These problems become apparent in the fields trying to address issues of the application of justice, which continue to challenge modern theories to re-evaluate their foundations. This problem affects the continuing concretion of processual theories of justice, as that of John Rawls or in the more concretely defined model of the capability approach by Martha Nussbaum.[88] They have shown: A global society is just only if it is equitable for all participants. This means that every person must be offered the best possible conditions under which to live according to their destiny. A just order is that which corresponds to the destiny of humanity, as understood in terms of its inherent dignity – a creature called to freedom, justice, and truth. This just order includes fundamental human rights, which secure the destiny inherent to the human condition as well as the conditions necessary to the individual's development. Most important among these conditions are the right to food, health serv-

87 Freud, Sigmund, "A Difficulty in the Path of Psycho-Analysis," in: *The Standard Edition of the Complete Psychological Works of Sigmund Freud*, XVII 1917–1919, London: Hogarth, 1978, 135–44.
88 Cf. Nussbaum, "Human Capabilities, Female Human Beings."

ices, and education as well as the more abstract idea that resources and opportunities must be distributed in accordance with the principle of equal opportunity.

Justice is the measure that must be levied against governing injustices. Humanity cannot distance itself from this task. First, this will require ecological justice. Secondly, a way for just allocations to be made by taking globalization and the historical debt of colonial exploitation into account, when action is taken to bring about circumstances that are more just while removing economic obstacles hindering a liberal world economy. Justice is thus expressed through the orderliness of society, of local and global economies, and in equitable human cohabitation around the globe.

The theological concept of justice contains an ethical dimension. Since justice is tied to the existence of a good order, the truth of the theological concept of justice becomes apparent when considering the issues of international justice. Justice can only be regarded as such if it is accompanied by mercy (in the sense of the Old Testament) and love (in the sense of the New Testament). This definition of justice is relevant for ethics. Justice, when understood as justification, carries a hermeneutical dimension that can serve as a guiding force for action. Considering the theological aspect of justification, which involves a reflection on the alien righteousness bestowed upon us, justice entails an obligation that impacts the way we understand its social aspects and claims. The hermeneutical achievement contained in a theologically inspired understanding of justice is what Christians can contribute to the discourse on social justice. For justification emphasizes the motivation and the binding force of actions by focusing upon the individual as a material concretion of justice and the experience of faith as a revelation of freedom. As such a revelatory experience, it refers to a transcendent horizon.

Justification, thus, cannot encourage deferring action and entrusting God with bringing about justice on earth. It necessitates a participation in the truth of God's justice as mercy. This truth of God's justice as mercy is visible in the attention given to the individual within a universal framework. The horizon of justice depicts the asymmetry between the universal and the individual, between God and humanity, between justice and freedom. Justification is the result of the insight into this relationship.

Freedom, as the effect of justice, becomes an expression of justification. Justification thus manifests itself as a modern conceptual horizon of justice. As opposed to an ultimate definition, which could not be attained without a definite horizon, it allows for a binding force tying together the individual concretions by acting as a frame and as a horizon. This is a guarantee of understanding the right to community in solidarity. It integrates the individual in his freedom and dignity. The experience of justification is an exposition of justice compatible with modernity since the individual defines the subject (as opposed to the universal). Thus, it allows for definitions only as a plausible relation of experiences but not as ultimate definitions. This experience shows: The world cannot become well-ordered solely by the means of a concept of justice understood in the sense of reciprocity. By its very nature, what is owed and deserved cannot be adequately provided and thus paid off. Joseph Pieper expressed this in the following way:

> Communal life will necessarily become inhuman if man's dues to man are determined by pure calculation. That the just man gives to another what is not due to him is particularly important since injustice is the prevailing condition in our world. Because men must do without things that are due to them (since others are withholding them unjustly); since human need and want persist even though no specific person fails to fulfill his obligation, and even though no binding obligation can be construed for anyone; for these very reasons it is not 'just and right' for the just man to restrict himself to rendering only what is strictly due.[89]

In a Christian understanding – and here, the direction of Thomas Aquinas is still valid – justice is not ours to produce, but it is given by God. However, we are meant to correspond to this gift through our freedom by which we answer to God's justice. Justice without mercy is cruelty. As Aquinas put it: "Seeking to preserve freedom and unity amongst humanity by mere justice is insufficient if love does not take root amongst them. Love is the fulfilment of the law."[90]

Biblical justice knows that it can only achieve its goals by going beyond oneself and towards the other. It knows that it cannot do so solely through its own strength but only according to the destiny of humanity that is set out towards dignity in the image of God. In this description and this demand, the concept of justice returns to its Hebrew meaning of *tsedaḳa:* In a biblical understanding, justice and mercy as well as justice and love are but two sides of the same coin. The recourse to the understanding of justice delivered by biblical Christology, which can be explained by the valuable *effect* it can have in the form of its nurturing community and the common good, can become a fruitful impulse for discussions on the issue of the foundation of justice in modernity. These effects tie the Christian accentuation of justice back to the cosmological accounts of Greek antiquity, allowing for it and the Platonic virtues to come together. Integrating justice into the representation of the good, true, and beautiful in the cardinal virtues of courage, prudence, and temperance.

As God lets his sun rise above all people, so the sun of justice does not allow us to give up on the search for a mutual understanding and consistent communica-

**89** Pieper, Josef, "Justice," in: Josef Pieper (ed.), *The Four Cardinal Virtues*, trans. Lawrence E. Lynch, New York: Harcourt, Brace & World, 1965, 43–113.
**90** Aquinas, Thomas, *Summa contra Gentiles*, ed. Anton C. Pegis, Notre Dame: University of Notre Dame Press, 1975, 3, 130.

tion between peoples, cultures, and religions. Even though this is a human task, it is still tied to a justice which can itself only be realized in the *eschaton:* When the works of creation can be recognized as "beautiful" and the work of God in humanity can be recognized as "good."

## Bibliography


Aquinas, Thomas, *The Summa Theologiae of Saint Thomas Aquinas: Latin-English Edition*, vol. 6: *Secunda Secundae, Q. 57–140*, Scotts Valley, CA: NovAntiqua, 2013.

Aquinas, Thomas, *Summa contra Gentiles*, ed. Anton C. Pegis, Notre Dame: University of Notre Dame Press, 1975.

Anselm of Canterbury, *Cur Deus homo: Why God became man*, trans. Edward Prout, London: Religious Tract Society, 1886.

Arendt, Hannah, *Essays in Understanding 1930–1954, Formation, Exile, and Totalitarianism*, ed. Jerome Kohn, New York: Schocken, 1994.

Aristotle, *Nicomachean Ethics*, ed. C.D.C. Reeve, Indianapolis [et al.]: Hackett, 2014.

Assmann, Jan, *Ma'at: Gerechtigkeit und Unsterblichkeit im Alten Ägypten*, Munich: Fink, $^{2}$1995.

Barth, Karl, *The Christian Life: Church Dogmatics IV,4. Lecture Fragments*, Grand Rapids, Mich.: Eerdmans Pub. Co., 1981.

Chryssavgis, Rev. Dr. John, "Toward A Social Ethos of the Orthodox Church, A New Document of the Ecumenical Patriarchate," published online: *Greek Orthodox Archdiocese Blog*, 29 May 2020, https://blogs.goarch.org/blog/-/blogs/toward-a-social-ethos-of-the-orthodox-church-a-new-document-of-the-ecumenical-patriarchate (accessed on 05.01.2024).

Camus, Albert, *The Myth of Sisyphus: And Other Essays*, New York: Vintage Books, 1961.

Dalferth, Ingolf, "Justification by Faith as Key to Understanding Human Existence," *The Japan Mission Journal* 71 (2017), 33–43.

Dreier, Ralf (ed.), *Gustav Radbruch – Rechtsphilosophie: Studienausgabe*, Heidelberg: Müller, 2003.

Dreier, Ralf, "Justice and Righteousness: V. Law," in: Hans Dieter Betz et al. (eds.), *Religion in Past and Present*, vol. 7, Leiden: Brill, 2010, 113–4.

Flaig, Egon, "Ehre gegen Gerechtigkeit: Adelsethos und Gemeinschaftsdenken in Hellas," in: Jan Assmann (ed.), *Gerechtigkeit: Richten und Retten in der abendländischen Tradition und ihren altorientalischen Ursprüngen*, Munich: Fink, 1998, 97–140.

Feyerabend, Paul, *Wider den Methodenzwang*, Frankfurt am Main: Suhrkamp, 1976.

Freud, Sigmund, "A Difficulty in the Path of Psycho-Analysis," in: *The Standard Edition of the Complete Psychological Works of Sigmund Freud*, XVII 1917–1919, London: Hogarth, 1955.

Gadamer, Hans-Georg, "Platons Denken in Utopien," *Gymnasium* 90 (1983) 434–55.

Gutierrez, Gustavo, "The Task and Content of Liberation Theology," in: Christopher Rowland (ed.), *The Cambridge Companion to Liberation Theology*, Cambridge: Cambridge University Press, 2007, 19–38.

Habermas, Jürgen, *Faktizität und Geltung: Beiträge zur Diskurstheorie des Rechts und des demokratischen Rechtsstaats*, Frankfurt am Main: Suhrkamp, 1992.

Habermas, Jürgen, *Between Facts and Norms: Contributions to a Discourse Theory of Law and Democracy*, Cambridge MA: MIT Press, 1996.

Hart, David Bentley/Chryssavgis, John (eds.), *For the Life of the World: Toward a Social Ethos of the Orthodox Church*, Brookline (Mass.): Holy Cross Orthodox Press, 2020. https://www.goarch.org/social-ethos?fbclid=IwAR2RSPrgYRhPfAgT9p2iIQkd9wqtOYJ74Gtjnpmyq9xYdxshwqr6U1FJFiY (accessed on 05.01.2024.)

Hauerwas, Stanley, *After Christendom? How the Church is to Behave if Freedom, Justice, and a Christian Nation are Bad Ideas*, Nashville: Abingdon Press, 1991.

Hobbes, Thomas, *Leviathan*, New York: Liberal Arts Press, 1958.

Holzleithner, Elisabeth, *Gerechtigkeit*, Vienna: Facultas, 2009.

Höffe, Otfried, *Political Justice: Foundations for a Critical Philosophy of Law and the State*, Hoboken: Wiley, 2010.

Huber, Wolfgang, *Gerechtigkeit und Recht: Grundlinien christlicher Rechtsethik*, Gütersloh: Gütersloher Verlagshaus, 2006.

Janowski, Bernd, "Die Tat kehrt zum Täter zurück: Offene Fragen im Umreis des 'Tun-Ergehen-Zusammenhangs'," *ZThK* 91 (1994), 247–271.

Janowski, Bernd, "Die rettende Gerechtigkeit: Zum Gerechtigkeitsdiskurs in den Psalmen, " in: Bernhard Greiner et al. (eds.), *Recht und Literatur: Interdisziplinäre Bezüge*, 239–255, Heidelberg: Winter 2010.

Ioanita, Viorel, "Rechtfertigung und Vergöttlichung des Menschen nach dem Apostel Johannes," in: Klaus Schwarz (ed.), *Rechtfertigung und Verherrlichung (Theosis) des Menschen durch Jesus Christus, Fifth bilateral theological dialogue between the Romanian Orthodox Church and the Evangelical Church in Germany from 18 to 27 May 1988 in Kirchberg Monastery*, Missionshandlung Hermannsburg, 1995.

Kant, Immanuel, *The Philosophy of Law: An Exposition of the Fundamental Principles of Jurisprudence as the Science of Right*, trans. William Hastie, Edinburgh: T&T Clark, 1887.

Kant, Immanuel, "Über das Misslingen aller philosophischen Versuche in der Theodizee," in: Immanuel Kant, *Schriften zur Anthropologie, Geschichtsphilosophie, Politik und Pädagogik*, 103–24, Darmstadt: Wissenschaftliche Buchgesellschaft, 1964.

Kant, Immanuel, *The Metaphysics of Morals*, trans. Mary J. Gregor, Cambridge: Cambridge University Press, 1996.

Khadduri, Majid, *The Islamic Conception of Justice*, Baltimore: Johns Hopkins University Press, 1984.

Kierkegaard, Søren, *The Concept of Anxiety: A Simple Psychologically Orienting Deliberation on the Dogmatic Issue of Hereditary Sin*, ed. and trans. Reidar Thomte, Princton: Princton University Press, 1980.

Koch, Bettina, "Johannes von Salesbury und die Nazari-Ismaeliten unter Terrorismusverdacht," *Zeitschrift für Rechtsphilosophie* (2013), 18–38.

Koch, Klaus, *Sdq im Alten Testament: Eine traditionsgeschichtliche Untersuchung*, Heidelberg: university publication, 1953

Korsch, Dietrich, *Glaubensgewissheit und Selbstbewusstsein: Vier systematische Variationen über Gesetz und Evangelium*, Tübingen: Mohr, 1989.

Kretschmar, Georg, "Rechtfertigung und Vergottung," in: Klaus Schwarz (ed.), *Rechtfertigung und Verherrlichung (Theosis) des Menschen durch Jesus Christus. Fifth bilateral theological dialogue between the Romanian Orthodox Church and the Evangelical Church in Germany from 18 to 27 May 1988 in Kirchberg Monastery*, Missionshandlung Hermannsburg, 1995.

Krämer, Gudrun, "Justice and righteousness: VIII. Islam," in: Hans Dieter Betz et al. (eds.), *Religion in Past and Present*, vol. 7, Leiden: Brill, 2010, 115–116.

Kriele, Martin, *Recht und praktische Vernunft*, Göttingen: Vandenhoeck und Ruprecht, 1979.

Locke, John, *The Second treatise of government: an essay concerning the true original, extent and end of civil government and a letter concerning toleration*, Oxford: Blackwell, 1956.
Luther, Martin, *Kirchenpostille*, WA 10/1, 155 – 161.206 f., Weimar: Hermann Böhlaus Nachfolger, 1910/1925.
Luther, Martin, *Kleiner Galaterkommentar* (1519), WA 2, 466 – 530, Weimar: Hermann Böhlaus Nachfolger, 1884.
Luther, Martin, *Dritte Disputation gegen die Antinomer*, WA 39/1,354 – 356.519 ff., Weimar: Hermann Böhlaus Nachfolger, 1926
Luther, Martin, *Tischreden*, WA TR 2, No.1234, 3 – 4, Weimar: Hermann Böhlaus Nachfolger, 1913.
Luther, Martin, *Disputatio de homine*, WA 39/1, 175 – 177, Weimar: Hermann Böhlaus Nachfolger, 1926.
Nietzsche, Friedrich, "Die fröhliche Wissenschaft," in: Giorgio Colli/Mazzino Montinari (eds.), *Nietzsche Werke: Kritische Gesamtausgabe*, vol. 2, 11 – 335, Berlin/New York: De Gruyter, 1967.
Nussbaum, Martha, "Human Capabilities, Female Human Beings," in: Martha Nussbaum/Jonathan Glover (eds.), *Women, Culture, and Development: A Study of Human Capabilities*, Oxford: Clarendon Press, 1995, 6 – 104.
Ockham, William of, *Super 4 libros sententiarum. In sententiarum*, Opera Plurima 3/4, Farnborough, Hants: Gregg Press, 1962.
Pieper, Josef, "Justice," in: Pieper, Josef, *The Four Cardinal Virtues*, trans. Lawrence E. Lynch, New York: Harcourt, Brace & World, 1965, 43 – 113.
Plato, *The Republic*, Chris Emlyn-Jones (ed.), Cambridge, Mass.: Harvard Univ. Press, 2013.
Rawls, John, *A Theory of Justice*, Cambridge: Belknap Press of Harvard University, 1971.
Rohrmoser, Günter, "Platons politische Philosophie," *Studium generale: Zeitschrift für interdisziplinäre Studien* 22 (1969), 1094 – 1134.
Rousseau, Jean-Jacques, *The social contract*, trans. Maurice Cranston, London: Penguin Books, 1968.
Salisbury, John of, *Policraticus: Of the Frivolities of Courtiers and the Footprints of Philosophers*, ed. and trans. Cary J. Nederman, Cambridge: CUP, 1990.
Sanders, Ed P., *Paul*, Oxford: Oxford University Press, 1991.
Scheler, Max, *The Human Place in the Cosmos*, trans. Manfred Frings, Evanston IL: NUP, 2009, 28 – 33.
Schillemeit, Jost (ed.), *Franz Kafka – Schriften, Tagebücher, Briefe: Kritische Ausgabe, Nachgelassene Schriften und Fragmente II*, Frankfurt am Main.: Fischer Verlag 1992.
Schmid, Hans Heinrich, *Gerechtigkeit als Weltordnung: Hintergrund und Geschichte des alttestamentlichen Gerechtigkeitsbegriffs*, BHTh 40, Tübingen: Mohr, 1968.
Schröter, Jens, "'The new perspective on Paul': Eine Anfrage an die lutherische Paulusdeutung?," *Lutherjahrbuch* 80 (2013), 142 – 158.
Sen, Amartya, "Capability and Well-Being," in: Amartya Sen/Martha Nussbaum (eds.), *The Quality of Life*, Oxford: Clarendon Press, 1993, 30 – 53.
Staniloae, Dumitru, *The Experience of God: Orthodox Dogmatic Theology*, vol. 2, The World: Creation and Deification, ed. and trans. Ioan Ionita, Brookline, Mass.: Holy Cross Orthodox Press, 2000.
Ulpianus, Domitius, *Liber primus regularum*, T. Honoré (ed.), Oxford: Oxford University Press, 1982.
Walzer, Michael, *Spheres of Justice*, Oxford: Robertson, 1983.
Weber, Max, *Politics as a Vocation*, repr. from Soc. Essays, New York: OUP, 1946.
Wiesel, Elie, *Night*, New York: Hill & Wang, 1960.
Wolter, Michael, "Das neutestamentliche Christentum und sein Gottesdienst," in: Gräb-Schmidt/Reiner Preul (eds.), *Marburger Jahrbuch Theologie XXX, Gottesdienst und Kirche*, Leipzig: EVA, 2018.

Wort des Rates der Evangelischen Kirche in Deutschland und der Bischofskonferenz zur wirtschaftlichen und sozialen Lage in Deutschland, *Für eine Zukunft in Solidarität und Gerechtigkeit*, Hannover/Bonn: Self-published, 1997.
Yong-Bock Kim, "Justice and righteousness: VII. Missiology," in: Hans Dieter Betz et al. (eds.), *Religion in Past and Present*, vol. 7, Leiden: Brill, 2010, 114–5.
Zenger, Erich, *Ein Gott der Rache? Feindpsalmen verstehen*, Freiburg im Breisgau: Herder, 2003.

## Suggestions for Further Reading

Härle, Wilfried, "Suum cuique, Gerechtigkeit und als sozialer und theologischer Grundbegriff," in: *ZEE* 41 (1997), 303–12.
Sen, Amartya/Nussbaumn, Martha (eds.), *The Quality of Life*, Oxford 1993.
Assmann, Jan, *Ma'at*, Munich, ²1995.
Frey, Christopher, et al. (eds.), *Gerechtigkeit – Illusion oder Herausforderung?*, Münster, 2006.
Loos, Friedrich / Schreiber, H. L. (eds.), "Recht/Gerechtigkeit," in: Otto Brunner et al. (eds.), *Geschichtliche Grundbegriffe*, Bd. 5, 2004, 245–313.
Heckel, Joachim, "Natur, Recht und christliche Verantwortung im öffentlichen Leben nach dem Leben Martin Luthers", in: *Zur politischen Predigt*, Hannover 1952.

Sabri Ciftci

# The Concept of Justice in Islam

## 1 Introduction

Justice is the most central concept of Islam.[1] Scriptural concepts such as the oneness of God (*tawḥīd*), vicegerency of man (*khalīfa*), and the promotion of public interest (*maṣlaḥa*) are all related to the conception of justice. The term *tawḥīd* means unity of God. It is a foundational principle of Islam that has implications for the organization of Islamic society.[2] Just as one God brings harmony, perfection, and justice to the cosmos, an Islamic society can become just if the community of believers becomes one. The prophetic community of the early period of Islam is seen as a unified society where perfect justice prevailed. The second concept, *khalīfa*, specifies that man is God's representative, i.e. his vicegerent, on earth.[3] This qualification elevates man to a special status. He is a being who holds free will and who is thus responsible for seeking justice for all humanity. The final concept, *maṣlaḥa* or public interest, was developed by Muslim jurists as a principle of Islamic law. *Maṣlaḥa* is closely related to another Islamic term, *iḥsān*, which means perfection, beauty, or goodness and these terms relate to social justice. Building on these notions, Islamic legal scholars provided religious justifications for their suggested methods of establishing justice through Islamic law principles. During the medieval period of Islam, *maṣlaḥa* occupied a central place in Islamic legal writings while philosophers and political theorists relied on such notions as *tawḥīd* and *khalīfa* to develop alternative conceptions of justice, especially in the political realm. Together, these three concepts provide a general framework defining the conceptions of Islamic justice.

This chapter will introduce the theoretical and practical underpinnings of Islamic conceptions of justice, with a special focus on social and political justice as the two most salient dimensions of Islamic justice. As will be demonstrated below,

---

1 Portions of this chapter previously appeared as chapters in my book *Islam, Justice, and Democracy*, titled "Historical and Conceptual Foundations of Justice Discourses in Islam" and "Islamist Justice Theory". Used by permission of Temple University Press. ©2022 by Temple University. All Rights Reserved.

2 al-Mawdudi, Abu al-A'la, "Islam in Transition: Muslim Perspective," in: John J. Donohue/John L. Esposito (eds.), *Islam in Transition: Muslim Perspective*, 253–61, New York: Oxford University Press, 1982 n.d.; Sedgwick, Mark, *Muhammad 'Abduh*, Oxford: Oneworld Publications, 2014.

3 Iqbal, Mohammad, *The Reconstruction of Religious Thought in Islam*, Lahore: Sh. Muhammad Ashraf, 1968.

https://doi.org/10.1515/9783110561692-004

a lively debate on free will and determination was initiated by the scholarly exchange regarding the notion of *khalīfa*, thereby shaping the founding principles of the respective conceptions of political justice. Competing discourses of social justice emerged from the discussion of *maṣlaḥa* as a legal principle of Islamic law. *Tawḥīd*, on the other hand, provided a general framework for Islamic justice principles and various conceptions of justice.[4]

This chapter places a special focus on social and political conceptions of justice and explores their historical trajectory from the beginning of Islam to the present. *Section 1* presents a brief and selective review of the theological and philosophical foundations of Islamic conceptions of justice. It attempts to show the linkages between Islamic social and political justice and their foundations. *Section 2* explores the lineages of political and social justice from the beginning of Islam to the end of the medieval period and introduces their legacy in modern times. *Section 3* examines modern conceptions of social and political justice in the context of Muslim responses to modernity and colonialism. It demonstrates how scriptural notions of Islamic justice were deployed by the 19th and 20th century modernists like Jamāl ad-Dīn al-Afghānī (1838–1897/1253–1314) and the Ottoman constitutionalists like Namık Kemal (1840–1888/1256–1306) to address the political, economic, and social problems of that time. *Section 4* looks at the conceptions of justice put forth by Islamism,[5] particularly focusing on Sayyid Quṭb (1906–1966/1324–1386) and ʿAlī Sharīʿatī Mazīnānī (1933–1977/1352–1397). These two intellectuals are chosen because they have developed comprehensive theories of justice and have had widespread influence on Islamism as well as Sunni and Shīʿa theories of justice. This section also presents a comparative overview of other justice theories, including the views of other Islamists like Abū l-Aʿlā Mawdūdī (1903–1979/1321–1399) of Pakistan and Ayatollah Rūḥollāh Mūsawī Khomeinī (d. 1989/1409) of Iran. *Section 5* provides a comparative account of Islamic, Christian, and Judaic conceptions of

4 A detailed account of the literature on Islamic justice conceptions is presented below. The authoritative work in this area is Majid Khadduri's Islamic Conception of Justice (Khadduri, Majid, *The Islamic Conception of Justice*, Baltimore, MD: JHU Press, 1984).

5 The author acknowledges the immense diversity within Islamist movements but does not provide a detailed assessment of this rich ideological landscape. It only focuses on select thinkers whose work lies at the intersection of justice and an Islamist worldview. Islamism is defined in a broad sense, following the conceptualization of Ismail Kara: "Islamism is a thought and a movement of the 19th and 20th century, which is the total sum of the political, intellectual and scholarly studies/quests that are highly activist and eclectic and aim to re-establish the dominance of Islam in society as a whole (belief, worship, ethics, philosophy, law, education) to save the Muslim world from the Western exploitation, oppressive and tyrannical rulers, imitation [of the West] and the superstitions in order to civilize, unite, and help develop it [the Muslim world]" (Kara, İsmail, *Türkiye'de İslamcılık Düşüncesi (I–II)*, İstanbul: Dergah Yayinlari, 2013, 17).

justice. While it does not provide a comprehensive comparison of the various conceptions of justice in Judaism, Christianity and Islam, it elaborates on their commonalities and differences and highlights the dynamic and context-bound evolution of these conceptions. *Section 6* examines the practical applications of political and social justice from an Islamic perspective. Finally, the *Conclusion* summarizes the main insights of this chapter, discusses its limitations, and presents some ideas for future research on the subject.

## 2 Theological and Philosophical Foundations of Justice in Islam

The Arabic word for justice, *ʿadāla* (عدالة) comes from the root *ʿadl*, which, in verb form, means to straighten, be equal, or balance.[6] There are several Qur'ānic concepts that each describe different aspects of justice. Among these are *qisṭ* (installment, fair share), *mīzān* (balance), *wasaṭ* (middle), and *istiqāma* (direction).[7] The opposite of justice is *jawr*. A literal translation would be oppression or tyranny. The Qur'ān describes an absence or lack of justice with such terms as *ẓulm* (wrongdoing, tyranny), *ṭughyan* (extremity), and *inḥirāf* (deviation).[8] *ʿAdl* is mentioned 24 times in 22 verses in the Qur'ān. Some examples include:[9]

> God witnesses that there is no deity except Him, and [so do] the angels and those of knowledge – [that He is] maintaining [creation] in justice. There is no deity except Him, the Exalted in Might, the Wise (3:18). O you who have believed, be persistently standing firm for God, witnesses in justice, and do not let the hatred of a people prevent you from being just. Be just; that is nearer to righteousness. And fear God; indeed, God is Acquainted with what you do (5:8),
> Indeed, God orders justice and good conduct and giving to relatives and forbids immorality and bad conduct and oppression. He admonishes you that perhaps you will be reminded (16:90). Indeed, God commands you to render trusts to whom they are due and when you judge between people to judge with justice (4:58).

Some of the Qur'ānic concepts describe justice as a moderate position between two extremes in that they imply balance (e.g., *wasaṭ, mīzān*) and direction (*istiqāma*).

6 Khadduri, *The Islamic Conception of Justice*, 6.

7 Ibid., 6; Mirakhor, Abbas/Hossein, Askari, *Conceptions of Justice from Islam to the Present*, Switzerland: Springer, 2020, 182–85.

8 Khadduri, *The Islamic Conception of Justice*.

9 The translations of the verses are taken from Sahih International at http://www.Qur'ān.com (accessed on February 20, 2024).

The Qurʾān also makes reference to disorderly or immoderate practices (e.g., *inḥirāf, tughyan*) that are the opposite of order, harmony, and balance. These concepts have practical implications for the implementation of justice in an Islamic society. For example, rulers are expected to act in moderation and not engage in tyranny (*ẓulm*) so that there may be order in society. Believers are discouraged from engaging in rebellious acts to avoid anarchy.[10] Justice will be realized when rulers and people act in harmony and moderation to create orderly social and political systems, especially according to the traditional Sunni political theory.[11]

Another term that is frequently used to describe justice is *ḥaqq*, a word that has multiple meanings, including truth and rights. The Qurʾān refers to *ḥaqq* as a quality of God that ensures order in the universe (23:71) and justice in the hereafter (21:47; 39:69). Mustafa Çağrıcı[12] views *ḥaqq* as a moral principle that requires individuals to be just toward other human beings regardless of their race, physical properties, and social status as seen in the Qurʾān (51:8, 4:3 and 3:75). Consequently, the notion of *haqq* is closely related to the Islamic conception of justice meant to promote a social order based on the principles of tolerance, equality, and moderation.[13] These values are also implied by *maṣlaḥa,* which occupies a central place in Islamic law.

Some scholars also cite *mīthāq* (the primordial covenant between God and humans) and *walāya* (the caring of God for his servants) as scriptural foundations for Islamic conceptions of justice.[14] Mirakhor and Askari[15] argue that *walāya* means the complete love and caring of God for his servants and the servants' unconditional obedience to him. This relationship empowers individuals to believe in God's justice and to strive to implement it through the power of God's love and care. The covenant, on the other hand, ensures that God, as the most just, will fulfill his promises to empower believers and help them establish justice. This account of justice is similar to the conception of justice stemming from the notion of *khalīfa,* as detailed below.

---

**10** Enayat, Hamid, *Modern Islamic Political Thought: The Response of the Shiʿi and Sunni Muslims to the Twentieth Century*, London: MacMillan, 1982.

**11** Ibn Taymiyya, *Against Extremisms, Taymiyyan Texts,* trans. Y. Michot. Beirut: Dar Albouraq, 2002.; Quṭb, Sayyid, *Social Justice in Islam*, trans. John B. Hardie, New York: American Council of Learned Societies, 1953.

**12** Çagrıcı, Mustafa, "Adalet," published online: *Türkiye Diyanet Vakfı İslam Ansiklopedisi*, Istanbul, 2010, https://islamansiklopedisi.org.tr/adalet#1-ahlak (accessed on 18.06.2024).

**13** Ersöz, Resul, "Kur'ân'a Göre 'Hakk' ve 'Adalet' Kavramları Bağlamında İslâm Toplumunun İctimâî Değerleri," *Afyon Kocatepe Üniversitesi Sosyal Bilimler Dergisi* 18, no. 2 (2016), 1–27.

**14** Mirakhor, Abbas/Askari, Hossein, *Conceptions of Justice form Earliest History to Islam*, New York, Palgrave-MacMillan, 2019, 181–214.

**15** Ibid., 183–90.

Muslim philosophers also rely on scriptural principles to define their conceptions of justice and derive prescriptions for a balanced, orderly society.[16] For example, according to the principle of *tawḥīd*, the whole of creation is a harmonious unity – from its smallest elements to its existence as a whole – thanks to God's justice. Muslim philosophers, thus, believe that justice is inherent in the creation of the universe and hence in man's nature who is the vicegerent of God on earth.[17] The virtues of moderation and balance appear prominently in many philosophical writings. Abū Yūsuf Yaʿqūb Ibn Isḥāq aṣ-Ṣabbāḥ al-Kindī (1399–1468/801–873) cites temperance or moderation (*iʿtidāl*) among the virtues of Islamic ethics, and for him, those who deviate from this balance fail to realize justice.[18] For Abū Naṣr Muḥammad al-Fārābī (1466–1544/870–951), justice is a constitutive principle of religion and morality along with temperance.[19] Human beings can achieve justice through a balance between the heart and mind that ensures moderate behavior. This resembles the justice in the virtuous city that brings its different parts together in a balanced manner.[20] It can be stated that the underlying principle of individual and societal balance in Fārābian philosophy is the omnipotence of God. He is fully capable of establishing justice and balance in the universe.

Islamic theologians also relied on the scripture to derive principles for an Islamic conception of justice.[21] The Muʿtazila movement has been especially influential in theological debates about justice. In fact, they were known as *ahl al-ʿadl wa-t-tawḥīd* (the people of justice and unity).[22] According to Muʿtazili thought, justice is one of the central concepts of Islam along with other scriptural principles. Their position begins with a rejection of the idea that God has attributes, a principle

---

**16** Çagrıcı, "Adalet," 342.

**17** Fakhry, Majid, *A History of Islamic Philosophy*, New York: Columbia University Press, 2004; Çagrıcı, "Adalet."

**18** On al-Kindi Cf. Atiyeh, George N., *Al-Kindi: The Philosopher of the Arabs*, Rawalpindi: Islamic Research Institute, 1966 and Adamson, Peter, "al-Kindi," in: Edward N. Zalta (ed.), *The Stanford Encyclopedia of Philosophy*, Spring 2020 edition, Stanford, CA: Stanford University, 2020, published online: https://plato.stanford.edu/archives/spr2020/entries/al-kindi/ (accessed on 02.02.2024).

**19** Al-Fārābī, *Al-Fārābī on the Perfect State: Abū Naṣr Al-Fārābī's Mabādi' Ārā' Ahl Al-Madīna Al-Fāḍila: A Revised Text with Introduction, Translation, and Commentary*, trans. Richard Walzer, New York: Oxford University Press, 1985.

**20** Ibid.

**21** Fakhry, *A History of Islamic Philosophy*; Mirakhor/Askari, *Conceptions of Justice from Earliest History*.

**22** Muʿtazilah was derived from the verb *iʿtazala*, literally "withdrew", referring to the separation of Wāṣil Ibn ʿAṭā' (d. 748) from his teacher Ḥasan al-Baṣrī (d. 728) to form a new school of thought. This movement is viewed as the rationalist school of Islamic theology (Cf. Campanini, Massimo, "The Muʿtazila in Islamic History and Thought," *Religion Compass* 6, no. 1 (2012), 41–50). On Muʿtazilah, also Cf., Fakhry, *A History of Islamic Philosophy*.

which constitutes the foundation for Islamic justice and implies that the principle of *tawḥīd* is of great significance as an all-encompassing element of their philosophy. Justice, in effect, is part of the essence of God and hence, by definition, God cannot commit an injustice. Furthermore, because human beings have free will and God cannot be unjust, the latter cannot be responsible for evil actions and injustices, yet God is, in theory, fully capable of evil. Finally, given God's absolute justice and man's free will, the Muʿtazilites contend that it is a duty upon all believers to command the good and forbid the evil (*al-amr bi-l-maʿrūf wa-n-nahy ʿani-l-munkar*).[23] Overall, the Muʿtazili justice theory has close resemblance to the primary framework of Islamic justice conception introduced in this chapter, including the principles of *tawḥīd* (resulting in God's absolute justice and harmony in the universe), *khalīfa* (resulting in free will of man), and the legal principle of *maṣlaḥa* (resulting in commandment of good and prevention of evil).

Muslim philosophers also drew on ancient Greek philosophy (especially *Nicomachean Ethics*) to develop conceptions of justice and morality.[24] al-Kindī, Abū ʿAlī Aḥmad b. Muḥammad Ibn Yaʿqūb Miskawayh ar-Rāzī (1526–1621/932–1030), Ibn Sīnā (1572–1628/980–1037), and Abū Ḥāmid Muḥammad Ibn Muḥammad aṭ-Ṭūsī al-Ghazālī (d. 1111/505) define justice as a combination of virtues like moderation, chastity, and wisdom.[25] Reason (*al-ʿaql*) emerges as an important element of the theories of justice in Islamic philosophy. For example, al-Kindī argues that reason requires justice and that it was given to man for him to learn about God and his perfect justice.[26] Abū Bakr ar-Rāzī (d. 925 or 935), too, believes that justice can be achieved by reason and views it in terms of personal justice, which involves virtues like modesty, compassion, and generosity.[27] As discussed below, modernist Islamists also understood reason to be a constitutive element of Islamic justice and in that they relied on the notions of *khalīfa* and free will. The medieval philosopher Rāghīb al-Iṣfahānī (d. 1108/502) proposed that justice is a virtue that is the sum of all good virtues, and as such, he employs the personalistic view of justice.[28] al-Fārābī departs from this view by providing an account of political justice moving

---

23 Campanini, "The Muʻtazila in Islamic History and Thought,"; Mirakhor/Askari, *Conceptions of Justice from Earliest History.*

24 Fakhry, *A History of Islamic Philosophy*; Mirakhor/Askari, *Conceptions of Justice from Earliest History to Islam.*

25 Khadduri, *The Islamic Conception of Justice*; Fakhry, *A History of Islamic Philosophy*; Mirakhor/Askari, *Conceptions of Justice from Earliest History.*

26 Mirakhor/Askari, *Conceptions of Justice from Earliest History*, 222.

27 Ibid., 227.

28 Mohamed, Yasien, "The Concept of Justice in Miskawayh and Isfahani," *Journal for Islamic Studies* 18 (1998), 51–111; Çagrıcı, "Adalet."; Gafarov, Anar, "Râğıb El-İsfahânî'Nin Insan Ve Ahlâk Anlayişi," Master Thesis, Istanbul: Marmara University, 2004.

beyond personal traits and places it within a just structure of government. This topic will be covered more broadly in *sections 2–4* regarding the historical origins and the evolution of the conception of political justice as it evolved from the early period of Islam to present.

In Islam, justice is also frequently viewed as equality in both an individual and a social sense where non-discrimination is an important aspect of social equality.[29] Economic egalitarianism and charity are seen as essential elements of social equality and a harmonious social order.[30] It is possible to find the origins of these ideas in Islamic philosophy, especially in Ibn Miskawayh's work. He promotes fairness and redistribution as important features of Islamic social justice because the former shows the existence of balance and the latter the establishment of moderation that can be achieved by curbing excessive spending or a redistribution of wealth.[31] The subsequent sections of this chapter elaborate on the ideas of order, distribution, and equality as components of Islamic conceptions of social justice. Limits on the scope of this chapter prevent a more detailed discussion of the theological and philosophical foundations of Islamic conceptions of justice. However, the conceptual field of justice and the ideas of Muslim philosophers have been foundational for the Islamic conception of justice.

## 3 Conceptions of Social and Political Justice in Islam

In Islam, God is the ultimate sovereign, the protector, and the sole provider thanks to his omnipotence and power.[32] These attributes also underlie the foundation of divine justice, which the faithful believe is perfect. The application of this perfect justice to worldly life, however, poses a challenge. The tension between divine justice and the real-world conditions that restrict its realization set off a continuous debate in Islamic political theory.[33] Scholarly research on Islamic justice employs different paradigms to explain the hold this controversy has on Islamic discourse. For example, Majid Khadduri views the development of Islamic conceptions of jus-

29 Mohamed, Yasien/Swazo, Norman K, "Contributing to Islamic Ethics," *American Journal of Islam and Society* 27, no. 3 (2010), i–xiv; Khadduri, *The Islamic Conception of Justice.*

30 Ciftci, Sabri, "Islam, Social Justice, and Democracy," *Politics and Religion* 12, no. 4 (2019), 549–76.

31 For a detailed account of Ibn Miskawaih's views on justice, Cf. Khan, M. S., *An Unpublished Treatise of Miskawaih on Justice* [Risāla fī māhiyat al-'adl li Miskawaih], Leiden: Brill, 1964.

32 Al-Mawdudi, "Islam in Transition: Muslim Perspective."

33 Khadduri, *The Islamic Conception of Justice*, 1–11.

tice as a dialectical process where two parties struggle to establish a paradigm of justice and eventually reach a synthesis. This theoretical synthesis becomes a source of new disagreement among scholars until its resolution leads to a new paradigm. Other scholars define justice in terms of liberal theories and compare Islamic conceptions of justice to Western theories of justice.[34] In these accounts, the question of a possible compatibility of Islamic and liberal conceptions of justice and the latter's evolution within a modern political framework take center stage.[35] Others have taken a value-based approach to locate their conceptions of justice in an Islamic jurisprudential framework.[36] Alternatively, justice is viewed as a religious virtue related to civic values, democracy, and political life in general.[37] Native theories of Islamic justice firmly ground their approach in scriptural concepts and broad Islamic worldviews. For example, Sayyid Quṭb (1906–1966/1324–1386)[38] develops an Islamic theory of justice based on the goal of creating solidarity and harmony in the Muslim community. Tunisian intellectual and activist Rāshid al-Ghannūshī (b. 1941), on the other hand, builds a theory of justice and democracy based on the vicegerency status of man, human dignity, and responsibility, all of which necessitates active participation of believers in political processes.[39]

Justice is a concept with many dimensions, including but not limited to its individual, political, social, legal, economic, commutative, and distributive facets. As discussed above, Muslim philosophers and theologians have elaborated on different individual aspects as well as developing comprehensive frameworks of justice. Over time and across different contexts, some dimensions of justice may have received more attention than others.[40] For example, in the West, the Industrial revolution created socioeconomic conditions that brought the distributive aspects of justice to the forefront.[41] Religion (Christianity) played a vital role in the reconci-

---

**34** Mirakhor/Askari, *Conceptions of Justice from Islam.*

**35** Kaminski, Joseph J, *Islam, Liberalism, and Ontology: A Critical Re-Evaluation*, New York: Routledge, 2021.

**36** Abou El Fadl, Khaled/Cohen, Joshua et al. (eds.), *Islam, and the Challenge of Democracy: A Boston Review Book*, Princeton University Press, published online: *JSTOR*, 2004, http://www.jstor.org/stable/j.ctt14bs1gz (accessed on 19.06.2024).

**37** An-Naim, Abdullahi Ahmed, *Islam and the Secular State*, Cambridge, MA: Harvard University Press, 2008.

**38** Quṭb, *Social Justice in Islam.*

**39** March, Andrew F, *The Caliphate of Man: Popular Sovereignty in Modern Islamic Thought* Cambridge, MA: Belknap Press, 2019.

**40** Maguire, Daniel C, "Religious Influences on Justice Theory," in Michael Reisch (ed.), *Routledge International Handbook of Social Justice*, 53–64, New York: Routledge, 2014.

**41** Lorenz, Walter, "The Emergence of Social Justice in the West," in Michael Reisch (ed.), *Routledge International Handbook of Social Justice*, 40–52, New York: Routledge, 2014.

liation of the social tensions resulting from the industrial revolution by providing a frame for secular conceptions of social justice. Social democracy and religiously inspired egalitarian ideologies such as liberation theology can be cited as manifestations of this trajectory.[42] Liberal ideology, also played an important role in reconciling the free-market ideas with socially just outcomes in the modern age.[43] The ideas of freedom and the distributive procedures that were reformulated from Christian theology into secular forms from the medieval to the modern period were especially significant for this development.[44]

While justice has many different aspects in Islam, throughout Islamic history, political and social justice emerged as its most salient dimensions. Such conceptions were especially consequential in shaping Islamic political theory and practice from the earliest period of Islam. Social justice came to be considered as equivalent to public interest and has underlined political legitimacy since the medieval period.[45] Conceptions of social justice gradually evolved within Islamic jurisprudence (*fiqh*) where Muslim jurisprudents defined social justice in relation to the end goals of divine law (*maqāṣid*). This concept marked the implementation of public interest in accordance with Islamic law.[46] Political justice theory, on the other hand, was developed by philosophers and advisors, who built specifically on the philosophy of al-Fārābī. Their writings later gave way to political advising literature, known as mirrors for princes.[47] As the Muslim Empire expanded and various rulers started to create an independent body of legislation (*qānūn*) next to the vast corpus of religious rulings, justice came to be associated with the qualities of the ruler and the compatibility between *qānūn* and *sharīʿa*. This approach is different from the justice conception of al-Kindī and Ibn Sīnā who endorse a rational and personalistic conception of justice rather than one focused on a ruler's quality and legal imperatives. Much later, following the first Muslim encounters with a triumphant West, traditional Islamists began to associate justice with religious renewal (*tajdīd*). Modernists turned to Western ideas such as popular sovereignty and constitutional government as a means to overcome the injustices in their so-

42 Smith, Christian, *The Emergence of Liberation Theology: Radical Religion and Social Movement Theory*, Chicago, University of Chicago Press, 1991; Gutiérrez, Gustavo, *A Theology of Liberation*, New York: Orbis Books, 1971.

43 Rawls, John, *A Theory of Justice*, Cambridge, MA: Harvard University Press, 2009.

44 Cf. the chapter by Gräb-Schmidt in this volume.

45 Ahmed, Shahab, *What Is Islam? The Importance of Being Islamic*, Princeton: Princeton University Press, 2016; Abdelkader, Deina, *Social Justice in Islam*, Herndon, VA: International Institute of Islamic Thought, 2000.

46 Abdelkader, *Social Justice in Islam*.

47 Ahmed, *What Is Islam?*

cieties. In these examples, we see the evolution of Islamic conceptions of justice in response to the changing social and political problems of a given time.

This section provides an account of the historical evolution of the social and political conceptions of justice in Islam. To understand the contemporary interpretations and applications of Islamic justice, it is necessary to visit the critical moments that shaped this core concept. Among many defining critical junctures, two moments have been the most consequential in shaping Islamic conceptions of justice and their long-lasting influence on Muslims' social and political preferences. The first of these moments occurred in the 7th century when the first civil war (*fitnah*) broke out and created political divisions amongst the members of the community in this early period of Islam. These divisions eventually gave way to the sectarian separation into the Sunni and Shīʿa camps.[48] The Mongol invasion of the 13th century during the decline of Abbasid rule marks a second instance of such an evolution. The interaction between scholarship and practical politics at this critical moment resulted in two distinct trajectories in the development of Islamic understandings of justice, political and social justice. While we should also consider the philosophical and mystic variants of justice[49] in the Islamic tradition, most other conceptions either attached themselves to political and social justice or they remained underdeveloped vis-à-vis these main trends. Various debates and struggles around political and social justice trajectories took place during the medieval and the modern period, creating continuities and variations in the notion of justice and its strategic deployment by rulers and scholars.

## 3.1 Lineages of Political Justice

The tension between the necessity of obedience and a duty to rebel against an unjust ruler is the central puzzle in need of solving when defining a conception of Islamic political justice. When looking to gain an understanding of the evolution of the concept of justice in Islam, it is of primary importance to acquaint oneself with two central factors: the founding principles of the prophetic community and the first major civil war, otherwise known as the first *fitna* (Battle of Siffin, 657). The prophetic community was essentially a political organization, yet it was built on religious moral principles. To describe this community, Patricia Crone[50]

---

**48** I use the term "early period of Islam" to refer to the period extending from *hijrah* (the migration of Prophet from Mecca to Medina in 622 AD) to the end of the Abbasid Golden Age (861 AD).
**49** Fakhry, *A History of Islamic Philosophy*; Khadduri, *The Islamic Conception of Justice*; Mohamed, "The Concept of Justice in Miskawayh and Isfahani."
**50** Crone, Patricia, *God's Rule: Government and Islam*, New York: Columbia University Press, 2004.

uses the metaphor of a caravan. Just as the members of a caravan move in one direction, the whole Muslim community (*umma*) moves toward the rightful path under the guidance of its leader. Because of these qualities, the prophetic community has been elevated to a special status as an ideal vision of a just society, a golden age to be imitated by subsequent generations.[51]

The first civil war began with a disagreement about who should succeed the Prophet Muhammad upon his passing in 632. We should look closely at the parties in this first civil war to better understand later discussions about political justice. The Battle of Siffin took place between the forces of ʿAlī b. Abī Ṭālib (d. 661/41), the son-in-law and cousin of Muhammad and the fourth caliph, and the governor of Damascus, Muʿāwiya I (d. 680/60) The latter built a parallel state in Syria and rejected the former's claim to the caliphate. When ʿAlī accepted arbitration to prevent a battle and to resolve the issue of who would be the next Caliph of the *umma*, a group known as al-Khawārij (those who defected or left) took a unique position in disagreement with both parties. For the Khawārij, arbitration meant the violation of God's rule, namely, that there is no sovereign other than God (*lā ḥukma ilā li-llāh*). According to the Khawārij, since sovereignty belongs to God, any other method, like arbitration, to select an *imam* (leader, ruler) is illegitimate.[52]

One long-lasting legacy of this early conflict is the sectarian division between Shīʿa and Sunni Islam, a division engendering different conceptions of justice over time.[53] The Shīʿa believed that a family relation to the Prophet is a necessary condition for becoming the leader of the *umma*. They argue that Muḥammad designated ʿAlī to be his successor and passed the vital knowledge for this task on to him. Thanks to this special relationship and the qualifications that came with it, the Imam (i. e. ʿAlī) was infallible and thus the only one who could bring justice to this world. This theme has been present in the *imamate* theories of different Shīʿa groups. The Sunni doctrine, on the other hand, gives some power to the Muslim community[54] and views its agreement as a prerequisite of justice when a new

---

**51** Ayoob, Mohammed, "Political Islam: Image and Reality," *World Policy Journal* 21, no. 3 (2004), 1–14.

**52** March, Andrew F, "Genealogies of Sovereignty in Islamic Political Theology," *Social Research: An International Quarterly* 80, no. 1 (2013), 293–320.

**53** The discussion in this section makes gross generalizations for the sake of simplicity and in order to set out the argument presented in this chapter. The *Shīʿa* and *Sunni* theories of Imamate involved deeper discussions and took centuries to consolidate (Cf. Hodgson, Marshall G S, *The Venture of Islam*, vol. 1, *The Classical Age of Islam*, Chicago: University of Chicago press, 1974; Enayat, *Modern Islamic Political Thought*).

**54** Enayat, *Modern Islamic Political Thought*.

leader is selected.[55] This doctrine has led some contemporary political theorists to define a political theology of Islam in terms of popular sovereignty.[56] The Khawārij strongly advocated for the *umma's* role in leader selection. For them, God is all-powerful and no man can consider himself a sole sovereign. Thus, the choice of a new leader cannot be the privilege of a few men. Since all believers are equal in Islam, all *umma* members have the right to select their leader. Furthermore, the community has the duty to remove a corrupt and unjust leader, because God could not have willed injustice by endorsing a tyrannical rule.

The conceptualizations of justice developed in the wake of this first schism also necessitated philosophical reflection on the relationship between predetermination and free will. The positions derived in this process were foundational to the development of different understandings of political justice. *Kalām* (Islamic scholastic theology) is the field where most of these debates unfolded.[57] The Khawārij were the first to use the notion of *qadar* (power) as a quality that all believers possess, including the ruler. For them, it was critical to hold any individual responsible for the injustices that he may commit, because man must bear consequences of his free will. In contrast, the Jabri school propagated predetermination and viewed human choice and responsibility as irrelevant and thus this line of questioning as a non-issue.[58] According to the Qadari School, free will is the foundation of political justice for two reasons. First, it obligates the ruler to act justly. Second, it places a responsibility on his subjects to elect a just imam and to depose an unjust ruler. One can argue that the Qadari school provided a religious justification for popular sovereignty and political accountability in Islam. The Jabri doctrine, in contrast, argued that all acts of the ruler should be deemed acceptable regardless of the justice clause, because they are predetermined. To demonstrate the validity of this view, Khadduri[59] cites a letter written by the Umayyad caliph al-Walīd Ibn Yazīd Ibn ʿAbd al-Malik (709–744/90–126) to his governors in which he explains his decision to appoint two of his sons as his successors. In this letter, Walīd presents the caliphate as a divine institution that ensures the implementation of order and justice. He argues that obedience to the caliph is necessary, because God predetermined everything and those who rebel will earn the displeasure of God.

The debate between the Qadari and Jabri schools was only a first iteration in a long line of diametrically opposed stances on the dichotomy between free will or predetermination with regard to the human individual and justice or oppression

55 Khadduri, *The Islamic Conception of Justice.*
56 March, Andrew F, *The Caliphate of Man.*
57 Fakhry, Majid, *A History of Islamic Philosophy.*
58 Khadduri, *The Islamic Conception of Justice*, 23.
59 Ibid., 25–26.

as ideals of political order. These disagreements concentrated on questions of creed and philosophy discussed in endless debates among *kalām* scholars, philosophers, Sufis, and theologians. For example, the rationalist Muʿtazila.[60] and traditionalist Ḥanbalis[61] found themselves at the center of a political crisis in the early 9$^{th}$ century during the reign of the Abbasid Caliph al-Ma'mūn (786–833/170–218). During various rebellions, caliph al-Ma'mūn made the ideas of the Muʿtazila movement the official doctrine of the caliphate in an effort to legitimize his political position. This position was based on a doctrine of governance that combined political and religious authority in the office of the caliphate. With support from Muʿtazila scholars, he started an inquisition (*al-miḥna*) against the opponents of this doctrine, particularly targeting Aḥmad Ibn Ḥanbal (780–855/163–241) and his followers. The main issue driving this policy was a disagreement on the concept of just government. For traditionalist scholars like Ibn Ḥanbal, it was imperative to maintain religious guidance in the face of divisions within the *umma*. The office of the caliphate was no longer qualified to provide religious guidance because the caliph had shown himself to be unjust and there were several individuals who claimed to be caliphs in different parts of the Muslim world. Ira Lapidus[62] argues that amid *al-miḥna*, Ibn Ḥanbal and like-minded scholars managed to increase the power of religious authority over the office of the caliphate by joining forces with rebellious groups and the public. This event is important, because it signifies the separation of religious and political authority and grants the former the power to hold the latter accountable in the name of justice.

Islamic conceptions of justice also influenced Muslim attitudes after the first civil war. Abdelwahab El-Affendi[63] argues that a specific tension came to define Muslim politics since the time of the Prophet. Some, which he dubs the ethicalists, held a puritanical worldview and desired to implement a just social order reminiscent of the ideal prophetic community (i.e., Medina model). Others, he classifies as realists, who strove to grab hold of political power with little regard for justice (i.e., Damascus model).[64] A similar cleavage is presented by Marshall Hodgson who states, "gradually the ideal of benevolent absolutism attached itself to the ca-

---

**60** *Muʿtazilites* are known as the rationalist school of Islamic theology (Fakhry, *A History of Islamic Philosophy).*

**61** The Ḥanbali school is one of the traditional Islamic schools of jurisprudence named after Aḥmad Ibn Ḥanbal (d. 855). It is known for its literalist interpretations of Islam and its reliance on the scripture and the *ḥadīth.*

**62** Lapidus, Ira M, "The Separation of State and Religion in the Development of Early Islamic Society," *International Journal of Middle East Studies* 6, no. 4 (1975), 363–85.

**63** El-Affendi, Abdelwahab, *Who Needs an Islamic State?*, London: Malaysia Think Tank, 2008.

**64** El-Affendi, *Islamic State*, 175–83.

liph's court, confronting the ideal of Islamic egalitarianism in the opposition."[65] The distinction between these groups was based on different interpretations of justice.

As the main religious minority that faced frequent repression, the Shīʿītes were instrumental in the development of a political theory of justice. These groups heavily relied on the influence of the discourses surrounding the injustices committed against the family of the Prophet in forming a unique theory of justice. Rebellion against tyranny is a continuous theme in Shīʿa political theory, resurfacing throughout the centuries, i. e. in the thought of ʿAlī Sharīʿatī or the Ayatollah Khomeinī, two ideologues of the Iranian revolution.

The weight of various Sunni groups in shaping an Islamic conception of justice is also noteworthy. As the Umayyad Empire expanded, various social hierarchies and inequalities were introduced between the Arab and the non-Arab population. This condition created a backlash from individuals who "envisaged a society which should embody justice on earth, led by the most pious among the Muslims."[66] Piety-minded leaders of the Sunni creed introduced a political theology that linked political behavior to the values of Islamic justice and thus justified rebellion against unjust rulers.[67] Thus emerged the principles of justice of the *piety-minded opposition.* Apart from egalitarian social commitments, they included such values as human dignity, denunciation of corruption, and the necessity of rebellion against unjust, tyrannical rulers. In the Shīʿīte tradition, atrocities committed against the family of the prophet and injustices and prosecution against Shīʿa groups brought forth the notion of *ẓulm.* While the search for justice was delayed until the return of the hidden imam according to the Shīʿīte creed, Khomeinī developed novel interpretations of Islamic justice to motivate a mobilization against tyranny in the modern age.[68]

Not infrequently, piety-minded leaders used their religious authority to constrain oppressive rulers[69] or even to lead rebellions against injustice.[70] An alternative vision encouraged obedience and restricted collective action against the ruler, however unjust he may be, to avoid anarchy reminiscent of the first *fitna.* Through-

---

**65** Hodgson, *The Venture of Islam*, vol. 1, 241.

**66** Ibid., 248.

**67** Ibid., 250.

**68** Khomeinī, Sayyid R.M, "Theory of Justice," trans. Hussein Karamyar, published online: *al-Islam.org*, https://www.al-islam.org/theory-justice-sayyid-ruhullah-musawi-Khomeinī , (accessed on 19.06.2024).

**69** Hodgson, *The Venture of Islam*, vol.1.

**70** Ibid.; Lapidus, Ira M, *A History of Islamic Societies*, New York: Cambridge University Press, 2002; Crone, *God's Rule.*

out the centuries, this duality either inspired revolutions or legitimized obedience to authoritarian rulers. For example, the Ottoman empire used Islamic credentials to encourage obedience among its unruly subjects by employing the services of Sufi dervishes and the religious bureaucracy to justify political actions.[71] More recently, Gulf monarchies like Saudi Arabia and the United Arab Emirates have been employing religious justifications concerning the preservation of the political order to discourage protests and opposition against the regime. In contrast, the rebellions carried by unorthodox mystic leaders in medieval Anatolia, modern rebellions against colonial powers in various parts of the Muslim world, and more recently the Arab Spring protests also drew on concepts of Islamic justice.[72] In short, the ideologies developed after the first schism in Islam became potent ideals that inform its notions of justice and their application in politics to this day.

## 3.2 Lineages of Conceptions of Social Justice

Social justice constitutes the second prominent dimension of justice that has its roots in the early and medieval Islamic periods. Islamic social justice encompasses the provision of social welfare and the protection of life, religion, property, and offspring.[73] These policy issues preoccupied religious scholars, especially from the 13th century onward, whose main ambition was to solve the problems of the declining Muslim society of the time.[74] Gradually, social justice in the form of the provision of social welfare came to be defined as the characteristic attribute of a just ruler. Since economic justice and a ruler's generosity toward his subjects are commonly regarded as religiously sanctified principles, they have also been used to justify authoritarian rule and to legitimize obedience to a benevolent tyrant.

A comprehensive conceptualization of Islamic social justice is provided by Islamic jurisprudential theory (*uṣūl al-fiqh*). Sunni schools of law (*madhāhib*)[75] pro-

---

71 Inalcik, Halil, *The Ottoman Empire: The Classical Age, 1300–1600*, trans. Norman Itzkowitz/Colin Imber, London: Weidenfeld and Nicholson, *1973*.

72 Quisay, Walaa/Parker, Thomas, "On the Theology of Obedience: An Analysis of Shaykh Bin Bayyah and Shaykh Hamza Yusuf's Political Thought," *MAYDAN*, 2019.

73 Abdelkader, *Social Justice in Islam*; Ahmed, *What Is Islam? The Importance of Being Islamic*, 2016.

74 Khadduri, *The Islamic Conception of Justice*.

75 Madhab (plural, Madhāhib) is the school of law that incorporates body of law, recommendations for rituals, and detailed descriptions of what is permissible or forbidden. Muslims adhere to one of the four Sunni schools, Mālikī, Shāfiʿī, Ḥanafī, and Ḥanbalī.

vide detailed jurisprudential prescriptions for social justice based on what is permissible and forbidden in Islam. These schools provide legal rulings to ensure the welfare of individuals and society according to the principles of Islamic law.[76] Towering religious scholars like al-Ghazālī (d. 1111/505) and Ibn Taymīya (1263–1328/661–728) developed sophisticated social justice theories based on religious rulings and the protection of life, progeny, religion, and intellect.[77] The main goal of the jurisprudents was to provide religious justifications and prescriptions for the provision of welfare to all according to Islamic law.

Islamic jurisprudential social justice conceptions and their practical applications gained widespread recognition during the political fragmentation and decline of the Islamic state from the 11th to 13th centuries. Since the central power of the Abbasid state had been weakened by the 11th century, various states and autonomous political entities began to rule over stretches of the vast Islamic empire. While there were periods of peace and prosperity, such as during the peak of the Seljuk State's reign, the standard of living in Muslim territories generally deteriorated resulting in religious and moral decay as well as a decrease in welfare. The Mongol invasion and the destruction of Baghdad in 1258 AD exacerbated these developments and had devastating effects on the security, order, and welfare of Islamic society. For religious scholars, establishing public order and guaranteeing the security and welfare of the *umma* were the most pressing issues of this period, a development that shifted their focus from political to social justice.[78]

The necessity to secure welfare and public goods as conditions of social justice was justified by scriptural principles, but its origins go back to the pre-Islamic notion of the *circle of justice*, which had already shaped government practices in the Middle East for centuries. Its origins reach back to the ancient wisdom of governance narrated in the oral literatures, folktales, and traditions of the East. It became the conceptual foundation for a literary tradition of political instruction intended to teach rulers how to implement justice and ensure welfare.[79] By and large, the circle of justice refers to complete harmony and justice among the sovereign, his army, the law, and his subjects. The following anonymous verses succinctly express this idea:

76 Abdelkader, Deina, *Social Justice in Islam.*
77 Ahmed, Shahab, *What Is Islam?*
78 Khadduri.
79 Darling, Linda T, *A History of Social Justice, and Political Power in the Middle East: The Circle of Justice from Mesopotamia to Globalization*, New York: Routledge, 2013; Thompson, Elizabeth F, *Justice Interrupted*, Cambridge, MA: Harvard University Press, 2013.

> The world is a garden, hedged in by sovereignty
> Sovereignty is lordship, preserved by law
> Law is administration, governed by the king
> The king is a shepherd, supported by the army
> The army are soldiers, fed by money
> Money is revenue, gathered by the people
> The people are servants, subjected by justice
> Justice is happiness, the well-being of the world.[80]

Or sometimes written in a simple way as follows:

> No power without troops,
> No troops without money,
> No money without prosperity,
> No prosperity without justice and good administration.[81]

The necessity of welfare provision under *sharīʿa* principles is particularly relevant to the circle of justice. In Islamic jurisprudential theory, the ruler's laws are an embodiment of the divine law. As Ahmed[82] succinctly puts it, "the ruler's *siyasat* [politics], then, is precisely the making of laws in accordance with the general principles of *shari'at* [sharīʿa] by observation and reason of what is necessary for the goal of human welfare in the context of the needs of the time and place." In addition, the protection of essential needs (life, progeny, and religion) and welfare provision were among the goals of Islamic law, the implementations of which scholars believed would bring about social justice.[83] Whenever the rulers failed in providing welfare and protecting their subjects, their acts were deemed to contradict public interest (*maṣlaḥa*) and the goals of divine law (or *maqāṣid al-sharīʿa*).

Concepts of social justice as developed in early and medieval Islamic jurisprudence have their roots in Islam's scriptural emphasis on benevolence and charity. In the Qur'ān, wealthy individuals are encouraged to pay a certain portion of their income (generally 2.5%) as *zakāt* (obligatory almsgiving) to those in need: "The good that you give should be to the parents, the close ones, the orphans, the needy and the homeless, and any good that you do, God is knowledgeable thereof."[84] There are many hadiths about *zakāt*, charity, and helping the needy. For example, it is reported in al-Bukhārī (d. 870/194) that the Prophet is heard saying:

---

**80** Darling, *A History of Social Justice*, 3.
**81** Ibid, 2.
**82** Ahmed, *What Is Islam?*
**83** Abdelkader, *Social Justice in Islam*; Ahmed, *What Is Islam?*
**84** Qur'ān, 2:215.

"God has made it obligatory for them to pay zakat from their property; it is to be taken from the wealthy among them and given to the poor."[85] 'Adī Ibn Ḥātim aṭ-Ṭā'ī (d. 687 or 688/67–8) reported that he heard the Prophet saying, "Save yourself from hell-fire even by giving half a date-fruit in charity."[86] In the early and modern periods of Islam, this strong emphasis on the individual responsibility for charitable giving and *zakāt* gave way to the collection and redistribution of *zakāt* by the state.[87]

Just as previously demonstrated with regard to the trajectory along which the understanding of political justice developed, the practices of social justice found in the prophetic community are foundational to a welfare-oriented model of social justice. The prophetic benevolence and the many stories about the second caliph ʿUmar b. al-Khaṭṭāb's (d. 644/23) justice, have been important elements of social justice theory. The second Caliph ʿUmar is best known for his iconic legacy as an ardent pursuer of justice. History books and folk culture are replete with stories that venerate ʿUmar's acts of justice. It is reported that in a letter sent to the governor of Basra, he said: "When people come to you for a hearing or when you gather a council, treat people equally. In this way, the weak will not despair of your justice. And the strong will not get the feeling that you may oppress others for your own gain."[88] In addition to pursuing political justice in his administration, ʿUmar also set an example for future generations with regard to economic justice through his charitable acts and distributive policies. The ideal of being a just ruler in ʿUmar's image has been an aspiration of many caliphs and sultans over the centuries. The *maẓālim* courts, an administrative court designed for hearing the grievances of ordinary people, were inspired by ʿUmar's administrative style. It has not been uncommon for rulers to show acts of generosity or to investigate into the affairs of their subjects by joining the crowds in the marketplace or wandering around the streets at night while hiding their identity, another practice of ʿUmar's. Sultans aspired to be just rulers by showing impartiality in their administration and caring for the welfare of their subjects. Since ʿUmar's reign, justice has been viewed as the primary virtue of Muslim rulers.

---

**85** al-Bukhari n.d., 2:24,537.

**86** Ibid., 2:24,498.

**87** Davis, Nancy J./Robinson, Robert V, "The Egalitarian Face of Islamic Orthodoxy: Support for Islamic Law and Economic Justice in Seven Muslim-Majority Nations," *American Sociological Review* 71, no. 2 (2006), 167–90.

**88** Balcı, İsrafil, "Umar (r.a): A Leader Crowned with Truth and Justice," *Life and Religion: A Publication of the Turkish Diyanet Foundation and the Istanbul Office of the Mufti*, Istanbul, 2013, published online: *Lastprophet.info*, https://www.lastprophet.info/the-companions/the-companions/925/umar-r-a-a-leader-crowned-with-truth-and-justice (accessed on 18.06.2024).

Meanwhile, building on this legacy, jurists developed flexible interpretations of Islamic law to address the social problems of their times. This is reflected in *uṣūl al-fiqh*, that incorporated an elaborate use of the principles of reasoning (*ijtihād*) and analogy (*qiyās*) and the dimension of the public interest (*maṣlaḥa*) in addition to the static sources of legislation.[89] In addition to the traditional sources of *sharīʿa*, including the Qurʾān, *sunnah*, and *ijmāʿ*, the scholars of four Sunni legal schools relied on these principles to issue religious rulings. There was disagreement amongst the schools regarding the extent to which these legal principles could be used to arrive at a judgement when a clear ruling could not be garnered from the first three sources alone. Among these legal principles, *maṣlaḥa* and the traditions of a society would especially be taken into account under *qiyās*. For the jurists, the principle of *maṣlaḥa* came to rest at the core of a conception of social justice that prioritizes social welfare and public goods.[90] There is a complex set of rules about how each *madhhab* applies the principle of *qiyās* and especially to *maṣlaḥa*. Imam Shafiʿī, for example, used *maṣlaḥa* when there was evidence supporting it in the text. Ḥanīfis expanded the application of *qiyās* to include anything that might promote public interest, while some jurists argued that *maṣlaḥa* could precede scripture. Notably, medieval scholar and jurist Ibn Taymīya developed an elaborate social justice theory focused on the provision of public goods, security, and economic justice.[91]

A just ruler is one who upholds virtue and feels bound by the principles of *sharīʿa* and could thus attain social justice. In practice, an implementation of social justice could be attained by means of a model of government that rests on the cooperation between religious scholars (*ʿulamāʾ*) and rulers.[92] Ahmet Kuru[93] argues that this notion resulted in the encroachment of secular law on religious law and the *ʿulamāʾ's* subordination to the sultans. Kuru's theory differs from that of Noah Feldman[94] who argues that the *ʿulamāʾ's* job is to constrain rulers and hold them accountable to Islamic law. This idea is most clearly described by Abdou Filali-Ansary as the "medieval compromise,"[95] which is an implicit agreement between rul-

---

89 Abdelkader, *Social Justice in Islam*; Ahmed, *What Is Islam?*

90 Abdelkader, *Social Justice in Islam*, 8–51. Abdelkader provides an excellent treatment of Islamic jurisprudence and the use of qiyās, maṣlaḥah, and other principles in her book *Social Justice in Islam*. I refer the reader to this book for a detailed account of the subject.

91 Khadduri, *The Islamic Conception of Justice*.

92 Ahmed, *What Is Islam?*

93 Kuru, Ahmet T, *Islam, Authoritarianism, and Underdevelopment: A Global and Historical Comparison*, New York: Cambridge University Press, 2019.

94 Feldman, Noah, *The Fall and Rise of the Islamic State*, Princeton: Princeton University Press, 2012.

95 Filali-Ansary, Abdou, "Muslims and Democracy," *Journal of Democracy* 10, no. 3 (1999), 27–28.

ers and the *'ulamā'* that places the former in charge of secular governance and leaves the implementation of justice and law in the hands of the latter. This compromise is the essence of the classical, medieval Islamic state. It made possible the implementation of *sharī'a* in the social, economic, and political realms and ensured a just social order alongside political legitimacy.

Islamic social justice theory is not exclusively the work of jurists to the extent that philosophers and scholars of ethics also contributed to this theory. They focused on the relationship between the virtues of a ruler and social justice. al-Fārābī's masterpiece *On the Perfect State* (*al-Madīna al-Fāḍila*) has been the definitive source for scholars of ethics, including Naṣīr ad-Dīn aṭ-Ṭūsī's (1201–1274/597–673) highly influential work *Akhlāq-i Naṣīrī*. For al-Fārābī, a just ruler should have certain qualities such as wisdom, love, fairness, good memory, and physical health. In his utopian notion of a virtuous city, the ruler's most important job is to implement justice. According to al-Fārābī, a ruler might achieve this goal by using his knowledge of Islamic law, the implementation of which would ensure the realization of public interest and justice.[96]

Building on al-Fārābī's ideas, the genre of didactic political literature, *mirrors for princes*,[97] was a guide for rulers for centuries, helping them to apply Islamic law and implement justice. A ruler can govern effectively by preserving religion, property, intellect, life, and lineage. Thus, the ruler must maintain the principles of the *sharī'a* in order to implement these policies, a conviction also shared by the jurists.[98] The welfare of the *umma* was also the most significant social justice issue for scholars like Ibn Taymīya and Ibn Khaldūn (1332–1406/732–809). Although Ibn Taymīya was a jurist and Khaldūn was a philosopher, both searched for religious justifications and positive rules to help implement social justice, which presumably were seen as solutions to the moral and social ills of a declining society.[99] A Ruler's engagement with the law was the most significant element of justice for these scholars. As Khadduri[100] states in his account of Ibn Taymīya:

> The unity of Religion and Law (state), which exists in principle, must be carried out in practice. Without the effective power (*shawka*) of the state, he [Ibn Taymiyya] held, religion and Law would be in danger. Conversely, without the constraints of the Law, the state (presided over by despotic rulers) degenerates into an unjust and tyrannical organization. Only in the pursuit of justice can the state be expected to fulfill the ends for which it was established. The justice that Ibn Taymiyya strove to achieve was obviously a new concept enshrined in the

**96** Al-Fārābī, *Al-Fārābī on the Perfect State.*
**97** Ahmed, *What Is Islam?*
**98** Fadl, *Islam, and the Challenge of Democracy*; Abdelkader, *Social Justice in Islam.*
**99** Khadduri, *The Islamic Conception of Justice.*
**100** Ibid., 179–80.

*siyasa shar'iyya* which might be called social justice, as its aims were to serve the public interest.

Although the proposed constraint on the ruler introduces political accountability into Ibn Taymīya's theory, his approach may also justify unconditional political obedience. If a ruler protects religiosity, prevents vice, and provides public goods, it would not be acceptable to rebel against him even if he were unjust. The Mongol invasion undermined the democratic potential of Ibn Taymīya's theory at the expense of unconditional obedience. The devastation brought on Muslim regions countered this potential by replacing the classical Islamic state with an absolutist model of governance. The codification of religious law and experimentation with new constitutional orders in Iran and Turkey[101] rendered both the Taymīyan model and the absolutist incarnations of Islamic statehood obsolete. New interpretations of both social and political justice now made the encounters with the West and modernity their point of departure. This development is particularly visible in the positions taken up by proponents of a constitutionalist movement and Islamists.[102]

# 4 Modernity and Islamic Justice

In the modern age, the confrontation between the West and the Muslim world has created tensions that engendered various responses from intellectuals. Given the West's economic and military superiority, a search for new standards of justice that could replace the political and social justice paradigms of the old was immediately launched. Traditional standards did not address the conditions that accompanied industrialization, colonialism, and the scientific revolution. As Khadduri[103] states, "Muslim thinkers began to reexamine the classical conception of justice when they became aware that its relevance to reality was significantly outdistanced by the material advantages which man derived from the standards of justice in Western society." To understand this search for new conceptions of justice, we need to examine the Muslim response to modernity and colonialism since the 18th century.

**101** Yavuz, M. Hakan, "Turkey: Islam without Shari'a?," in Robert W. Hefner (ed.), *Shari'a Politics: Islamic Law and Society in the Modern World*, Bloomington: Indiana University Press, 2009.
**102** Gellner, Ernest, "Islam and Marxism: Some Comparisons," *International Affairs* 67, no. 1 (1991), 1–6.
**103** Khadduri, *The Islamic Conception of Justice*, 195–96.

## 4.1 Modernist Islam and Justice

The early origins of contemporary Islamist movements can be traced back to the 18th-century renewal and reformism movements (*tajdīd wa-l-iṣlāḥ*).[104] *Tajdīd* is not exclusively a modern movement or merely a response to the Western encroachment on the Muslim world. We can trace back its origins to the medieval period. Islamic scholars like al-Ghazālī and Ibn Taymīya were known as *mujaddids* (person involved in the renewal of the religion). Thus, the medieval period had its own change makers. Like the modernists later on, these scholars were responding to a dramatic change in socio-economic conditions. Their goal was to counter the rising influence of new interpretations of Islam which they viewed as contrary to the "pure" message of the Qurʾān and the tradition of the prophet Muhammad.[105] Just like these early reformers, the revivalists and later the modernists were also dealing with new economic and political conditions. In their case, these changes were the result of modernization and colonialism. The puritan revivalists of the 18th century, such as Muḥammad Ibn al-Wahhāb (1703–1792/1115–1206) in Arabia, had also criticized new interpretations of Islam current in their lifetime, which were inspired by the veneration of saints and shrines in Shiism and Sufism. Justice (and the lack thereof) was one of the principal preoccupations of the scholars of renewal.

The search for a new paradigm of justice originated from the problems posed by dramatic changes in the global economy. The increasing share of Western countries in global trade and the European colonialism of the 19th century shattered the belief in Muslim superiority in the Islamic world. This crisis of confidence was caused by the European subjugation of the Muslim populations in Asia, Africa, and the Middle East and the significant cultural shock it had entailed for Muslims. The need for a response to colonialism was one of the main triggers of the modern revivalist and modernist Islamic movements. This distinct point of departure meant that these movements differed clearly from the classic renewal movements of the medieval age.[106] The significant socio-economic transformations accompanying colonial rule since the 18th century had created a set of deep ideational, cultur-

---

**104** Lapidus, Ira M, "Islamic Revival and Modernity: The Contemporary Movements and the Historical Paradigms," *Journal of the Economic and Social History of the Orient* 40, no. 4 (1997), 444–60; Ayoob, Mohammed, "Challenging Hegemony: Political Islam and the North–South Divide," *International Studies Review* 9, no. 4 (2007), 629–43.

**105** Ibid.

**106** Lapidus; Ayoob, Mohammed, *The Many Faces of Political Islam: Religion and Politics in the Muslim World*, Ann Arbor: University of Michigan Press, 2009; Ciftci, Sabri, *Islam, Justice, and Democracy*, Philadelphia, PA: Temple University Press, 2022.

al, and social crises throughout the Muslim world. Particularly significant was the feeling that injustice had taken hold. Consequently, in search of justice, Muslim intellectuals began their search for an Islamic answer fit to correct the apparent decline vis-à-vis European civilization. Since modernization and colonialism had shattered traditional concepts of Islamic justice, a Muslim response to this challenge came in the form of the revival and reform of religion. Thus, an absence of "true" religion was identified as the reason for the losses incurred by colonialism.

A long-lasting consensus, referred to as the Sunni-Sharīʿa-Sufi synthesis,[107] had been the status quo in the Islamic world. It informed the paradigm of Islamic social and political justice from the 13th to the 18th centuries and was first questioned by two scholars from South Asia [Sayyid Aḥmad Barelwī (1786–1831/1200–1247) and Shāh Walī Allāh of Delhi (1703–1762/1115–1176)] looking to remedy the decline of the Islamic civilization. Their solution was twofold. First, they called for a puritanical understanding of religion that prioritized a return to the "true" and "pure" meaning of the Qurʾān and *sunna*, the implementation of true *sharīʿa*, and an acceptance of the referential authority of the four schools of law. Second, they called for religious reform in order to safeguard Islam's relevance and to find solutions to the problems of Muslims in the face of colonialism, modernity, and changing socio-economic conditions. These scholars frequently used the classical sources of Islam. Accordingly, they reverted to the traditional notions of justice developed during the early and medieval period.

A second Islamic response emerged in the late 19th century in Russia, Asia, and the Ottoman Empire. The modernist Islamist movement led by Jamāl ad-Dīn al-Afghānī and his disciple Muḥammad ʿAbduh (1849–1905/1265–1323) was part of this second revivalist wave. The main goal of these scholars was to show that Western science, technology, rationality, and its political structure are compatible with Islam.[108] Some modernists, like Muḥammad ʿAbduh, also attempted to show that Islamic law is compatible with natural law and consequently with justice and freedom.[109] Some of the Islamic modernists were also political activists who strove to fight Western imperialism by mobilizing the masses through pan-Islamist ideologies and constitutionalist movements. It is this latter group that has developed new paradigms of justice, as discussed in detail in this section.

---

**107** Lapidus, "Islamic Revival and Modernity."

**108** Ayoob, *The Many Faces of Political Islam*; Keddie, Nikki R, *An Islamic Response to Imperialism: Political and Religious Writings of Sayyid Jamāl al-Dīn al-Afghānī*, vol. 586, Berkeley, CA: University of California Press, 1983.

**109** Sedgwick, Mark, *Muhammad ʿAbduh*; Khadduri, *The Islamic Conception of Justice.*

These new Islamic theories of justice were inextricably modern and at once firmly committed to main streams of Islamist thought. Because Islamist ideology moved between a progressive and traditional pole, it included both traditional conceptions of justice based on principles of the prophetic community, the medieval Islamic state, and traditional jurisprudence, on one hand, and modern conceptions that involved references to natural law and democracy, on the other.[110] Those who interpreted traditional conceptions of justice invoked the values of the so-called *golden age*, a period during the time of the Prophet Muḥammad that represented a puritanical understanding of religion. Such a move encouraged a return to the "true Islam" of Muḥammad and the *rāshidūn caliphs* (the first four caliphs) as a perfect embodiment of justice. Traditionalists were also greatly inspired by the Sunni jurisprudents and their justice conceptions, particularly by Ibn Taymīya's theory of social justice. The modernist camp, on the other hand, used the legal methods of *ijtihād* and *qiyās* and employed novel interpretations of Islam. This approach allowed them to combine political justice conceptions that relied on the free will of man with the responsibility of the *umma* members to appoint or remove a ruler. Thus, an old idea came to be expressed in constitutionalist terms.[111]

It should be noted that the traditionalist ideology of Islamic modernists was by no means anti-modern. In fact, the proponents of this camp were as modern in their practice and strategies as they could be. They were traditional only in their religious outlook. By and large, Islamist modernists could not escape the tension between the old and the new and tried to find a compromise between modernity and tradition. This tension is especially visible in the works of ʿAbduh who left an ambiguous legacy that was taken up by both traditional and secular modernist thinkers of subsequent generations. Rashīd Riḍā (1865–1935/1282–1354), a disciple of ʿAbduh, greatly influenced 20th century Islamism. His thought eventually evolved toward a traditional understanding in support of scriptural literalism. This perspective provides the main background for political Islamism and modern theories of justice.

In the traditional as well as the modernist camp, most Islamists rejected the wholesale application of Western standards. The primary concern for revivalists and reformists was the compatibility of Western (secular) standards and the Qur'ān, or rather, whether revelation could be understood to encompass Western science and rationality. al-Afghānī believed that domestic despotism and foreign powers created injustices against the Muslim people by undermining their free

110 Ayoob, *The Many Faces of Political Islam*; Moaddel, Mansoor, *Islamic Modernism, Nationalism, and Fundamentalism: Episode and Discourse*, Chicago: University of Chicago Press, 2005.
111 Ciftci, *Islam, Justice, and Democracy*.

agency and social welfare. Because Muslim rulers submitted to foreign powers, their dignity was harmed and their legitimacy undermined.[112] This outcome stood in contradiction to the values of Islamic political justice. To remove these injustices, he argues, Muslim rulers should implement political reform and allow for the participation of their people in public affairs through elected assemblies according to the Islamic *shūrā* or consultation principle.[113] This policy would help the rulers gain legitimacy and earn public support against foreign powers. Only then, al-Afghānī believes, could Muslims rulers join forces as a Pan-Islamist force to end foreign domination.[114] By and large, al-Afghānī's conception of justice resembles Islamic political justice in the sense that man is given choice and responsibility in accordance with his vicegerency status. People, that is believers, should have the right to elect their rulers in democratic elections. This is the modern path to implementing political justice.

al-Afghānī's disciple ʿAbduh largely followed his master, but he took a different approach to justice. He was a judge and hence more interested in procedural justice. This led him closer to classical legal theory, but he also believed that one cannot ignore the Western conception of justice and its standards. His main contention was that Western science and ideas were not necessarily incompatible with Islam. Therefore, interpreting Islamic law in the light of reason is not add odds with Islamic principles.[115] With this approach, ʿAbduh was employing the jurisprudential methods of *ijmāʿ* and *qiyās* while also considering Western standards to develop an Islamic justice conception appropriate for his time.

## 4.2 Constitutionalism and Justice

From South and Central Asia to Africa and the Ottoman capital, Muslim encounters with the West caused revivalist and reformist movements to flourish. While modernist intellectuals were instrumental in developing new theories of justice that reconciled Islamic principles with Western ideas, it was the constitutionalists who had carefully designed new incarnations of an Islamic conception of justice.

The point of departure for the constitutionalists was the same as it was for revivalists and reformists: the search for a response to the West's ascendance. As the Ottoman elite became increasingly aware of the economic and political decline of the state vis-à-vis the European powers, they implemented various reforms to save

112 Keddie, *An Islamic Response to Imperialism*; Ciftci, *Islam, Justice, and Democracy.*
113 Khadduri, *The Islamic Conception of Justice*, 197.
114 Keddie, *An Islamic Response to Imperialism*; Khadduri, *The Islamic Conception of Justice*, 198.
115 Khadduri, *The Islamic Conception of Justice*, 199.

the state. Diplomats and students who traveled to European countries to learn about Western civilization believed that freedom and a constitutional government would be a cure-all to the problems of their time. Initial reforms were miniscule, top-down, and they did not undermine either the power of the Sultan or that of the traditional institutions. However, an important group of 19th-century intellectuals, the *Young Ottomans*, proposed political strategies inspired by Western political models, especially those inspired by the notion of popular sovereignty, in order to bring change.[116]

There were several top-down attempts to institute constitutional government in the Ottoman capital and its periphery, including the *tanẓīmāt* reforms, the convening of an elected parliament by the Khedive of Egypt, and the declaration of a constitution by the Tunisian ruler Khayr ad-Dīn Pāshā (d. 1890/ 1307).[117] More significant in paving the way for future popular mobilization was the Ottoman constitutionalist movement that was inspired by the concepts of popular sovereignty and executive accountability a small group of elites whose influence outsized its numbers.[118] This movement eventually gave way to a short-lived constitutional monarchy, *Meşrutiyet*, in 1876. Notably, Ottoman reformism inspired similar movements in other parts of the Middle East, especially the Iranian constitutionalist movement of 1905–1911.

Constitutionalism had a significant influence on the development of a new paradigm of justice. This paradigm incorporated ideas of freedom and popular sovereignty, and it was greatly inspired by the Islamic notion of justice. The transformation of the constitutional revolutions from the project of a small elite to widespread popular mobilization – supported by discourses on justice – is a highly significant development in the history of the Middle East in the 20th century. For example, the ʿUrābī revolt in Egypt (1879–1882) was initially carried out by military officers against the government, but it later inspired ordinary citizens and spread to the streets of Egypt. In Iran, the 1905 Constitutional Revolution had a broad base formed by a coalition of religious scholars, merchants, and professionals. The leaders of these groups managed to mobilize the masses utilizing the language of Islamic justice and exploiting the prevalence of anti-imperialism among

116 Mardin, Serif, The *Genesis of Young Ottoman Thought: A Study in the Modernization of Turkish Political Ideas*, Syracuse, NY: Syracuse University Press, 2000.

117 Tanẓīmāt is the period of reforms that began in 1839 and ended when the first constitutional government took office in 1876. The reforms were based on Western political institutions and aimed at modernizing the structure of the Ottoman state, cf. Lewis, Bernard, "Why Turkey Is the Only Muslim Democracy," *Middle East Quarterly* 1, no. 1 (1994), 41–49.

118 Lewis, Bernard, The *Emergence of Modern Turkey*, New York: Oxford University Press, 1961; Mardin, *The Genesis of Young Ottoman Thought.*

the public.[119] For example, public anger against the economic concessions given to the imperial powers by the Qajars led to the Tobacco Protest (1890–1891) in Iran.[120] Similarly, the protest of Ottoman intellectuals' against financial and military imperialism were significant rallying points for the constitutionalist movements of the age. When people chanted *ḥurrīya* (freedom) in the streets of the Ottoman Empire, they were clearly calling for justice and an end to Western as well as domestic oppression. Religion also played a role in this development with its discourses on justice serving as a glue capable of binding different classes together. Thus, it should not come as a surprise that religious scholars like Muḥammad ʿAbduh and Iranian religious scholars were among the leaders of the constitutionalist revolutions.[121]

The success of these constitutionalist movements was greatly dependent upon their leaders' ability to mobilize the public to strive toward new political ideals such as freedom. By and large, their success owed itself to their ability to locate constitutionalism and freedom in the framework of traditional ideologies more familiar to the public, especially drawing on Islamic conceptions of just government. These movements successfully conveyed the idea to the public that popular sovereignty, freedom, and constitutional government are not foreign ideas to Islam, but rather elements of Islamic government. In other words, the popular support for constitutionalism that gave way to widespread mobilization in the first constitutionalist movements of the Middle East was the product of a creative intellectual strategy that justified such notions as accountability, executive constraints, and freedom by using Islamic conceptions of justice.

Religious modernists like al-Afghānī, ʿAbduh, and Muḥammad Iqbāl (1877–1938/1294–1357) argued that belief in science and the idea of progress are intrinsic to Islam and it did not take much to add democracy to this list.[122] Because justice has been a central problematic area in Islamic political theory since its foundation, it was convenient to make frequent references to justice in explaining, to the public, the need for modernizing reforms and constitutionalism. These references were not solely based on political justice conceptions, but they also involved ideas related to the goals of *sharīʿa* aiming to establish social welfare. As such,

119 Thompson, *Justice Interrupted.*

120 Keddie, Nikki R, *Religion and Rebellion in Iran: The Tobacco Protest of 1891–1892*, London: Frank Cass, 1966.

121 Abrahamian, Ervand, *Iran between Two Revolutions*, Princeton: Princeton University Press, 1982; Thompson, *Justice Interrupted.*

122 Keddie, *An Islamic Response to Imperialism*; Moaddel, *Islamic Modernism, Nationalism, and Fundamentalism*; Ayoob, "Political Islam: Image and Reality."

modernists and constitutionalists also propagated Islamic social justice to demand good government, welfare services, and provision of public goods.

A brief account of the ideas of Namık Kemal, a famous poet, playwright, and ardent supporter of Ottoman constitutionalism, will help demonstrate this last point. In an influential essay titled *And Seek their Council in the Matter*, Kemal reconciled Western ideas with the requisites of Islamic law to present solutions for the Ottoman Empire's decline.[123] He blamed its decay on its lack of freedom and a constitution. For him these deficits were incompatible with Islamic teaching because God created man to have agency as his representative on earth and hence people deserve the freedom to choose their own government. This argument is significant because it places Kemal in the same camp with the trajectory of Islamic political justice developed by the Qadari school. Contrary to the political quietism of the school of predetermination, on this account, the public should have a say in political matters, especially when choosing institutions that safeguard individual freedoms. As Kemal[124] states, "therefore, just as all individuals have the natural right to exercise their own power, so too conjoined powers naturally belong to all individuals as a whole, and consequently, in every society, the right to sovereignty belongs to the public."

In one variant of Sunni political theology, sovereignty belongs to the *umma* – the global community of Muslims. The public is responsible for choosing an imam, but they still retain the power to hold the ruler accountable and the right to depose him if injustices emerge.[125] Kemal believes that power should not be given to an absolute ruler who has no constraints on his power and may thus give way to injustice.[126] To ensure that the state will abide by the principles of justice, Kemal proposed that the state's executive and administrative duties should be transparent and subject to scrutiny and that the legislative function be given to an elected, representative body. In his essay, he also investigates the causes behind the state's decline, including inefficient government, corruption, and failing economic policies. These issues are closely related to Islamic conceptions of social justice. The vision developed by traditional jurisprudents that necessitates the protection of religion, life, and progeny and the provision of social welfare is especially close to his own. Once again, Kemal returns to constitution as a panacea. For him, all of the problems named above could be addressed by the institution of a constitutional regime

**123** Wa-shāwirhum fi l-amri (Qur'ān, 3:159).
**124** Kemal, Namik, "And Seek Their Council in the Affairs," Charles Kurzman (eds.), *Liberal Islam: A Source Book*, 114–48, New York: Oxford University Press, 1998.
**125** Khadduri, *The Islamic Conception of Justice*; Enayat, *Modern Islamic Political*; March, *The Caliphate of Man.*
**126** Kemal, "And Seek Their Council in the Affairs," 146.

that relies on the principles of executive accountability and popular sovereignty.[127] Overall, Kemal justified the instalment of a constitutional regime by reverting to the Islamic principles and addressed the practical challenges facing the state as impediments to the implementation of justice.

Kemal was not alone in reconciling Western ideas with Islamic theories of justice. His work exemplifies an intellectual strategy that was also seen in Egypt during the ʿUrābī revolt and in Iran during the Constitutionalist Revolution of 1905. During the age of early constitutionalist movements in the Muslim world, it was essential to convince the public of the compatibility of Western political institutions with Islam. Intellectuals could have used the framework provided by the *circle of justice* to explain this proposition to the public, as it was well understood by the people.[128] However, a second element was needed to create popular mobilization. The intellectuals of the constitutionalist movements had to inspire the masses by linking these abstract ideas to real-life problems to make them comprehensible to ordinary people. As a result, they discussed corruption, inefficient government, poverty, economic decline, lack of freedom, and inequality and linked these notions to Islamic justice. In other words, the constitutionalist movements needed leaders who could utilize the traditional language familiar to the public to motivate the masses. These leaders emerged throughout the 20th century in various uprisings, such as Aḥmad ʿUrābī (1841–1911/1257–1329) in Egypt, Mīrzā Seyyed Muḥammad Ṭabāṭabāʾī (1842–1920/1258–1338) in Iran, and Halide Edib Adıvar (1884–1964/1301–1384) in the context of war of liberation in Turkey.[129]

These constitutionalist movements employed a strategy that attributed the social and political problems of the day to the decline of the ideals implied by the *circle of justice.* As both Thompson and Darling[130] argue, the *circle of justice* lost its prominence as a political idea in the modern era, however, the underlying principles concerning the provision of public goods, security, and social justice continued to thrive in the nationalist, liberal, socialist, and Islamist ideologies of the 20th century. As the Middle East descended into authoritarianism in the aftermath of the Second World War, the ideals stemming from Islamic conceptions of justice survived in popular usage. These ideals included freedom, human dignity, and general welfare, all of which are essential to Islamic political and social justice.

The constitutional arrangements marrying Islamic principles with modern ideas were not always accepted without reproach. The main point of contention was the application of secular standards that were deemed incompatible with

**127** Ibid., 145–48.

**128** Darling, *A History of Social.*

**129** Thompson, *Justice Interrupted.*

**130** Darling, *A History of Social Justice*; Thompson, *Justice Interrupted.*

Islam in the political sphere, and they met with significant public resistance. There was a great backlash from different parts of the Muslim world when Mustafa Kemal Atatürk (d. 1938/1357), the founder of modern Turkey, abolished the caliphate in 1924, symbolically embedding its power in the Turkish parliament. Kemal's reforms went even further. He employed policies that aimed to forcibly enact secularization in the social realm and eventually made Turkey the first Muslim country to completely accept secular standards. Others kept Islamic as well as some secular standards in their formulas of political justice without going to the extent of the Kemalist reforms. The unchanging influence of more traditional conceptions of justice and the simultaneous appeal of new ideas originating from the West merged into an uneasy synthesis between Islamic law and modern ideas. As Khadduri[131] succinctly puts it, "this resulted in the establishment of two levels of political justice without any serious effort to harmonize them. The office of Imamate remained in theory, but no agreement was reached to enthrone an Imam." Egyptian intellectual ʿAlī ʿAbd ar-Rāziq (1888–1966/1305–1386) tried to resolve this duality by making the case for the abolition of the caliphate and proposing a secularization of the standards of justice in Islamic constitutions. He argued that the caliphate lacked a binding religious foundation, and that questions of governance and justice should be addressed through human deliberation and reason, rather than through a presumed divine sanction. He believes that while the Prophet used political authority during his lifetime when it was necessary, his mission was strictly religious. Furthermore, the prophet's special mission as the spiritual and political leader of the *umma* ended with his death. Beginning with the first caliph Abū Bakr, the office was limited to the political realm, and a religious quality was assigned to it only by later generations. ʿAbd ar-Rāziq also introduced a theory of the practical implementation of social justice akin to Ibn Khaldūn's welfare-oriented social justice paradigm. He argues that only the principles of faith are timeless. All other matters should be taken as secular and thus as subject to change.[132] Therefore, any developments that cause harm to the welfare of a society should be dealt with according to the needs of the society.

In conclusion, while traditional interpretations of Islam informed the Islamic conceptions of justice developed by modernists, the latter also relied on scriptural principles but interpreted them in new ways. For example, *ʿadāla* came to be equated with freedom in the constitutionalist positions. Other readings took *ʿadāla* to mean the Qurʾānic principle of *al-amr bi-l-maʿrūf wa-n-nahy ʿani-l-munkar* and

131 ʿAbd ar-Razīq, ʿAlī, *al-Islām wa-uṣūl al-ḥukm: Baḥth fi-l-khilāfa wa-l-ḥukūma fi-l-Islām* (Islam and the Foundations of Governance: Research on the Caliphate and Governance in Islam), Bayrūt: Dār Maktabat al-Ḥayāh, 1978; Khadduri, *The Islamic Conception of Justice*, 202.
132 Khadduri, 203–4.

gave it a modern reading in the form of good governance, social welfare, and provision of public goods. A dynamic interpretation of justice based on Qur'ānic notions also informs more recent developments in Islamist thought and this will be examined in the next section.

## 5 Islamism and Justice

The analysis up to this point introduced the scriptural, philosophical, and legal foundations of a variety of conceptions of justice. Previous sections also demonstrated that among different aspects of justice the social and political dimensions of Islamic justice conceptions took center stage in Islam. Debates about political justice relate to the disagreement about leader selection in the early Muslim community and the resulting political divisions. In the medieval period, the focus shifted toward social justice and the welfare of the community to address the decline in Muslim society at the time. Within the Islamic social justice paradigm, economic justice encouraging egalitarian distribution and charity are especially important. Throughout Islamic history, the prophetic community has been treated as the perfect example for the embodiment of Islam's economic justice model. Alongside Muḥammad, the second caliph ʿUmar is presented as an ideal ruler who was always just in his social and political dealings. Modern Islamists have used this legacy and the new justice paradigms of modernist scholars to develop a new Islamic theory of justice. In doing so, they have provided new interpretations of the Qur'ānic terms concerning justice to address the problems of their respective contexts. For example, the notion of *tawḥīd* has inspired early and contemporary Islamists to develop comprehensive social systems based on the ideal of a harmonious and unified society.[133] Some scholars used the principle of *shūrā* to justify pluralistic ideas in Islam. They equated justice with freedom and democracy.[134] Rebellion against *ẓulm* (tyranny) has been an important ideological principle employed by Islamists like ʿAlī Sharīʿatī.[135] Man's status as vicegerent (*khalīfa*), another Qur'ānic term, led Tunisian Islamist al-Ghannūshī to describe justice in terms of human dig-

---

**133** Al-Mawdudi, "Islam in Transition: Muslim Perspective"; Iqbal, *The Reconstruction of Religious Thought in Islam.*

**134** Kemal, Namık, "And Seek Their Council in the Affairs,"; Sachedina, Abdulaziz, *The Islamic Roots of Democratic Pluralism*, New York: Oxford University Press, 2001; Fadl, *Islam, and the Challenge of Democracyk.*

**135** Sharīʿatī , Ali, "Red Shi'ism (the Religion of Martyrdom) vs. Black Shi'ism (the Religion of Mourning)," published online: *Iran Chamber Society*, https://www.iranchamber.com/personalities/aSharīʿatī /works/red_black_shiism.php (accessed on 19.06.2024).

nity and free will, two principles that also underly democratic ideals.[136] As we can see here, there is certainly a vast intellectual field of Islamists who employ the scriptural and traditional sources of Islam to develop solutions for the problems of modernity, particularly those concerning justice and democracy. Within this field, Sayyid Quṭb and ʿAlī Sharīʿatī stand out for their comprehensive theories of justice.

The following section sets out to explain the foundations of Islamist approaches to justice by focusing on the philosophies of Sayyid Quṭb and ʿAlī Sharīʿatī. It also introduces a brief review of other contemporary Islamists' views on justice to put Quṭb and Sharīʿatī's thoughts into perspective. Quṭb and Sharīʿatī acknowledge the traditional conceptions of justice and focus on Qurʾānic terms like *tawḥīd* and *ẓulm* to develop their own. While Quṭb seeks justice in the unity and harmony of the society in accordance with the *tawḥīd* principle, Sharīʿatī rebels against *ẓulm* or tyranny. His critique of tyranny is the centerpiece of his political philosophy. As depicted below, it remains unclear how these concepts can help to achieve justice in practice or how they could be realized in an Islamic society. Both authors assign a central role to man as *khalīfa* and as an agent striving to establish justice. Specifically, free human agency and benevolent or charitable acts are constitutive principles of the Islamist conception of social justice put forth in their philosophies. In addition, just like the modernists a century earlier, both scholars respond to the current challenges Muslim societies are facing by proposing Islam as the sole panacea to modern social ills.

Before providing a systematic discussion of Quṭb's and Sharīʿatī's social justice theories, we must compare Islamist conceptions of religion and justice to their counterparts in Western thought. Liberal justice theories are strictly secular paradigms based on a consensus about minimally acceptable rights and economic distribution.[137] In contrast, the Islamist conception avoids the religious-secular binary and uses scriptural principles in an encompassing way to provide solutions to worldly injustices. While liberal theories of justice have also drawn on Christian ideals of justice and natural law,[138] in Islam, religious principles have remained much more salient in shaping theories of justice. The active engagement of free and conscious individuals as a central factor in the implementation of social and political justice is an important premise of Islamist conceptions of justice. In his seminal study of the Islamic state, Abdullahi Ahmed an-Naim[139] states,

136 Tamimi, Azzam, *Rachid Ghannouchi: A Democrat within Islamism*, New York: Oxford University Press, 2001; March, *The Caliphate of Man.*
137 Rawls, *A Theory of Justice*; Lorenz, "The Emergence of Social Justice in the West."
138 Maguire, Daniel C., "Religious Influences on Justice Theory."
139 An-Naim, *Islam and the Secular State*, 1.

"this emphasis on the agency of the human subject in determining what justice means for her, and striving for realizing her own conception, leads me to focus on Muslims as believers seeking justice, rather than speaking of Islam as a religion." This insight is similar to the implications that emanate from the scriptural notion of *khalīfa.* In the same vein, this section shows that conceptions of Islamist justice are not merely sophisticated ideals but have widespread practical implications for the socio-political realm thanks to the active role assigned to Muslim agency.

## 5.1 Sayyid Quṭb: Religious Law and Social Justice

The Egyptian scholar, teacher, and activist Sayyid Quṭb is best known as the ideologue of the Egyptian Muslim Brothers. He is also widely regarded for his ideas inspiring radical Islamist movements and Salafi Jihadism. He was the leading member of the Muslim Brothers in 1950s and 1960s, a large Islamist organization that was active in society and represented the main opposition against an authoritarian regime. He viewed Egypt's secular society and the ruling regime as un-Islamic and strived to educate a vanguard generation that would establish an Islamic order. He was imprisoned and executed by the Egyptian regime for plotting an assassination against the Egyptian President Jamāl ʿAbd an-Nāṣir (1918–1970/1336–1390) in 1966. The author of more than two dozen books and numerous articles, Quṭb developed his theory of social justice in *Social Justice in Islam, Milestones,* and in his Qur'ānic exegesis, *In the Shade of the Qur'ān.* In his conception of justice, Quṭb places Islamic law at the center of a harmonious society where economic and political justice prevail.[140] This brings him closer to the classical jurisprudential view that gives priority to the law and legal principles in defining the Islamic conception of justice, but his approach remains modern. He also provides a sharp criticism of Western societies because, in his view, they are too materialistic and thus neglect the spiritual side of man. Consequently, he provides a native justice theory and delineates it from the Western and Christian conceptions of justice. However, it can be stated that his account of Western and Christian ideas is rudimentary and does not fully recognize the depth of these traditions in developing dynamic conceptions of justice.

Quṭb's seminal work, *Social Justice in Islam,* was published in 1949, in the aftermath of the World War II and at the dawn of the Cold War. At that time, capital-

**140** March, Andrew F. "Taking People as They Are: Islam as a 'Realistic Utopia' in the Political Theory of Sayyid Quṭb," *American Political Science Review* 104, no. 1 (2010): 189–207.

ism and communism were regarded as two competing economic systems represented by democratic regimes on the one hand and communist regimes on the other. Against these alternatives, Quṭb presented an Islamic system combining both material and spiritual values. As detailed below, the Quṭbian theory of social justice relies on the twin pillars of an inner purification of man and lawfulness within the community. In an Islamic society, freedom of conscience, emancipation, and charitable acts play a central role in upholding these pillars.

The principle of *tawḥīd* plays a vital role in Quṭb's social justice theory.[141] It should be noted that long before Quṭb and Sharīʿatī, Muslim philosophers and early 20th century Islamists like Muhammad ʿAbduh also understood *tawḥīd* to be a fundamental principle that underlies the organization of social, economic, and political life.[142]

In *Social Justice in Islam*, Sayyid Quṭb defines Islamic justice in rather broad terms in order to take into account interactions among such concepts as God, the universe, life, and mankind. In this complex picture, *tawḥīd* is the primary element that connects everything and creates a meaningful whole of these broad concepts. In Quṭb's[143] words, "because, the universe is a unity emanating from a single Will; because man is himself a part of the world, dependent upon and related to all the other parts; and because individuals are as atoms, dependent upon and related to all the other parts; and because they must have the same dependence upon, and relation to, one another."

This approach lays the groundwork for distinguishing Quṭb's Islamic conception of justice from concepts developed in Western civilization. He talks about essential dualities present in Christianity and modern Western civilization like the separation of religion and state or the divide between the material and the spiritual. In Islam, unity replaces this duality thanks to *tawḥīd*, which is like a glue that holds everything together. The human person also represents a unity, but it is made of differing desires. In its servitude to God (*ʿubūdīya*) and through its prayers, humanity joins in unity with God.[144]

The resolution of dualities in human and society thanks to the *tawḥīd* principle has important implications for the Islamic conception of social justice, which Quṭb develops by highlighting the tension between the material and spiritual. According to Quṭb, social justice need not only address either the material needs of

**141** The following discussion builds on Quṭb's *Social Justice in Islam* and several works of Sharīʿatī's. I make conservative use of citations by reserving them for direct quotes and when a discussion heavily relies on the terminology of the text.

**142** Sedgwick, *Muhammad ʿAbduh.*

**143** Quṭb, *Social Justice in Islam*, 41.

**144** Quṭb, *Social Justice in Islam*, 41.

the individual as in communism and capitalism or the spiritual needs as in Christianity. Life consists not only of material desires. It also consists of, "mercy, love, help, and a mutual responsibility [...] There are, then, these two great facts. The absolute, just, and coherent unity of existence, and the general mutual responsibility of individuals and societies. On these two facts Islam bases its realization of social justice, having regard for the basic elements of the nature of man, yet not unmindful of human abilities."[145] This account relies on a rudimentary and inaccurate representation of Christianity. When we regard the Christian tradition more closely, we can find a sophisticated model of social justice based on the principle of love. The Christian account of justice does consider both material and spiritual needs. In fact, Christian conceptions of justice have inspired egalitarian social democratic models and liberation theology.[146]

In his account of social justice, Quṭb also refers to a cosmic balance, a perfectly harmonious social order where neither the needs of man nor the welfare of society are neglected. In contrast to communism, Islamic justice does not require absolute economic equality because individuals differ in their material and spiritual endowments. Quṭb also recognizes *ḥaqq* (rights, deserving), a right that comes with hard work, and the ideal of equal opportunity as essential pillars of Islamic social justice.[147] While *ḥaqq* is important, too great an emphasis on worldly life is not in accordance with the Islamic faith. Islam also demands for every individual to gain moral competence by freeing himself from the constraints of material needs. In Quṭb's words, Islam "prescribes the claims of the poor upon the wealth of the rich, according to their needs, and according to the best interests of the society, so that social life may be balanced, just, and productive."[148]

How can one establish this balance between the individual and society? Is this vision nothing but a utopian dream? To answer this question, Quṭb elaborates on the principles of social justice and assigns a central role to human agency in order to show the possibilities of a harmonious, just society. For Quṭb, three principles are critical in establishing Islamic social justice: absolute freedom of conscience, the complete equality of all men, and a firm mutual responsibility within society or solidarity.[149] All three require the active involvement of human agency. Given these principles, social justice depends on the fulfillment of man's spiritual and material needs. For Quṭb, there should be an inner conviction of the value of social

**145** Ibid., 45.
**146** Maguire, "Religious Influences on Justice Theory"; Smith, *The Emergence of Liberation Theology*; Gutierrez, *A Liberation Theology*.
**147** Quṭb, *Social Justice in Islam*, 47–48.
**148** Ibid, 49.
**149** Quṭb, *Social Justice in Islam*, 52.

justice (as in Christianity) rooted in the spiritual. On the material side, an individual should be willing to pay the costs of this conviction and be ready to defend social justice (as in socialism).[150] Quṭb's attribution of the material and the spiritual to socialism and Christianity respectively relies on a caricaturized depiction of both. In reality, both socialism and Christianity have sophisticated conceptions of justice that consider the material needs as well as the need for fulfillment as relevant factors in an individual's existence. This stylized portrayal has nonetheless had a lasting impact. We can trace its influence down to the ideology of present-day Islamist groups and political parties.[151]

Another weakness of Quṭb's theory lies in the naivety of his assumption that a community of believers will unconditionally accept his variant of the Islamic worldview. After all, his conception rests on the inner conviction of individuals. Without their application of Islamic social justice, the theory has no bearing. For Quṭb, this conviction is reliant on man obtaining a profound freedom of conscience, "by freeing the human conscience from servitude to anyone except Allah and from submission to any save Him."[152] Here, Quṭb employs scriptural terms like *tawḥīd*, and *rizq* (provision) to build his conception of justice. First, God's unquestionable oneness holds a monopoly as the sole provider (*ar-Razzāq*) and this leads to a direct relationship between God and his servant. The belief that God is the sole provider of mankind results in a psychology of existential security that frees man from his existential fears and his related anxieties. Since exclusive servitude requires the individual to believe that any other creature is incapable of hindering any part of God's provision, this frees the individual from the anxiety of earning a livelihood. For Quṭb,[153] this mechanism "strengthens the human heart and human conscience; it sets the poor man who is anxious over his livelihood on a level with a man who thinks that his provision is in his own hand, to be won with all his strength and resource." He acknowledges that freedom of conscience is not immune to social and material forces. However, when Islam intervenes, it will reduce the effect of material values, put these values in the proper place, and equip man with dignity.[154]

The realizability of the second foundational principle of social justice, equality, is dependent upon the extent to which man can free himself from the fears surrounding his need to earn his livelihood and avoid poverty.[155] In an Islamic out-

**150** Ibid., 53.
**151** Ciftci, *Islam, Justice, and Democracy.*
**152** Quṭb, *Social Justice in Islam*, 55.
**153** Ibid., 59.
**154** Ibid., 60.
**155** Quṭb, 68.

look, equality derives from the God-given nobility of man and rests on the idea that humanity is one in its origins. Quṭb supports this idea by citing a famous *ḥadīth:* "All people are equal as the teeth of a comb."[156] Just as he did with regard to other elements in his justice theory, Quṭb conceptualizes equality in reference to the all-encompassing nature of Islam. Equality becomes possible when Islam removes the duality between the material and the spiritual.[157] Here, Quṭb seems to neglect the real-life hinderances to establishing equality and justice. Rather, he focuses on abstract ideals to build a just, Islamic society. Unemployment and poverty posed significant problems in Egypt at the time. The patriarchal culture prevented women's empowerment and hindered gender equality. He acknowledged these issues as problems of ignorance (*jāhilīya*) and conceptualized a social system that he hoped could both improve the existing Islamic order and build on Islamic principles. However, his belief that belief in the Islamic faith would bring justice and equality without clearly laid out policy solutions was not realistic. This approach also missed the historical fact that the Prophet Muḥammad's success was based on his firm resolve not only on the propagation of faith principles but to address the socioeconomic problems of Arabic society.

Another pillar of the Quṭbian justice system is the principle of mutual responsibility that necessitates solidarity among the members of an Islamic society. According to Quṭb, while Islam helps an individual obtain freedom and equality, it also places some restraints in the form of mutual responsibility to ensure the welfare of all members of an Islamic society.[158] For him, every individual has a duty toward the social welfare and safety of others. The responsibility to prevent vice is a duty required of all members of an Islamic society because the whole community will be harmed if evil takes root. Society, in turn, has a responsibility to help its poor and destitute members as prescribed in the scripture and by the Prophet Muḥammad. According to Quṭb,[159] "the whole Islamic community is one body, and it feels all things in common; whatever happens to one of its members, the remainder of its members are also affected." Once again, Quṭb's account neglects the socioeconomic reality in this third pillar of justice. His social system can easily be a utopian society that is authoritarian in nature.[160] In his thought, there is a real danger of subduing individual freedom at the benefit of the promotion of societal good, a danger that might undermine Quṭb's three pillars of justice that rely on individual freedom.

---

**156** The Prophet Muhammad, as recorded in al-Qudai, Musnad al-Shihab, I, 145.

**157** Quṭb, *Social Justice in Islam*, 79.

**158** Quṭb, *Social Justice in Islam*, 86.

**159** Ibid., 90.

**160** March, "Taking People as They Are."

Quṭb is aware that establishing a just society will require a more comprehensive model of justice that moves beyond the mere distribution of material wealth. At a minimum, legal measures are necessary to implement social justice, such as the laws allowing the state to collect and distribute *zakāt* or the state's promotion of charity. Islamic law, too, requires these acts to promote the implementation of distributive justice. It appears as though Quṭb was aiming to establish a material basis for his ideal society by enforcing charitable acts through the coercive power of Islamic law. The failure of state-sanctioned *zakāt* collection in several Arab-majority societies in the 20$^{th}$ century[161] makes Quṭb's ideal vision less convincing. Thus, it appears Quṭb is aware that a material basis that is provided through economic and legal tools is necessary but not sufficient to build a just society. He introduces the idea of voluntary charitable acts, which are not externally imposed with a law and are not restricted to a fixed rate, to fill the gaps in his theory. Unlike *zakāt*, charity is not institutionalized but rather left to the discretion of the individuals. For Quṭb, charitable acts are the essential foundation of Islamic social justice, because they are the central mode in which the individual's mutual responsibility and solidarity are expressed.[162] With this idea, Quṭb's ideal society becomes reliant on the voluntary act of individuals. A foundation based solely on individual willpower is likely to be shaken by human greed and self-interest. Therefore, unlike Rawls, the liberal theorist who utilizes the idea of a social contract,[163] Quṭb cannot sufficiently address the destructive consequences of self-interest and insecurity.

Quṭb deals with the destructive consequences of human nature by widening the scope of charity beyond monetary giving. Charity is not only about helping the poor or distributing material wealth – any act of kindness toward his neighbors, society, or the environment counts. A believer's engagement in charitable acts ensures the inner purification of their conscience and strengthens their belief in solidarity. The psychological mechanism highlighted here stems from the notion of sacrifice. Since human nature is inclined toward selfishness and a love of money, the charitable act works its way toward the purification of human consciousness by helping the man give up what is dear to him thus has a powerful grip on him. Therefore, charity as a voluntary act is a prerequisite of justice.[164]

The existing political and economic system should also be compatible with the ideals of Islamic social justice. With regard to governance, Quṭb[165] introduces his

161 Kuran, Timur, *Islam and Mammon*, Princeton: Princeton University Press, 2010.

162 Quṭb, *Social Justice in Islam*, 99.

163 Rawls, *A Theory of Justice.*

164 Quṭb, *Social Justice in Islam*, 99–102.

165 Ibid., 119–20.

political theory of Islam by setting out three principles: "justice on the part of the rulers, obedience on the part of the ruled, and consultation between ruler and ruled." Rulers should implement and maintain complete political equality regardless of origin, race, and religion. In exchange, the ruled should be obedient to the ruler, but this is not unconditional. Obedience should not derive from a ruler's privileges or his outstanding qualities. Instead, a ruler only deserves obedience when he adheres to Islamic law. Quṭb[166] goes so far as to argue that it is necessary to get rid of a ruler when he abandons the law. In placing such a limitation on the ideal of obedience, his position is not without proximity to those of the Kharijites and some Sunni scholars.[167] Finally, there is the consultation between the ruler and the ruled. While Quṭb's political model is clearly defined, his ideas are reminiscent of those scholars' views who propose that Islam can play a positive role in the foundation of pluralistic institutions.[168]

In the economic sphere, Quṭb invokes the well-known legal maxim that "there should be neither harming [*ḍarar*] nor reciprocating harm [*ḍirār*] (*lā ḍarar wa-lā ḍirār*)."[169] Within this general maxim, both law and inner conviction are required for social welfare. This purely normative framework does not ensure that distributive justice and charitable acts will actually take place. Therefore, Quṭb introduces additional principles that ensure the compatibility between an Islamic economic system and social justice. Islam accepts private ownership and wealth; however, this does not entail a freedom to economic irresponsibility. There are certain restrictions placed on the disposal of wealth because "property belongs to society and is merely administered by an individual, so that if he leaves no issue, the property reverts to its original ownership by the community."[170] This understanding of property differs from communism in that property rights are firmly established in Islam. The owner, however, is the steward of their private property and is required to use it for the good of society after meeting his/her needs. This restriction on the use of property is necessary because Islam forbids the lavish spending and wastefulness seen in capitalist systems. According to Quṭb, the prevalence of a wasteful lifestyle can destroy society and create great injustices.[171]

---

**166** Ibid., 121.

**167** Ibid., 124.

**168** Iqbal, *The Reconstruction of Religious Thought*; Rahman, Fazlur, "The Principle of 'Shura' and the Role of the Umma in Islam," *American Journal of Islamic Social Sciences* 1, no. 1 (1984): 1–1; Fadl, *Islam, and the Challenge of Democracy*.

**169** Imam Nawawi, n.d. 32.

**170** Quṭb, *Social Justice in Islam*, 134.

**171** Ibid., 150–62.

Is Quṭbian social justice a utopian fantasy or can it become the foundation for a real-world transformation? To answer this question, we need to study the role of the prophetic community in Quṭb's writings. Quṭb anchors his theory in the practice of social justice during the early period of Islam, especially the time of Muḥammad and the first four caliphs. Islam's just order, according to Quṭb, was in place even after the death of the Prophet during the reign of the caliphs Abū Bakr (d. 634/13), ʿUmar, and ʿAlī. However, due to the third caliph's [ʿUthmān (d. 644/23)] nepotist rule, who favored his clan and inclined toward greed and corruption, Islamic political practice strayed from the spirit of Islam. His special blame falls on the governor of Damascus and the main challenger to the caliphate, Muʿāwīya, for corrupting Islam's true spirit and introducing a model of governance incompatible with Islamic social justice. "The greatest crime of Muʿāwīya, therefore, was that he destroyed the spirit of Islam at the very beginning of his reign by a complete suppression of its moral elements."[172] To him, this was the result of some unfortunate events that resulted in the failure to select ʿAlī as the caliph. These developments brought the system of justice that had been so well-established in the Muslim community during the time of Muhammad to an end.

However, this historical transformation is not taken as a sign for a downward trajectory of an ever-deteriorating presence of justice in Islamic societies. Quṭb believes that Islam's spirit and the practice of justice have always remained present and were simply dormant at times. He uses the examples of ʿAlīs fight against Muʿāwīya, the rebellions against the Umayyads, and the later example of ʿUmar b. ʿAbd al-ʿAzīz (d. 720/102)[173] to show that ideal models of Islamic social justice continued to exist in different periods. The best embodiment of a practical application of justice, in effect, appears to be the second caliph, ʿUmar. He had not only had the necessary inner conviction, but he actually managed to establish justice through charity and a perfect implementation of the *sharīʿa*. Quṭb provides many examples demonstrating how ʿUmar helped the poor, distributed all of his wealth in acts of charity, put the public interest above his own personal gain, and always applied the law equally regardless of race, religion, or origin. A similar treatment can be seen in his account of Abū Bakr and ʿAlī, but he most frequently cites stories about ʿUmar to demonstrate the true meaning of Islamic social justice.[174]

Several issues arise in Quṭb's theory of justice. First, the historical accuracy of the notion of early Islam as an ideal society has been questioned by historians of Islam as social divisions were not uncommon even at the time of the prophet and

---

**172** Ibid., 215.

**173** ʿUmar Ibn ʿAbd al-ʿAzīz (682–720 AD) was an Umayyad ruler who was praised as a just and devout ruler.

**174** Quṭb, *Social Justice in Islam*, 205–10.

became even more prominent thereafter.[175] Second, Quṭb's explanation that justice ended and conflict emerged in the early Islamic community due to random occurrences does not account for the failure of prophetic vision immediately after Muhammad's death. Quṭb's own theory of justice sets out to describe the transformation of the individual and society on the model of the Prophetic community, but without a vision of how one might bring the individuals brought up in existing societies to act against their own self-interest. He thus describes what a perfect society would look like but does not tell us how we might get there. This issue has been the main point of contention amongst liberal justice theorists in their efforts to provide consistent philosophical answers and policy solutions to address problems of self-interest, fairness, and altruism.[176] Third, Quṭb leans toward idealism and does not deal with the economic problems of his time. In one way, his vision lacks a material base from which to address salient policy issues. His attempt to establish social justice in society by building solidarity through religiously induced voluntary acts and the coercive power of the Islamic law results in a utopian vision of an authoritarian quality. Notwithstanding these reservations, Quṭb's justice theory provides a comprehensive view of Islamic justice conception, and it has had a significant influence on Islamist movements.

Another prominent theoretician who developed an Islamic conception of justice is the Iranian thinker ʿAlī Sharīʿatī. In his work, he views the law with suspicion. For Sharīʿatī, its coercive power may be abused by despotic regimes to serve their interests. Sharīʿatī focuses on Islam's spirit and chooses to present the noble struggle of ʿAlī, not ʿUmar, as the ultimate example of Islamic social justice.

## 5.2 Sharīʿatī, Rebellion, and Justice

ʿAlī Sharīʿatī is an Iranian sociologist and intellectual whose ideas have inspired democratic and revolutionary movements in Iran and beyond. He came from a clerical family and earned his doctorate at the University of Paris. An intellectual and social activist, he inspired and participated in anti-regime protests. Although exiled and later assassinated by the regime in 1977, his ideas continue to influence Islamist movements today. Sharīʿatī 's ideas are shaped by both Eastern and Western philosophers. His writings on justice reflect the influences of Fanon (1925–1961), Marx (1818–1883), Islamic scholars, and his own reading of the history of

175 Crone, *God's Rule*; Hodgson, Marshall G. S., The Venture of Islam, vol. 2, *The Expansion of Islam in the Middle Periods*, Chicago: University of Chicago Press, 1974; Lapidus, *A History of Islamic Societies.*

176 Rawls, *A Theory of Justice.*

Shiʿism. Inspired by Marx's historical materialism, Sharīʿatī provides a dialectical account of Islam, history, and class struggle to provide a comprehensive theory of justice. According to Abrahamian,[177] Sharīʿatī rejects the institutionalized Marxism of the communist and socialist parties and views Marx as "predominantly a social scientist revealing how rulers exploited the ruled, how the laws of "historical determinism" – not "economic determinism" – functioned, and how the superstructure of any country, particularly its dominant ideology and political institutions, interacted with its socioeconomic infrastructure." This outlook has had a significant influence on social justice-oriented Islamists who promoted the idea of Islamic socialism in the Muslim world.[178] A selective and critical reading of Marx and Western philosophers underlies Sharīʿatī's vision of Islam as a revolutionary ideology. Despite this radical outlook, one can trace the resemblance of his thought system to that of Quṭb, especially through their joint emphasis on *tawḥīd* and human agency as factors in establishing social justice.

*Tawḥīd* plays a central role in Sharīʿatī's social justice theory. In a lecture titled *Worldview of Tawḥīd*,[179] Sharīʿatī contrasts the *tawḥīdi* worldview (monotheism) with *shirk* (polytheism) using a dialectical framework. For Sharīʿatī, *tawḥīd* is an essential principle of faith that has a direct impact on the social and political order. *Shirk* is a worldview that involves a multiplicity of gods, which results in societal inequality. *Tawḥīd* or monotheism, on the other hand, provides motivation for the historical struggles of the oppressed masses against tyranny (*ẓulm*). In the *tawḥīdi* view, the physical and social world is seen as a harmonious unity. Just as *tawḥīd* does not accept the idea of a duality between the body and spirit or of a contradiction between man and nature, the *tawḥīdi* worldview does not accept class differences, divisions between the rulers and the oppressed, or racial and economic contradictions in the social realm:

> One further consequence of the worldview of *tawḥīd* is the negation of the dependence of man on any social force, and the linking of him, in exclusivity and in all his dimensions, to the consciousness and will that rule over being. *Tawḥīd* bestows upon men independence and dignity. Submission to Him alone – the supreme norm of all being impels man to revolt against all lying powers, all humiliating fetters of fear and greed.[180]

177 Abrahamian, Ervand, "Ali Shariati: Ideologue of the Iranian Revolution," *Merip Reports* 102 (1982): 24–28.

178 Nurtsch, Ceyda, "The Koran and Social Justice. Interview with Turkish Theologian Ihsan Eliacik," published online: *Qantara* 2014, https://qantara.de/en/article/interview-turkish-theologian-ihsan-eliacik-koran-and-social-justice (accessed on 14.06.2024).

179 Shariati, Ali, "Worldview of Tawhid," in *On the Sociology of Islam*, trans. Hamid Algar. Berkeley: Mizan Press, Shaban, 1398 h.

180 Shariati, "Worldview," 87.

In contrast, the assumption of foundational contradictions in the *shirk* worldview cause real-world problems. The distinction between *tawḥīd* and *shirk* touches on the duality of materialistic and religious visions that we encountered in the Quṭbian philosophy. This duality also manifests itself in differing social orders and economic and political systems. Sharīʿatī argues that humanity has always been divided into two opposing poles. For Sharīʿatī,[181] "the pole that represented corruption, crime, exploitation, ignorance, slavery, racism, imaginary virtues, and impediments to human progress, has always been at odds with justice, human consciousness, growth, and those who struggle to unite humanity."

Sharīʿatī reconstructs the story of Cain and Abel to further elaborate the consequences of this duality. Abel is a herdsman who represents a phase in human history during which man's livelihood depended on hunting and gathering. Cain was a farmer, and, in Sharīʿatī's view, he represents a phase in which private property was introduced, and with it, the danger of monopolies appeared. Sharīʿatī states, "all men are of Abelian' character because resources are equally at everyone's disposal. Individualism, individual ownership, monopoly, "mine", and "yours" have not yet developed in man. On the other hand, Cain exemplifies an order in which a person fences a piece of land, tags his name to it, and begins to exploit and enslave others."[182]

Sharīʿatī's reading of Abel and Cain's story gives significant insight into his conception of Islamic justice. Monotheism promotes a harmonious state of order and thus brings about a just society. In contrast, a polytheist order creates an inherent duality that is reflected in the individual and leads to a hierarchical social system. In this system, a subjective polytheistic religion is disguised as true religion to justify objective inequalities. In effect, most of human history can be understood as a struggle between monotheist religion and polytheist religion rather than as a struggle between religion and non-religion.[183] Declaring the principle of *tawḥīd* to be the most suitable means by which to implement justice and harmony in an Islamic society is not new approach. Numerous philosophers and intellectuals, including Quṭb, have taken the same approach.[184] However, Sharīʿatī's approach differs from those of other scholars, especially that of Quṭb, in a significant way. He places a clear emphasis on political activism and aims to use this principle to motivate revolutionary acts to replace the existing order with a monotheistic one. In con-

**181** Shariati, Ali, "World Vision," in: *Man and Islam*, trans. Fatoallah Marjani, New Jersey: IPI Press, 1981, Cf. Kindle locations, 586–88.

**182** Shariati, "World Vision," Cf. Kindle Locations 608–18.

**183** Shariati, Ali, *Religion vs Religion*, Chicago: ABC International Group, 2003.

**184** Iqbal, *The Reconstruction of Religious Thought*; Al-Mawdudi, "Islam in Transition"; Quṭb, *Social Justice in Islam*.

trast, Quṭb developed an abstract notion of justice using the *tawḥīd* principle to establish an Islamic order through religious education and was less interested in revolutionary acts.

Like Quṭb, Sharīʿatī also believes that human agency and freedom are essential components of Islamic justice. A revolution against the oppressors that aims to institute justice and equality will be realized when man acts with free will as the vicegerent of God.[185] Sharīʿatī reconstructs the myth of creation in the Qurʾān to support this claim in the following way. God created man from mud and breathed his soul into him, making him two-dimensional. Thus, man swings between the lowliness of mud and the lofty ideals that he has received from the spirit of the Lord.[186] A believer can aim to bring justice into the world by virtue of being a free and responsible agent (spiritual dimension). In both Quṭb's and Sharīʿatī's conceptions of justice, human beings are free to make conscious choices as vicegerents of God to establish justice.[187] This has also been a prevalent theme in the works of other Islamists from the 19th century to the present including those of Kemal, al-Mawdūdī, Ghannūshī, and Ramadan.[188]

Yet, bringing justice to the world is not an easy task as man is confined to four prisons preventing him from realizing his potential. These prisons are nature, history, society, and the self.[189] Through learning and science, man can free himself of the first three limitations; however, it is more difficult to escape the prison of the self. Here, Sharīʿatī makes a distinction between *insān* and *bashar*, the two Qurʾānic terms used to describe human beings. *Bashar* is the biological creature, a "being", whereas *insān* is man in a state of "becoming" that brings forth an extraordinary creature with unique properties and significant potential.[190] In Sharīʿatī's words:[191]

> Ensan [insān] has three characteristics: a) he is self-conscious, b) he can make choices; and c) he can create. All of man's other characteristics derive their origin from these three. We are, therefore, Ensan [insān] relative to the degree of our self-consciousnesses and our creativity. Accordingly, when the characteristics of an ideal Ensan [insān] is clarified, we must try to identify the factors that hinder man in his becoming, and by removing them we can pursue our inherent and instinctive movement in the process of becoming an Ensan [insān].

---

**185** Shariati, Ali, "Man and Islam."

**186** Shariati, Cf., Kindle Locations 391–93.

**187** Shariati, Ali, "Modern Man and His Prisons," in *Man and Islam*, trans. Fathollah Marjani, New Jersey: IPI Press 1981.

**188** Kemal, "And Seek Their Council in the Affairs"; Tamimi, *Rachid Ghannouchi*; Ramadan, Tariq, *Islam, the West and the Challenges of Modernity*, trans. Said Amghar, Leicester, UK: The Islamic Foundation, 2009.

**189** Shariati, "Modern Man and His Prisons."

**190** Shariati, "Man and Islam"; Shariati, "Modern Man and His Prisons."

**191** Shariati, "Modern Man and His Prisons," Kindle Locations 1157.

To recap, Sharīʿatī believes that Western civilization can release man from his first three prisons (nature, history, and society) by using scientific knowledge and providing material needs.[192] Saving man from the prison of the self, however, poses quite different challenges. As human beings gain material comfort, they inevitably arrive at the alternative between futility and rebellion, which directs man to asceticism and subjectivity. Hence, approaches like existentialism or the Hippie movement had significant appeal in the West. This fundamental lack of meaning in modern societies confronts us with the question: How can man, as a free and responsible agent, make a difference? For Sharīʿatī, this is possible only when one accepts a higher goal that can help man negate his self. Just like Quṭb, Sharīʿatī believes that *īthār* (benevolence, selflessness) can help *bashar* transform into becoming *insān*. With love and benevolence, argues Sharīʿatī, man can become an agent of change, a responsible individual struggling for equality and justice.[193]

The *tawḥīdi* worldview brings about a just society free from transgression and oppression. In this society, prosperity comes from religious, not materialistic values. In keeping with this principle, Sharīʿatī aims to rejuvenate the role of religion in instituting justice in such a society: "if religion does not work before death, it certainly will not work after it."[194] Unlike Quṭb, Sharīʿatī's proposed social order is not an unrealistic utopia. It is a system inspired by historical materialism and it promises full equality and freedom to its citizens while taking real world conditions into account.[195]

Sharīʿatī uses events and characters from the time of Muḥammad and the four *rashidūn* caliphs to set out an ideal model of social justice. In his account, particular historical figures function as ideal embodiments of *insān* because of their commitment to the goal of a just Islamic order. Figures like Muḥammad, ʿUmar, and Abū Dharr (d. 652/32) engage in the historical dialectic of justice and constantly oppose social polytheism, oppression, and inequalities.[196] The most apparent manifestation of this opposition can be found in the struggle of *tawḥīd* against *shirk*, ʿAlī against Muʿāwīya, red Shīʿism (the religion of martyrdom) against black Shīʿism (the religion of mourning), the working-class against the capitalists, and the oppressed against their despotic oppressors. Such dualities pit one's preference for

---

**192** This paragraph provides a general overview of Shariati's influential essay titled Modern Man and His Prisons.

**193** Shariati, "Modern Man and His Prisons," Cf. Kindle Locations 1379–1380.

**194** Shariati, Ali, *Eslam-Shenasi (Islamology)*, Tehran: Ershad, 1971, 79.

**195** Danesh, Maryam/Hassan, Abniki, "The Relation between Liberty and Justice in Ali Shariati's Political Thought," *International Journal of Political Science* 5, no. 9 (2015), 1–8.

**196** Shariati, Ali, "Red Shi'ism (the Religion of Martyrdom) vs. Black Shi'ism (the Religion of Mourning)," n.d.

piety, ethics, equality, and justice against corruption, tyranny, exploitation, and aristocracy.

In *The Reflections of a Concerned Muslim on the Plight of Oppressed People*, Sharīʿatī portrays the Prophet Muḥammad as a simple man who is himself one amongst the poor and weak, someone who rebels against the aristocracy and who struggles to empower ordinary people.[197] In this shepherd-like role, Muḥammad, argues Sharīʿatī, established a just and equitable society ruled by one who considered himself not as above but as one of the weak and poor. However, this society was eventually destroyed by the oppressive rulers.[198] To Sharīʿatī, this process started with the denial of ʿAlī's right to be the successor of the Prophet. Meccan aristocrats, especially the Umayyad family, transformed this prophetic society and replaced its just order with one of inequity and a simple, pious way of life with one of luxury. According to Sharīʿatī, the isolation of ʿAlī, who was the embodiment of the spirit of this religion, after the death of the Prophet, "is a sign that justice is separated from religion."[199] Sharīʿatī describes this stage as an "inclination of Islam to the right," where the masses leave the scene to the aristocrats and clergymen.[200] ʿAlī is portrayed as the ultimate leader that is capable of re-instituting the just system of the Prophetic community.

In *And Once Again Abu Dharr*, Sharīʿatī presents the story of Abū Dharr to demonstrate how ordinary people can struggle against injustices. Abū Dharr was one of the companions of the Prophet Muḥammad and he was well known for his egalitarian views. Above all, Abū Dharr desired to bring about a return to the piety of the Prophet's age, and to that end, he engaged in a one-person rebellion against the Umayyad aristocracy. In his struggle he had to oppose class discrimination and to fight *kinz* (accumulation of wealth) in order to establish justice. Abū Dharr always reminded his followers of the simplistic, egalitarian, ethical, and pious life of the Prophet.[201]

To sum up, Sharīʿatī favors a system established upon the principles of the *tawḥīdi* worldview. The empowered and emancipated man is transformed from *bashar* to *insān* and is placed at the center of this just social order. With absolute freedom, *insān* struggles to establish equality and a just social order where class differences are minimal and where neither excess nor social hierarchy distort

197 Shariati, Ali, "Reflections of a Concerned Muslim on the Plight of Oppressed People," published online: *Shariati.com*, http://www.shariati.com/kotob.html (accessed on 14.06.2024).

198 Shariati, "Reflections of a Concerned Muslim."

199 Shariati, Ali, "And Once Again Abu Dharr," n.d.; Shariati, "Reflections of a Concerned Muslim."

200 Shariati, "And Once Again Abu Dharr," Part 5, published online: *Shariati.com*, http://www.shariati.com/kotob.html (accessed on 14.06.2024).

201 Shariati, "And Once Again Abu Dharr," part 5.

the unity of society. Neither economic greed nor tyranny can persist in this society. This system is built on the power of human agency to overcome its obstacles through divine instructions, free will, and benevolence. Unlike Quṭb, and some of the other Islamists, Sharīʿatī's conception of justice is firmly embedded in a socioeconomic context. It also relies on a novel interpretation of the scripture in the light of historical materialism. Informed by the Shīʿa creed, it provides a theory of justice with a clear focus on the fight Muslim agency must face against injustice and tyranny. It also takes human nature into consideration in its conceptualization of justice, an outlook that moves Sharīʿatī closer to the contractarian view of justice.

## 5.3 Analysis of Islamist Theories of Justice

Any theory of Islamic justice should acknowledge a critical division that emerged in the early period of Islam. It originally manifested itself in the first civil war and evolved into an ideological division between those who value piety and good morals and their realist-minded counterparts for whom obtaining power is the most important goal.[202] The time of the first community of believers has been praised as a golden age that represents the embodiment of Islamic justice. In spite of this seemingly unquestioned consensus, Quṭb and Sharīʿatī have different assumptions and draw different conclusions about justice as we can see in their use of examples taken from this historical period. This divergence shows that the idea of a golden age of a unified harmonious Islamic social order is a myth rather than historical fact. Given the divisions and conflicts within this society, it is obvious that Islamist justice theory must deal with the practical impossibility of creating a completely just society. Sharīʿatī's view has a materialistically grounded base that allowed him deal with this issue, but Quṭb's account lacks any materialistic foundation. Sharīʿatī recognizes the socio-economic conditions that inhibit the realization of justice and recommends political action to bring about change. Quṭb emphasizes an abstract notion of Islamic law and does not explain how his vision of social justice can be realized.

One major difference between liberal and Islamist theories of justice concerns their respective premises about the ownership and disposal of private property. The Islamist view diverges radically from the former in that all wealth and resources belong to God and to humanity as a whole. This difference has important implications for economic distribution. First, while Quṭb believes that the right to pri-

---

202 El-Affendi, *Who Needs an Islamic State?*, 171–83.

vate property is legitimate in Islam, the disposal of property is constrained by social responsibility. An individual is not free to waste his wealth with a luxurious lifestyle because all wealth (*mulk*) belongs to God, and it should be used to promote the welfare of all. According to Quṭb, the use of public treasure (*bayt al-māl*) for social welfare during the prophetic age is the model to be emulated. For Sharīʿatī, class differences and inequalities are a result of *kinz* (accumulation of wealth), and they are the foundation of a polytheist worldview. Public treasure should not be used for personal gain, a lesson that can be learned by the example of the reign of ʿUthmān and Muʿāwiya. However, the dominant paradigm in Islamic history regarding the use of public treasure has come to be of quite a different nature than that of the idealized Prophetic community. The corruption and exploitation of public funds for personal gain became the model employed by later rulers. The struggle between realists seeking a power grab and ethicalists who strive to establish justice[203] was already present in the prophetic community and has continued to shape Muslim politics over time. In fact, the worldly pragmatist's understanding of public funds has been the dominant paradigm. Both Quṭb and Sharīʿatī seem to be siding with the ethicalists camp, but only the latter appears to recommend concrete social action to reach this goal. While Quṭb makes reference to this early period to justify the unconditional application of religious law, Sharīʿatī applies a Marxist framework to political theology to justify the idea of rebellion against tyranny.

Quṭb and Sharīʿatī have developed sophisticated political philosophies that directly address social and political justice as constitutive elements of Islamic society. However, neither addressed the alternative vision of justice presented by Western liberal thinkers. Sharīʿatī applied the Marxist vision of justice to Islamic conceptions but not their liberal counterparts. Furthermore, their accounts of Christianity and Judaism do not recognize the sophisticated conceptions of justice developed by scholars of these faiths.

Notwithstanding these limitations, Quṭb and Sharīʿatī have had a significant influence on Islamist intellectuals and movements since the 1980s across Muslim-majority societies. While other prominent Islamists also assign a central role to justice, they either do not put justice at the center of their inquiry or they fail to develop a complete theory of justice like Quṭb and Sharīʿatī do, save al-Ghannūshī. Pakistani scholar al-Mawdūdī, for example, drastically shaped Quṭb's ideas about the blueprint of Islamic society. He introduced the concept of Theo-democracy to offer a native governance model based on integration of Islamic law and

203 El-Affendi, *Who Needs an Islamic State?*

popular sovereignty.[204] While justice and benevolence are central values in al-Mawdūdī's thought, unlike Sharī'atī, he is far from being a revolutionary.[205] He emphasized justice as a central virtue of Islamic society but did not present a complete theory of justice like Quṭb.

Another scholar that should be mentioned is the Iraqi scholar Muḥammad Bāqir aṣ-Ṣadr (1935–1980/1354–1400), who criticized capitalism and socialism in order to develop a native Islamic theory of economics. aṣ-Ṣadr views justice as the second principle of Islam after *tawḥīd* and usually defines it as economic justice. It should be noted that his account of economic justice is embedded within the broader conception of justice that is integral to Islamic society. as-Sadr's most notable contribution to justice theory is his strong advocacy for democracy. Like other scholars, he derives the Islamic roots of democracy and popular sovereignty from man's status as an earthly vicegerent. He believes that this status makes all members of *umma* equal and gives them the power and the right to govern their political affairs within a democratic system.[206]

We should also mention two other scholars who have left a significant mark on the Islamist landscape, Rāshid al-Ghannūshī and Said Nursi (1877–1960/1294–1380). The Tunisian intellectual and party leader al-Ghannūshī views justice as the end goal of an Islamic political system. Like Quṭb and Sharī'atī, man's vicegerency is the starting point for Ghannūshī, who derives principles of dignity, agency, and responsibility from this position in order to develop an Islamic model of democracy compatible with the notion of Islamic justice.[207] This model relies on the active participation of Muslims through the notion of *bay'a* (allegiance) and an active engagement of community members in making and interpreting Islamic law. With this framework, he seems to be bringing together the abstract Quṭbian notions of justice and Sharī'atī's action-based model with its focus on the implementation of justice. Ghannūshī's most significant contribution is his political theology of popular sovereignty that suggests the participation of all *umma* members in the political process as well as the interpretation of

---

**204** Al-Mawdudi, "Islam in Transition," *253–61.*

**205** Nasr, Seyyed Vali Reza, *Mawdudi and the Making of Islamic Revivalism*, New York: Oxford University Press, 1996.

**206** Al-Rikabi, Jaffar, "Baqir Al-Sadr and the Islamic State: A Theory for 'Islamic Democracy'," *Journal of Shi'a Islamic Studies* 5, no. 3 (2012), 249–75; Jamalzadeh, Naser, "Sociopolitical Justice in Three Jurisprudential, Philosophical and Sociological Approaches," *Islamic Political Thought* 2, no. 1 (2015), 7–42.

**207** Tamimi, *Rachid Ghannouchi*; March, *The Caliphate of Man.*

*sharīʿa.*[208] The end goal of his theory is the creation of a virtuous and just society.[209]

Said Nursi of Turkey, a prominent scholar and activist who has had a lasting legacy in the Turkish Islamist landscape, is best known for his spiritual guidance on the Nurcu groups and especially the Gülen movement.[210] During the early years of his life, which he dubs as the period of "Old Said," he participated in the struggle against the Ottoman Sultan Abdulhamid II by joining the Committee on Union and Progress, the main opposition party.[211] This was part of his quest for democracy and justice in which he saw the declining Ottoman Empire and Western incursion as his central antagonists. In the Turkish Republic, he took a different approach and started to write commentaries of the Qur'ān in an attempt to preserve the Islamic element within Turkish identity. His main goals at the time were to counter the positivist and anti-religious ideology of the Western-minded, secular elite by training individuals in their faith, which he viewed as the quintessential means by which to protect religion in the modern age. Although Nursi does not offer a complete theory of Islamic justice, his writings and actions reflect the weight Nursi assigned to this concept.[212] Nursi's theory of justice relies on the idea of an interrelationship between God, cosmos, and man. His position differs from the political philosophies of Quṭb and Sharīʿatī in its political implications and its lack of concrete prescriptions for an Islamic political system. He argues that a Muslim can become conscious after understanding the purpose of creation. Only when they gain an understanding of true faith, can individuals create a virtuous and just community. His main contention is that to empower the faithful through a strengthening of their belief will help to emancipate the individual to fight positivism and bureaucratic structures (i.e., secular Western Turkish state). In this point, he is close to the Quṭbian theory of justice grounded in the education of believers in Islam as a panacea for *jāhilīya.* Like Sharīʿatī and Quṭb, Nursi's theory of justice also values emancipation and empowerment of the self through a

**208** March, *The Caliphate of Man.*

**209** This brief overview hardly captures the sophisticated political philosophy of al-Ghannūshī. Two excellent and detailed accounts of al-Ghannūshī are Andrew March's, *The Caliphate of Man*, and Azzam Tamimi's *Rachid Ghannouchi: A Democrat within Islamism.*

**210** Yavuz, M Hakan, *Toward an Islamic Enlightenment: The Gülen Movement*, New York: Oxford University Press, 2013; Markham, Ian S./Suendam, Birinci Pirim, *An Introduction to Said Nursi: Life, Thought and Writings*, New York: Routledge., 2011.

**211** Vahide, Sukran, *Islam in Modern Turkey: An Intellectual Biography of Bediuzzaman Said Nursi*, Albany, NY: SUNY Press, 2012.

**212** Nursi, Said, *Risale-i Nur Külliyati*, vol. 2, Istanbul: Nesil, 1996.

thorough reinterpretation of the scripture and religion.[213] At the same time, his actual life exemplifies a struggle fought for justice and democracy.

Within the Shīʿite tradition, Ayatollah Khomeinī has developed a theory of justice inspired by the massacre of Karbala and the persecution of Shīʿite scholars and people throughout history. Khomeinī used this framework to invoke historical traumas in the context of the Shah's repressive regime. He placed particular emphasis on the notion of *ẓulm* to invite people to rebel in the wake of the Iranian Revolution. Khomeinī defines *ẓulm* broadly as oppression or transgression against oneself or others. *Ẓulm* is the opposite of justice, and its existence justifies rebellion against tyrants. The same ideology has also been used to foment anti-Americanism as a rallying point in Iran. With this theory of justice, Khomeini inspired millions in Iran to mobilize for revolution, and his influence spread throughout the Muslim world as an ideology against injustice.[214]

Finally, a contemporary Islamist from Turkey, İhsan Eliaçık, who inspired the newly formed Islamist groups in Turkey, has introduced an Islamic "justice state" theory. His thoughts reflect a strong influence of contemporary Islamists from the Middle East. He wrote in the context of Turkey's integration into the neoliberal global order at the hands of an Islamist government. Eliaçık believes that just as divine justice is one and brings balance to the universe, a political system based on justice can bring unity and prosperity to the world.[215] This theory's underlying logic is not new because numerous theologians, philosophers, and intellectuals have inferred the notions of justice and harmony from the *tawḥīd* principle as discussed in this chapter. Eliaçık's original contribution lies in his attempt to make justice the foundation of the modern state. He states, "it should be evident that the unity of existence leads to right and justice (*hak* ve *adalet*). Just as cosmic justice creates a unity of existence, can there be any method other than political and social justice to unite humanity? [...] What else can be the state's *raison d'etre* other than justice?" Eliaçık develops his theory of "justice state" as an alternative to the theocratic and secular models of statehood. His model is based on a unity of the state and religion according to a novel secular arrangement. In Eliaçık's words,[216]

> in the Turkish case, state-religion relations can be formed in the following way: 1. The state would have no power and responsibility in religious creed and religious duties, 2. The state

213 Yavuz, M Hakan, *Islamic Political Identity in Turkey*, New York: Oxford University Press, 2003.
214 Khomeini, "Theory of Justice."
215 Eliaçık, İhsan, "Sivil Dönüşüm," *Değişim*, 1997, 44–44; Eliaçık, İhsan, "Adalet 'Kozmos'un Temelidir," *Bilgi Ve Düşünce*, 2003, 58–63.
216 Eliaçık, İhsan, "İslam Uygarlığı Tarihten Mi Çekiliyor?," *Bilgi Ve Düşünce*, 2003, 58–63.

can be responsible for the moral aspects of the religion, 3. The state would sometimes be responsible according to some aspects of religious law.

It seems Eliaçık is trying to curb the influence of the state on the principles of faith and the implementation of Islamic law, an important departure point from Quṭb. His ideas resemble those of an-Naim.[217] He proposes a secular state that does not interfere in religious creed or Islamic law and rather provides a democratic environment facilitating the civic reasoning of believers. Eliaçık views the justice state that has a limited role in matters of religious creed as the best means for restoring Islam's primacy in modern society.

Overall, this brief review of Quṭb, Sharīʿatī, and other prominent Islamist intellectuals demonstrates the main contours of Islamist theories of justice. In general, Islamist political philosophy grounds its theories of justice in a cosmological worldview related to the principle of *tawḥīd.* The totality of existence connects man to nature, the universe, and his creator within a unified, just order. There is general agreement amongst Islamist thinkers that individuals have free will and that they can emancipate themselves as God's vicegerents within the cosmology of existence. However, Islamist theories of justice differ in their scope and focus. For example, aṣ-Ṣadr is mainly concerned with economic justice, though he does endorse the struggle for democratic institutions. Nursi's main goal is to initiate a bottom-up process to empower the individual to create a just society. al-Mawdūdī aims to develop a blueprint for an Islamic social and political system that involves elements of a democratic system. While all of these scholars assign importance to the notion of justice, unlike Quṭb and Sharīʿatī, none of them provide a complete theory of justice connecting the cosmological, individual, and system-wide aspects of justice. The only exceptions to this pattern are Eliaçık and Ghannūshī, whose comprehensive justice theories inspired the new Islamist movements in Turkey and Tunisia.

## 6 A Comparative Perspective on the Islamic Conception of Justice

At this point, it is helpful to return to the broader conception of Islamic justice and to compare it to theories of justice in liberal, Christian, and Judaic traditions. The review of the traditional and modern roots of Islamic conceptions of justice and the Islamist scholars' views reveals that Islamic justice theory is markedly differ-

217 An-Naim, *Islam and the Secular State.*

ent from the liberal theories of justice. The first difference concerns the underlying worldviews. In liberal justice theories, the right to private property and to freely dispose of this property unequivocally function as the foundational principle. The main issue these theories are confronted with concerns the search for an agreeable formula of economic distribution and the challenge posed by the question of the most efficient use of property to promote the common good. The answers range from utilitarian worldviews or communitarian solutions to the ideal of a procedurally produced consensus that is acceptable to all individuals regardless of their real-life conditions.[218] In Islamic social justice theories, however, all property belongs to God. He has given this property to humanity as a whole and only the members of the *umma* can establish economic justice by following the law given by God. The challenge posed by Islamic thought lies in the question of how one might establish a just order according to God's will. To achieve the same, the incompatibility between the perfect justice of the divine and its supposedly flawed worldly variants must be harmonized. Since no distinction is made between the realm of religion and that of worldly affairs in the classical Islamic approach, the starting point for Islamic justice theory lies in its criticism of the materialistic worldview.

Distributive justice is an important end goal, but it does not present the main problem for Islamist social justice theory. Political justice and the establishment of a just society through the voluntary mobilization and charity of the individual take the center stage in Islamic conceptions of justice. This does not necessarily entail a utopian vision, yet some Islamists end up with such a vision based on their construction of the prophetic community in idealistic terms. To emulate the prophetic community, which is seen as the most perfect manifestation of justice, a constant struggle against oppression and an inner purification of the soul accompanied by the flawless implementation of Islamic law is required.

Just as the human emancipation theories of Amartya Sen and other Western thinkers,[219] the Islamic conception of *khalīfa* treats freedom and choice as foundational to justice. From the beginning, the Qadari school, its later incarnations like the Muʿtazilah, and present-day Islamists built their conception of Islamic social justice on the presence of individual dignity. Man as vicegerent of God has freedom and thus choice and this capacity is regarded as the central trait from which to turn every man into an agent of justice according to Islamist justice theory. The

**218** Rawls, *A Theory of Justice*; Smith, *The Emergence of Liberation Theology*; Lorenz, "The Emergence of Social Justice in the West."

**219** Sen, Amartya Kumar, *The Idea of Justice*, Cambridge, MA: Harvard University Press, 2009; Welzel, Christian/ Inglehart, Ronald/Kligemann, Hans-Dieter, "The Theory of Human Development: A Cross-cultural Analysis," *European Journal of Political Research* 42, no. 3 (2003), 341–79.

doctrine of the vicegerency of man is the principal foundation from which to educate Muslim agency in the spirit of emancipation. In effect, whether the goal is creating a republic of virtue, a just society, or democracy, Islamists consider free will as a building block of justice.

The broader Islamic conception of justice also shares some similar tenets with Christianity and Judaism. Firstly, all three monotheistic religions grant justice a central role in their belief system. In these faiths, justice is viewed as a path to salvation, peace, and prosperity and it is seen as a universal value to be transmitted throughout the world.[220] In addition, charity and economic distribution are important elements of justice in Judaism, Christianity, and Islam.

The Hebrew word for justice is *tsedaḳah*, a lofty goal pursued by the prophets. Many verses from the Old Testament confirm the centrality of justice as a religious concept:

> Justice shall redeem Zion (Isa. 1:27).
> Justice and justice alone, you should pursue, so that you may live (Deut: 16:20).

In Judaism, there is no guarantee that justice will be achieved, but its pursuit is significant. There is visible doubt concerning the possibility of achieving true justice in Judaism as can be seen in the controversial Rabbinic debates concerning this issue.[221] These debates bear some similarities to the debates about the meaning of justice from the early period of Islam between the Qadari and Jabri schools and later among Kalām scholars and philosophers.[222] We also see a similar tendency between Islam and Judaism to consider economic monopolies undesirable. When explaining Sabbatical and Jubilee years in Judaism, Botwinick argues that these principles aim to prevent economic monopolies.[223] In Islam, excessive wealth is equally unacceptable as it undermines social justice. Islamists like Sadr, Quṭb, and Sharīʿatī discourage the accumulation of wealth and invoke Islam's emphasis on economic justice. Another similarity between Judaic and Islamic conceptions of justice is the primacy of law. The law is considered to be the foundation of justice in Islamic jurisprudence theory. Similarly, its understanding of law is central to the monotheistic project of Judaism. In this aspect, both traditions clearly differ from Christianity. St. Paul proclaims love to be the organizing principle of faith and justice in Christianity, an innovation with significant practical implications.

---

**220** Maguire, "Religious Influences on Justice Theory." Also Cf. chapters by Botwinick and Gräb-Schmidt in this volume.
**221** Cf. the chapter by Botwinick in this volume.
**222** Fakhry, *A History of Islamic Philosophy*; Khadduri, *The Islamic Conception of Justice.*
**223** Cf. chapter by Botwinick in this volume.

As Botwinick states,[224] "Judaism, in contrast to this programmatic formulation by St. Paul, by focusing upon law and making the elaboration of law and compliance with it central to its monotheistic project, has the opportunity to place in circulation values and standards that can serve as a critique of existing political, economic, and social arrangements."[225]

The centrality of the law in Islam also has a formative effect on social life as it is the law that prescribes the protection of public interest and welfare of the *umma*. Through the protection of life, religion, progeny, and intellect and through the provision of public goods, the jurisprudential principle of *maṣlaḥa* can be used to criticize existing socio-economic and political systems and to advance the well-being of a Muslim society. In a similar fashion, Judaic law and its interpretations view justice as the promotion of the good of society.

Just as the conceptual development of Islamic justice is inspired by critical moments in history such as the first civil war or the Mongol invasion, significant events underlie the evolution of the conception of justice in Judaism. For example, the Exodus and the Covenant play a central role in generating debates about the meaning and pursuance of justice in Judaism.[226] The Covenant on Mount Sinai is significant because it enters a human community into an agreement with God, but it also prescribes certain ethical and juridical standards which are foundational to the Judaic conception of justice. These standards include the provision of protections for the weak, charitable giving to the poor, and the establishment of fair courts. In this manner, the Judaic conception of justice is closely related to the Islamic conception which views justice as a broad principle organizing social, economic, and political life.

The Christian conception of justice also shares core values with Judaism and Islam, but it differs from both in some ways. For example, the Biblical conceptions of justice have entered into a constructive dialogue with both ancient and modern conceptions of justice.[227] In traditional Christianity, justice is seen as *suum cique* (to each what is due) and it is defined by the life and experience of Jesus Christ. Justice becomes intelligible by God's loving self-revelation in Jesus. God's justice is basically the character of God, and it becomes an example for humanity.[228] Similar to Islamic justice, the Biblical conception of justice treats God's justice as the most superior form of justice and makes clear that his justice precedes all earthly justice.

---

**224** Ibid.
**225** Ibid.
**226** Ibid.
**227** Cf. the chapter by Gräb-Schmidt in this volume.
**228** Ibid.

The Christian conception of justice is dynamic, and it evolved over time to respond to the changing socioeconomic conditions its believers found themselves in. For example, distributive justice and freedom emerged as the most significant elements of Christian justice and they contributed to the rise of the welfare state and liberation theology.[229] Both phenomena were built on Catholic theology and evolved in response to social injustices. Liberation theology seeks to realize Christian justice in everyday struggles and to empower weak individuals.[230] Christian values of mercy, love, and charity along with the Catholic principle of subsidiarity were foundational to the welfare policies of Christian democratic parties in Europe.[231] More recently, the Christian conception of justice evolved to address global injustices and inequities.[232] Islamic conceptions of justice are equally dynamic and they have evolved over time to address similar grievances, but political justice took an important role next to distributive justice. Sharīʿatī 's justice theory is the best example of such dynamism.

Overall, there are similarities in the conceptions of justice in the three monotheistic religions, including the supremacy of God's justice and the importance of the pursuance of justice. While social justice matters a great deal in Judaism and Islam, its application to social life is more pronounced in Christianity. The Islamic conception of justice, on the other hand, originated as a political concept but social justice gained in importance over time. Islam is a religion that encompasses all aspects of life and this can be most clearly seen in the application of justice in a broad fashion to social and political problems.

# 7 Practical Applications of Islamic Justice

Islamic conceptions of justice have implications for a range of issues, including democracy, mass mobilization, Islamist parties, welfare regimes, and international relations. As stated previously, the origins of the Islamic conception of justice are political. Accordingly, there is a close association between attitudes toward different conceptions of justice and Muslim political preferences. For example, there is a common misperception that Islam and democracy are antithetical to each other.[233] In contrast, some scholars argue that mercy and justice as core values

---

229 Maguire, "Religious Influences on Justice Theory."
230 Smith, *The Emergence of Liberation Theology.*
231 Maguire, "Religious Influences on Justice Theory."
232 Cf. Gräb-Schmidt in this volume.
233 Kedourie, Elie, *Democracy and Arab Political Culture*, Washington, DC: Washington Institute for Near East Policy, 1992.

of Islam's ethico-political system engender pluralistic ideas.[234] As vicegerent of God on earth, man has a responsibility to pursue justice. This is where democracy becomes an appealing regime for pious Muslims because the greatest likelihood for the implementation of justice may be found in democracy.[235] While there is no guarantee that justice will always be served in democratic systems, at a minimum, democracy provides an institutional basis for fulfilling the primary responsibility of man as vicegerent of God on earth; namely, the pursuance of justice as directed in many verses in scripture.

The association between justice and democracy is not merely a theoretical exercise to satisfy intellectual curiosity. It has practical implications. In *Justice Interrupted: The Struggle for Constitutional Government in the Middle East*, Elizabeth Thompson[236] challenges the conventional view that Islam and liberal democracy are antithetical. She argues that the people of the Middle East have initiated revolts at different times since the 1850s in the name of justice and the rule of law, but the domestic autocrats and the foreign powers complicit in repressive regimes silenced these democratic demands. From the *'Urābī rebellion* in Egypt (1879–1882) to the Arab Spring, democratic movements and popular struggles for justice have been the rule rather than the exception in the Muslim world.

The Arab Spring is the latest manifestation of how discourses on Islamic justice can become politically consequential. The mass uprisings in the Arab region took many by surprise in 2011. Mohamed Bouazizi, a street vendor in Tunisia, unleashed a popular wave on December 17, 2010, when he set himself on fire protesting the repression and corruption in his country. The spark in Tunisia quickly led to mass mobilization campaigns in the streets and squares of the Arab-majority countries. During these protests, people were chanting for freedom, the fall of the regime, and more importantly social justice. The protesters who took part in the Arab Spring wanted political and social justice against corrupt and inefficient governments. Implementing political justice would have put an end to corruption and held authoritarian leaders accountable, or so the protesters believed. The protesters also called for social justice in the form of an end to unemployment, poverty, and other problems that especially affected the younger generation in the region. Religion mattered in these uprisings because the demands for social justice were religiously inspired. Like all major faiths, Islam promotes justice, and this may motivate devout individuals to change the world around them according to

---

**234** Fadl, *Islam, and the Challenge of Democracy.*
**235** Ibid, 6.
**236** Thompson, *Justice Interrupted.*

the principles of their faith.[237] In other words, religious belief and the values it promotes have informed political grievances by shaping perceptions of injustices in the Arab Spring.[238]

Conceptions of Islamic justice have also informed the ideology and behavior of contemporary Islamist movements beyond the Arabic-speaking countries. For example, Turkey's new Islamist movements aligned with the opposition groups at the *Gezi Parkı* protests in 2013 and they employed Islamic justice discourses to support a formidable challenge against the Islamist government led by Justice and Development Party (*Adalet ve Kalkınma Partisi* (AKP)). The Labor and Justice platform and the Anti-capitalist Muslims (ACMs) were among the oppositional Islamist movements. They were inspired by the writings of influential Islamist intellectual İhsan Eliaçık, who has written extensively about social justice and the political role of justice in an Islamic government.[239] The clash of two Islamist camps in Turkey can be seen as a new incarnation of the historic cleavage in Islamic history between ethically-minded pious individuals and those who seek power at the expense of religious principles.[240] One camp, the new Islamist movements, highlight such values as good morals, justice, and human dignity and put these values at the center of their criticism of AKP's neo-liberal policies, which they deem to be corrupt and unjust. Their charity activities aim to establish justice for the most marginalized segments of Turkish society, explicitly including immigrants.

Islamic social justice theory can also provide insights about Islamist party programs and help us to explain the political strategies of these parties from their own perspective. It is often noted that many Islamist parties around the world use the word "justice" in their names or put special emphasis on this concept in their party programs. This provides a basis for popular mobilization and political strategies geared toward economic and political justice. Social justice and welfare provision also matter a great deal to religious groups in the Muslim world. When governments fail to provide social services, religious groups assume this responsi-

237 Ciftci, *Islam, Justice, and Democracy*; Ciftci, "Islam, Social Justice, and Democracy," *Politics and Religion* 12, no. 4 (2019): 549–76.

238 Hoffman, Michael/Amaney, Jamal, "Religion in the Arab Spring: Between Two Competing Narratives," *The Journal of Politics* 76, no. 3 (2014), 593–606.

239 Eliaçık, İhsan, *Adalet Devleti: Ortak İyinin İktidarı*, Istanbul: İnşa Yayınları, 2015.

240 Hodgson, The Venture of Islam, vol. 1; Emre, Akif, "'Müslümancılık' Ya Da Klan Siyaseti," *Haber*, 7, August 2008; Yenigun, Halil I., "The New Antinomies of the Islamic Movement in Post-Gezi Turkey: Islamism vs. Muslimism," *Turkish Studies* 18, no. 2 (2017), 229–50.

bility.[241] As declared, social justice and welfare service provision are among the primary policy goals of Islamist political parties. Some scholars point to an Islamist electoral advantage due to Islam's focus on economic justice and the social service orientation of Islamist parties.[242]

Islamist justice theory can provide the conceptual tools for understanding the prevalence of anti-imperialist ideologies and anti-Americanism in majority-Muslim societies. While not all anti-imperialist and anti-American individuals are religious or Islamists, or vice versa, research shows that religion and Islamist cues have significant effects on these attitudes.[243] In the 1960s and 1970s, Islamist justice discourses were used to confront Communist ideology. The cooptation of various Islamist groups by the existing regimes in Indonesia, Egypt, and Turkey was supported by a predeterminate and *fitnah*-averse Sunni conception of justice.[244] The criticism of Western civilization and the call for a native theory of justice in the political philosophies of Quṭb and Sharīʿatī provide important clues about the origins of anti-imperialist preferences in the Muslim world. Furthermore, Sharīʿatī's application of historical materialism to Islamic concepts is especially valuable for understanding various uprisings and religious labor movements in the Islamic periphery. Additionally, violent extremist groups also justify their actions and recruit members by spreading a religious ideology that promises to correct injustices.[245] Finally, an attitude of anti-globalization and a call to search for social justice amid increasing global inequality have both been frequently voiced by the Islamists of our time.[246]

While the values of Islamic justice and the related preferences and orientations can be foundational for pluralistic ideas, the same forces may also justify authoritarianism. In fact, the latter path has conveniently legitimized forms of authoritarian and unjust rule, which have been the prevailing model of governance for much of Islamic history. Relatedly, Islamic rulers of the past have tended to prioritize order and security as preconditions of Islamic social jus-

---

**241** Masoud, Tarek, *Counting Islam: Religion, Class, and Elections in Egypt*, New York: Cambridge University Press, 2014; Cammett, Melani, *Compassionate Communalism: Welfare and Sectarianism in Lebanon*, Ithaca: Cornell University Press, 2014.

**242** Pepinsky, Thomas B. et al., "Testing Islam's Political Advantage: Evidence from Indonesia," *American Journal of Political Science* 56, no. 3 (2012): 584–600.

**243** Ciftci, Sabri/J O'Donnell, Becky/Tanner, Allison, "Who Favors Al-Qaeda? Anti-Americanism, Religious Outlooks, and Favorable Attitudes toward Terrorist Organizations," *Political Research Quarterly* 70, no. 3 (2017), 480–94, published online: http://www.jstor.org/stable/26384918 (accessed 17.06.2024).

**244** Ayoob, "Challenging Hegemony"; Ciftci, *Islam, Justice, and Democracy*.

**245** Ciftci/O'Donnell/Tanner, "Who Favors Al-Qaeda?".

**246** Eliaçık, *Adalet Devleti*.

tice in order to gain legitimacy as benevolent but authoritarian rulers. This tendency has and is still being used by authoritarian rulers in contemporary Muslim politics. Middle Eastern states, for example, deployed Bismarckian welfare policies in the 1960s and 1970s to help authoritarian survival.[247] The so-called "rentier states" have been known to utilize distributive policies to quiet dissent in the past.[248] More recently, the oil-rich monarchies have upped their tactical use of welfare provision. In the wake of the Arab Spring, improvements to social security, salary increases, and free educational perks were put in place in order to buy the loyalty of their citizens and to quell the demands for democracy.[249] Religious justifications are equally pervasive as exemplified by the support voiced for the Saudi rulers by religious scholars or the Mauritanian Shaykh Maḥfūẓ Ibn Bayyah's (b. 1935) fatwas legitimizing the authoritarian policies of the United Arab Emirates.[250]

In sharp contrast to such practices, Muhammad is viewed as a revolutionary and a social justice warrior, who established the "ideal Muslim community" and cherished political and economic egalitarianism. Some later incarnations of Islamic governance models, however, favored benevolent dictators because they adhered to the widely held belief that a pious ruler would ensure the welfare of the Muslim community by upholding God's justice on earth. In this model, positions of political quietism and obedience came to prominence due to the alliance of rulers and religious scholars. This position was most succinctly expressed by the great medieval theologian Ibn Taymīya: Sixty years with a tyrannical imam are better than one night without an imam.[251]

# 8 Conclusion

Justice is the central concept of Islam's ethico-political system, yet systematic studies about the historical evolution and conceptual underpinnings of this concept are rare. This essay attempted to fill this gap. By and large, Islamic justice conceptions

247 Owen, Roger, *State, Power, and Politics in the Making of the Modern Middle East*, London: Routledge, $^{3}$2004.

248 Beblawi, Hazem/Giacomo, Luciani, *The Rentier State*, New York: Routledge, 2015.

249 Murphy, Caryle, "Saudi King Unveils Massive Spending Package," published online: *The National* (Abu Dhabi), 2011, www.thenational.ae/news/world/saudi-king-unveils-massive-spending-package#page2 (accessed on 17.06.2024).

250 Quisay and Parker, "Thought, On the Theology of Obedience," *MAYDAN*, 2019. Ibn Bayyah is a traditional scholar of Mauritanian origin with significant credentials in the field of uṣūl al-fiqh. He has close ties to the monarchs in Saudi Arabia and the UAE.

251 Ibn Taymiyya, *Against Extremisms*.

are rooted in Qur'ānic terms such as *tawḥīd* and *khalīfa*. *Tawḥīd* means unity of God and it functions as an organizing principle to structure society in a way that inspires order, harmony, and justice. *Khalīfa* is a concept that expresses the special status of man as vicegerent of God and thus gears the capacities of free will and human responsibility toward the cause of justice. Alongside these two concepts, other terms are used in the Qur'ān to describe different aspects of Islamic justice like balance, direction, and rights. Still other verses refer to tyranny, misguidance, and extremities as the opposite of justice. This chapter provided an account of how such scriptural foundations informed various trajectories of justice in the age of the Prophet, the ensuing theological and philosophical debates of the medieval era, and the intellectual Islamist debates of modern times. It showed that the concept of justice is constantly evolving in response to the changing contexts it is called to answer to.

Scriptural foundations of Islamic conceptions of justice are not sufficient on their own to grasp the complex nature of justice in Islam. Critical events in Islamic history and responses to socioeconomic developments have been instrumental in shaping the discourse on Islamic justice, most prominently its social and political justice dimensions. Philosophers, jurists, and intellectuals tailored the Islamic conception of justice to fit the needs of their respective times. An inherent tension characterized these endeavors. Islamic justice conceptions swung between discourses of order and freedom. On one side of the coin, the Qur'ānic terms used to describe justice imply balance, moderation, and harmony. On the other side, they necessitate initiative and an agency to bring change and correct injustices. From the beginning of Islam to the present-day, this tension has constituted the core of Islamic justice theory. The dialectic of these opposing sides gave way to an ever-changing conception of Islamic justice. Most recently, this tension and attempts at resolving it are seen in the works of Islamists. This chapter also attempted to provide the first systematic overview of this rich history. Yet, the study of this subject is in its infancy, and it requires further analysis. Future studies could focus on the multilayered dialectic unfolding between scriptural foundations and their context, discourses of order and those of freedom, and the justification of the status quo as opposed to a longing for change in the Muslim world to provide a fuller account of Islamic conceptions of justice.

Of its various possible dimensions, social and political justice moved to the center in the development of the Islamic conceptions of justice. The prophetic community has been presented as the ideal model of social and political justice to be emulated by later generations of Muslims. Hidden behind an idealized image of unity, prosperity, and equality within this community are the political struggles that sharply divided the *umma*. The first civil war and the philosophical debates that generated from this somewhat unexpected conflict were the first manifestation of realist politics. This development brought with it a new model of justice based on the idea of obedience to a ruler for the good of the Muslim community. The distinction between the parties involved this first conflict and in the later incarnations of similar divisions established a dichotomy of order and freedom, consensus and tyranny, and democracy and authoritarianism as two separate manifestations of the Islamic paradigm of justice. Whenever Islamic society and the state went into decline or when they were challenged by external forces, philosophers, scholars, and intellectuals came to redefine and reconceptualize the Islamic conception of justice around these dichotomies, especially with respect to social justice. Human dignity and public interest are two ideals that have corresponded to the inherent tension between free will and order, the two sides of the Islamic conception of justice. More recently, Islamists redefined the Islamic conception of justice in response to the encroachment of modernity and Western colonialism on the Muslim world. The challenge from the West necessitated that scholars revisit the foundations of the ideal prophetic community to make sense of it in a new context, this time marrying the scriptural foundations of justice and notions of a prophetic golden age to modern ideas like freedom and democracy.

The pattern of change and invention in the evolution of Islamic conceptions of justice can help us understand the current challenges Islamic societies and Muslims living outside predominantly Muslim countries more generally are facing due to the political and economic consequences of globalization. Conflict, poverty, underdevelopment, and massive migration are some of the outcomes of globalization that have come to weigh heavily on some corners of the Muslim world. The Muslim response to this most recent challenge comes in various forms including extremist violence, calls for an Islamic society of good morals, and Muslim democracy. All of these responses place the Islamic conception of justice at the center of their social designs. With respect to Muslim democracy, we are already witnessing a new iteration of the previously established cleavage appearing in the Muslim world. This phenomenon is most visible in Turkey, a society which has experienced secular and religious modes of democracy as well as episodes of authoritarianism all within the last half century. This cleavage manifests itself in two alternative visions of Islamism voiced by the realist and ethicalist interpretations.[252] The substance of the debate concerns justice and its reinvention. Scriptural, traditional, and modernist conceptions are being fused to gain new concepts of Islamic justice. The proponents of the realist camp, presumably represented by political Islamists, have focused their efforts on welfare programs and institutionalized charity as convenient tools to grasp political power. To that end, they did not hesitate to

252 Yenigun, "The New Antinomies of the Islamic Movement in Post-Gezi Turkey."

integrate into the global neoliberal order and justified it with a religiously inspired conception of social justice. In contrast, those concerned with ethical values and human dignity, the ethical camp, became fierce critics of this order and aligned with the most impoverished segments of the society, including workers, members of the precariat, the unemployed, and migrants.[253] Their criticism was unequivocally grounded in an Islamic conception of justice based on the notion of *khalīfa*, the responsibility of believers to fight oppression, and the centrality of justice to Islamic faith.

We can expect that for the whole Muslim world, and not only for Turkey, the challenge posed by globalization and the neoliberal economic order will be the new frontline of the struggle between the rival conceptions of justice laid out in this chapter. This time around, we might very well see a deeper engagement with liberal and socialist theories of justice as well as the Christian and Judaic conceptions of justice. Islam has always managed to respond to the various challenges it has faced by transforming and reinventing its native conceptions. On the economic front, economic inequality creates a tension between those in control of economic resources who possess great wealth and those who are in danger of losing a standard of life that befits their human dignity. Conceptions of Islamic social justice might be reinvented to provide religiously inspired policy solutions countering this economic tension. On the political front, the struggle between a popular quest for democracy and the elitist desire for power might come to be the main stage on which this latest reinvention of the concept of political justice in Islam is carried out.

# Bibliography

Abdelkader, Deina, *Social Justice in Islam*, vol. 8, Herndon, VA: IIIT, 2000.

ʿAbd ar-Razīq, ʿAlī, *al-Islām wa-uṣūl al-ḥukm: Baḥth fi-l-khilāfa wa-l-ḥukūma fi-l-Islām* (Islam and the Foundations of Governance: Research on the Caliphate and Governance in Islam), Bayrūt: Dār Maktabat al-Ḥayāh, 1978.

Abrahamian, Ervand, *Iran between Two Revolutions*. Princeton: Princeton University Press, 1982.

Abrahamian, Ervand, "Ali Sharīʿatī: Ideologue of the Iranian Revolution," *Merip Reports* 102 (1982), 24–28.

Adamson, Peter, "al-Kindi," in: Edward N. Zalta (ed.), *The Stanford Encyclopedia of Philosophy*, Spring 2020 edition, Stanford, CA: Stanford University, 2020, published online: https://plato.stanford.edu/archives/spr2020/entries/al-kindi/ (accessed on 02.02.2024).

Ahmed, Shahab, *What Is Islam? The Importance of Being Islamic*, Princeton: Princeton University Press, 2016.

253 Eliaçık, İhsan, "The Koran and Social Justice, Interview with Turkish Theologian."

al-Mawdudi, Abu al-A'la, "Islam in Transition: Muslim Perspective," in: John J. Donohue/John L. Esposito (eds.), *Islam in Transition: Muslim Perspective*, 253–61, New York: Oxford University Press, 1982 n.d.

al-Rikabi, Jaffar, "Baqir Al-Sadr and the Islamic State: A Theory for 'Islamic Democracy'," *Journal of Shi'a Islamic Studies* 5, no. 3 (2012), 249–75.

an-Naim, Abdullahi Ahmed, *Islam and the Secular State*, Cambridge, MA: Harvard University Press, 2008.

Atiyeh, George N., *Al-Kindi: The Philosopher of the Arabs*, Rawalpindi: Islamic Research Institute, 1966.

Ayoob, Mohammed, "Political Islam: Image and Reality," *World Policy Journal* 21, no. 3 (2004), 1–14.

Ayoob, Mohammed, *The Many Faces of Political Islam: Religion and Politics in the Muslim World*, Ann Arbor: University of Michigan Press, 2009.

Ayoob, Mohammed, "Challenging Hegemony: Political Islam and the North–South Divide," *International Studies Review* 9, no. 4 (2007), 629–43.

Balcı, İsrafil, "Umar (r.a): A Leader Crowned with Truth and Justice," *Life and Religion: A Publication of the Turkish Diyanet Foundation and the Istanbul Office of the Mufti*, Istanbul, 2013, published online: *Lastprophet.info,* https://www.lastprophet.info/the-companions/the-companions/925/umar-r-a-a-leader-crowned-with-truth-and-justice (accessed on 18.06.2024).

Beblawi, Hazem/Giacomo, Luciani, *The Rentier State*, New York: Routledge, 2015.

Çagrıcı, Mustafa, "Adalet," published online: *Türkiye Diyanet Vakfı İslam Ansiklopedisi*, Istanbul, 2010, https://islamansiklopedisi.org.tr/adalet#1-ahlak (accessed on 18.06.2024).

Cammett, Melani, *Compassionate Communalism: Welfare and Sectarianism in Lebanon*, Ithaca: Cornell University Press, 2014.

Campanini, Massimo, "The Mu 'tazila in Islamic History and Thought," *Religion Compass* 6, no. 1 (2012), 41–50.

Ciftci, Sabri/J O'Donnell, Becky/Tanner, Allison, "Who Favors Al-Qaeda? Anti-Americanism, Religious Outlooks, and Favorable Attitudes toward Terrorist Organizations," *Political Research Quarterly* 70, no. 3 (2017), 480–94, published online: http://www.jstor.org/stable/26384918 (accessed on 19.06.2024).

Ciftci, Sabri, "Islam, Social Justice, and Democracy," *Politics and Religion* 12, no. 4 (2019), 549–76.

Ciftci, Sabri, *Islam, Justice, and Democracy*, Philadelphia, PA: Temple University Press, 2022.

Crone, Patricia, *God's Rule: Government and Islam*, New York: Columbia University Press, 2004.

Danesh, Maryam/Hassan, Abniki, "The Relation between Liberty and Justice in Ali Sharīʿatī 's Political Thought," *International Journal of Political Science* 5, no. 9 (2015), 1–8.

Darling, Linda T, *A History of Social Justice and Political Power in the Middle East: The Circle of Justice from Mesopotamia to Globalization*, New York: Routledge, 2013.

Davis, Nancy J/Robinson, Robert V, "The Egalitarian Face of Islamic Orthodoxy: Support for Islamic Law and Economic Justice in Seven Muslim-Majority Nations," *American Sociological Review* 71, no. 2 (2006), 167–90.

El-Affendi, Abdelwahab, *Who Needs an Islamic State?,* Malaysia Think Tank London, 2008.

Eliaçık, İhsan, "İslam Uygarlığı Tarihten Mi Çekiliyor?," *Bilgi Ve Düşünce*, 2003, 58–63.

Eliaçık, İhsan, "Adalet 'Kozmos'un Temelidir," *Bilgi Ve Düşünce*, 2003, 58–63.

Eliaçık, İhsan, "Sivil Dönüşüm," *Değişim*, 1997, 44–44.

Eliaçık, İhsan, *Adalet Devleti: Ortak İyinin İktidarı*, İstanbul: İnşa Yayınları, 2015.

Emre, Akif, "'Müslümancılık' Ya Da Klan Siyaseti," *Haber* 7, August 2008.

Enayat, Hamid, *Modern Islamic Political Thought: The Response of the Shi 'i and Sunni Muslims to the Twentieth Century*, London: MacMillan, 1982.

Ersöz, Resul, "Kur'ân'a Göre 'Hakk' ve 'Adalet' Kavramları Bağlamında İslâm Toplumunun İctimâî Değerleri," *Afyon Kocatepe Üniversitesi Sosyal Bilimler Dergisi* 18, no. 2 (2016), 1–27.
Abou El Fadl, Khaled/Cohen, Joshua et al. (eds.), *Islam, and the Challenge of Democracy: A Boston Review Book*, Princeton University Press, published online: *JSTOR*, 2004, http://www.jstor.org/stable/j.ctt14bs1gz (accessed on 19.06.2024).
Fakhry, Majid, *A History of Islamic Philosophy*, New York: Columbia University Press, 2004.
Al-Fārābī, *Al-Fārābī on the Perfect State: Abū Naṣr Al-Fārābī's Mabādi' Ārā' Ahl Al-Madīna Al-Fāḍila: A Revised Text with Introduction, Translation, and Commentary*, trans. Richard Walzer, New York: Oxford University Press, 1985.
Feldman, Noah, *The Fall and Rise of the Islamic State*, Princeton: Princeton University Press, 2012.
Filali-Ansary, Abdou, "Muslims and Democracy," *Journal of Democracy* 10, no. 3 (1999): 18–32.
Gafarov, Anar, "Râğıb El-İsfahânî'Nin Insan Ve Ahlâk Anlayişi," Master Thesis, Istanbul: Marmara University, 2004.
Gellner, Ernest, "Islam and Marxism: Some Comparisons," *International Affairs* 67, no. 1 (1991), 1–6.
Gutiérrez, Gustavo, *A Theology of Liberation*, New York: Orbis Books, 1971.
Hodgson, Marshall G S, The Venture of Islam, vol. 1, *The Classical Age of Islam*, Chicago: University of Chicago Press, 1974.
Hodgson, Marshall G S, The Venture of Islam, vol. 2, *The Expansion of Islam in the Middle Periods*, Chicago: University of Chicago Press, 1974.
Hoffman, Michael/Amaney, Jamal, "Religion in the Arab Spring: Between Two Competing Narratives," *The Journal of Politics* 76, no. 3 (2014), 593–606.
Ibn Taymīya, Taqī ad-Dīn, *Against Extremisms, Taymiyyan Texts*, trans. Y. Michot. Beirut: Dar Albouraq, 2002.
Inalcik, Halil, *The Ottoman Empire: The Classical Age, 1300–1600*, trans. Norman Itzkowitz/ Colin Imber, London: Weidenfeld and Nicholson, 1973.
Iqbal, Mohammad, *The Reconstruction of Religious Thought in Islam*, Lahore: Sh. Muhammad Ashraf, 1968.
Jamalzadeh, Naser, "Sociopolitical Justice in Three Jurisprudential, Philosophical and Sociological Approaches," *Islamic Political Thought* 2, no. 1 (2015), 7–42.
Kaminski, Joseph J, *Islam, Liberalism, and Ontology: A Critical Re-Evaluation*, New York: Routledge, 2021.
Keddie, Nikki R, *Religion and Rebellion in Iran: The Tobacco Protest of 1891–1892*, London: Frank Cass, 1966.
Keddie, Nikki R, *An Islamic Response to Imperialism: Political and Religious Writings of Sayyid Jamāl al-Dīn al-Afghānī*, vol. 586, Berkeley, CA: University of California Press, 1983.
Kedourie, Elie, *Democracy and Arab Political Culture*, Washington, DC: Washington Institute for Near East Policy, 1992.
Kemal, Namık, "And Seek Their Council in the Affairs," Charles Kurzman (eds.), *Liberal Islam: A Source Book*, 114–48, New York: Oxford University Press, 1998.
Khadduri, Majid, *The Islamic Conception of Justice*. Baltimore, MD: JHU Press, 1984.
Khan, M. S, *An Unpublished Treatise of Miskawaih on Justice* [Risāla fī māhiyat al-ʿadl li-Miskawaih], Leiden: Brill, 1964.
Khomeinī, Sayyid R.M, "Theory of Justice," trans. Hussein Karamyar, published online: *al-Islam.org*, https://www.al-islam.org/theory-justice-sayyid-ruhullah-musawi-Khomeinī , (accessed on 19.06.2024).
Kuran, Timur, *Islam and Mammon*, Princeton: Princeton University Press, 2010.

Kuru, Ahmet T, *Islam, Authoritarianism, and Underdevelopment: A Global and Historical Comparison*, New York: Cambridge University Press, 2019.
Lapidus, Ira M, “The Separation of State and Religion in the Development of Early Islamic Society,” *International Journal of Middle East Studies* 6, no. 4 (1975), 363 – 85.
Lapidus, Ira M, *A History of Islamic Societies*, New York: Cambridge University Press, 2002.
Lapidus, Ira M, “Islamic Revival and Modernity: The Contemporary Movements and the Historical Paradigms,” *Journal of the Economic and Social History of the Orient* 40, no. 4 (1997), 444 – 60.
Lewis, Bernard, “Why Turkey Is the Only Muslim Democracy,” *Middle East Quarterly* 1, no. 1 (1994), 41 – 49.
Lewis, Bernard, *The Emergence of Modern Turkey*, New York: Oxford University Press, 1961.
Lorenz, Walter, “The Emergence of Social Justice in the West,” in: Michael Reisch (ed.), *Routledge International Handbook of Social Justice*, 40 – 52, New York: Routledge, 2014.
Maguire, Daniel C, “Religious Influences on Justice Theory,” in: Michael Reisch (ed.), *Routledge International Handbook of Social Justice*, 53 – 64, New York: Routledge, 2014.
March, Andrew F, “Taking People as They Are: Islam as a ‘Realistic Utopia’ in the Political Theory of Sayyid Quṭb,” *American Political Science Review* 104, no. 1 (2010), 189 – 207.
March, Andrew F, *The Caliphate of Man: Popular Sovereignty in Modern Islamic Thought*, Cambridge, MA: Belknap Press, 2019.
March, Andrew F, “Genealogies of Sovereignty in Islamic Political Theology,” *Social Research: An International Quarterly* 80, no. 1 (2013), 293 – 320.
Mardin, Serif, *The Genesis of Young Ottoman Thought: A Study in the Modernization of Turkish Political Ideas*, Syracuse, NY: Syracuse University Press, 2000.
Markham, Ian S/Suendam, Birinci Pirim, *An Introduction to Said Nursi: Life, Thought and Writings*, New York: Routledge, 2011.
Masoud, Tarek, *Counting Islam: Religion, Class, and Elections in Egypt*, New York: Cambridge University Press, 2014.
Mirakhor, Abbas/Askari, Hossein, *Conceptions of Justice form Earliest History to Islam*, New York: Palgrave-MacMillan, 2019, 181 – 214
Mirakhor, Abbas/Askari, Hossein, *Conceptions of Justice from Islam to the Present*, Switzerland: Springer, 2020, 182 – 85.
Moaddel, Mansoor, *Islamic Modernism, Nationalism, and Fundamentalism: Episode and Discourse*, Chicago: University of Chicago Press, 2005.
Mohamed, Yasien/Swazo, Norman K, “Contributing to Islamic Ethics,” *American Journal of Islam and Society* 27, no. 3 (2010), i–xiv.
Mohamed, Yasien, “The Concept of Justice in Miskawayh and Isfahani,” *Journal for Islamic Studies* 18 (1998), 51 – 111.
Murphy, Caryle, “Saudi King Unveils Massive Spending Package,” published online: *The National* (Abu Dhabi), 2011, www.thenational.ae/news/world/saudi-king-unveils-massive-spending-package#page2 (accessed on 18. 06. 2024).
Nasr, Seyyed Vali Reza, *Mawdudi and the Making of Islamic Revivalism*, New York: Oxford University Press on Demand, 1996.
Nursi, Said, *Risale-i Nur Külliyatì*, vol. 2, Istanbul: Nesil, 1996.
Nurtsch, Ceyda “The Koran and Social Justice. Interview with Turkish Theologian Ihsan Eliacik,” published online: *Qantara* 2014, https://qantara.de/en/article/interview-turkish-theologian-ihsan-eliacik-koran-and-social-justice (accessed on 14. 06. 2024).

Owen, Roger. *State, Power, and Politics in the Making of the Modern Middle East.* 3rd ed. London: Routledge, 2004.
Pepinsky, Thomas B. et al., "Testing Islam's Political Advantage: Evidence from Indonesia," *American Journal of Political Science* 56, no. 3 (2012), 584–600.
Quisay, Walaa/Parker, Thomas "On the Theology of Obedience: An Analysis of Shaykh Bin Bayyah and Shaykh Hamza Yusuf's Political Thought," *MAYDAN*, 2019.
Quṭb, Sayyid, *Social Justice in Islam*, trans. John B. Hardie, New York: American Council of Learned Societies, 1953.
Rahman, Fazlur, "The Principle of 'Shura' and the Role of the Umma in Islam," *American Journal of Islamic Social Sciences* 1, no. 1 (1984), 1–9.
Ramadan, Tariq, *Islam, the West, and the Challenges of Modernity*, trans. Said Amghar, Leicester: UK: The Islamic Foundation, 2009.
Rawls, John, *A Theory of Justice*, Cambridge, MA: Harvard University Press, 2009.
Sachedina, Abdulaziz, *The Islamic Roots of Democratic Pluralism*, New York: Oxford University Press, 2001.
Sedgwick, Mark, *Muhammad ʿAbduh*, Oxford: Oneworld Publications, 2014.
Sen, Amartya Kumar, *The Idea of Justice*, Cambridge, MA: Harvard University Press, 2009.
Sharīʿatī, Ali, *Eslam-Shenasi (Islamology)*, Tehran: Ershad, 1971.
Sharīʿatī, Ali, *Man and Islam*, trans. Fathollah Marjani, New Jersey: IPI Press [Kindle Edition], 1981.
Sharīʿatī, Ali, "Red Shi'ism (the Religion of Martyrdom) vs. Black Shi'ism (the Religion of Mourning)," published online: *Iran Chamber Society*, https://www.iranchamber.com/personalities/aSharīʿatī/works/red_black_shiism.php (accessed on 19.06.2024).
Shariati, Ali, "Reflections of a Concerned Muslim on the Plight of Oppressed People," published online: *Shariati.com*, http://www.shariati.com/kotob.html (accessed on 14.06.2024).
Sharīʿatī, Ali, "World Vision," in *Man and Islam*, trans. Fatoallah Marjani, New Jersey: IPI Press 1981.
Sharīʿatī, Ali, "Worldview of Tawhid," in *On the Sociology of Islam*, trans. Hamid Algar, Berkeley: Mizan Press, Shaban, 1398 h.
Sharīʿatī, Ali, *Religion vs Religion*, Chicago: ABC International Group, 2003.
Shariati, Ali, "And Once Again Abu Dharr," Part 5, published online: *Shariati.com*, http://www.shariati.com/kotob.html (accessed on 14.06.2024).
Sharīʿatī, Ali, "Modern Man and His Prisons," in: *Man and Islam*, trans. Fathollah Marjani, New Jersey: IPI Press 1981.
Smith, Christian, *The Emergence of Liberation Theology: Radical Religion and Social Movement Theory*, Chicago: University of Chicago Press, 1991.
Tamimi, Azzam, *Rachid Ghannouchi: A Democrat within Islamism*, New York: Oxford University Press, 2001.
Thompson, Elizabeth F, *Justice Interrupted*, Cambridge, MA: Harvard University Press, 2013.
Vahide, Sukran, *Islam in Modern Turkey: An Intellectual Biography of Bediuzzaman Said Nursi.* Albany, NY: SUNY Press, 2012.
Welzel, Christian/Inglehart, Ronald/Kligemann, Hans-Dieter, "The Theory of Human Development: A Cross-cultural Analysis," *European Journal of Political Research* 42, no. 3 (2003), 341–79.
Yavuz, M. Hakan, *Islamic Political Identity in Turkey*, New York: Oxford University Press, 2003.
Yavuz, M. Hakan, "Turkey: Islam without Shari'a?," in Robert W. Hefner (ed.), *Shari'a Politics: Islamic Law and Society in the Modern World*, 146–78, Bloomington: Indiana University Press, 2009.
Yavuz, M Hakan, *Toward an Islamic Enlightenment: The Gülen Movement*, New York: Oxford University Press, 2013.

Yenigun, Halil I, "The New Antinomies of the Islamic Movement in Post-Gezi Turkey: Islamism vs. Muslimism," *Turkish Studies* 18, no. 2 (2017), 229 – 50.

## Suggestions for Further Reading

Abdelkader, Deina, *Social Justice in Islam*, Herndon, VA: International Institute of Islamic Thought, 2000.

Abou El Fadl, Khaled, *Islam and the Challenge of Democracy: A Boston Review Book*, Princeton: Princeton University Press, 2004.

al-Fārābī, *Al-Fārābī on the Perfect State: Abū Naṣr Al-Fārābī's Mabādi' Ārā' Ahl Al-Madīna Al-Fāḍila: A Revised Text with Introduction, Translation, and Commentary*, Oxford University Press, 1985.

an-Na'im, Abdullahi Ahmed, *Muslims and Global Justice*, Philadelphia: University of Pennsylvania Press, 2011.

Askari, Hossein/Mirakhor, Abbas (eds.), *Conceptions of Justice from Islam to the Present*, Cham: Springer, 2020.

Ciftci, Sabri, *Islam, Justice, and Democracy*, Philadelphia, PA: Temple University Press, 2021.

Darling, Linda T., *A history of social justice and political power in the Middle East: The circle of justice from Mesopotamia to globalization*, New York: Routledge, 2013.

Khadduri, Majid, *The Islamic Conception of Justice*, Baltimore, MD: JHU Press, 1984.

Khan, M. S., *An Unpublished Treatise of Miskawaih on Justice* [Risāla fī māhiyat al-'adl li-Miskawaih], Leiden: Brill, 1964.

Quṭb, Sayyid, *Social Justice in Islam*, trans. John B. Hardie, Oneonta, NY: Islamic Publications International, 2000

Catharina Rachik and Georges Tamer

# Epilogue

What is justice? This question, as the articles in this volume illustrate, cannot be adequately answered in a single sentence. In Judaism, Christianity, and Islam,[1] justice is intricately tied to a spectrum of theological conceptions. These conceptions are structured within a framework that encompasses legal, moral-ethical, and social dimensions. A distinctive characteristic of justice across these three traditions is its relational nature: it is consistently framed in reference to God's justice as the ultimate measure for worldly justice.

But what is God's justice? Throughout the history of these religious traditions, theologians have struggled to understand God's nature and the rationale for divine action in human history. Some have portrayed God as a strict judge who enforces divine law without deviation, while others have emphasized his compassion and mercy. Still, some perspectives even view divine judgment as retributive or vengeful. Another line of thought has posited that God's justice is ultimately incomprehensible to human understanding, raising questions about whether God is bound by his own laws or transcends them entirely. The challenge for many within these traditions remains the tension between God's moral nature and humanity's moral empowerment, which leads to a crucial question: how can an understanding of divine justice inform human justice?

Understanding this complex dynamic – the divine-human relationship and its implications for human morality – is crucial to understanding the concept of justice as it is conceived in each tradition. This chapter begins by summarizing the conceptions of justice in Judaism, Christianity, and Islam. It then examines the commonalities and differences among these religions, beginning with an exploration of divine justice. This discussion is framed around the example of Abraham's plea for Sodom, a narrative present in the scriptures of all three traditions. Each religion acknowledges the covenant God made with Abraham, and we will explore how this covenant is understood within each tradition and how it shapes their respective conceptions of justice.

In Genesis 18, Abraham not only appeals to God to judge justly but also implores him to act mercifully toward Sodom. This narrative raises a central question: how are mercy and justice intertwined in Judaism, Christianity, and Islam,

1 It should be noted that these religions are not monolithic entities, but rather comprise a multitude of diverse schools of thought. In order to facilitate comparison between the various religions, we will present the ideas put forth by a number of influential theologians, representing different historical contexts.

https://doi.org/10.1515/9783110561692-005

and what implications does this relationship have for the human pursuit of justice? Building on this foundation, the chapter concludes by examining social justice, focusing on the concept of charity as a practical expression of justice. This analysis considers how the interplay between justice and compassion informs the religious imperative to build equitable societies and care for the vulnerable.

# 1 The Concept of Justice from a Jewish Perspective

In his article, Aryeh Botwinick examines justice as a core principle within Judaism, exploring its foundations, historical evolution, and philosophical complexities. Justice, rooted in biblical texts and rabbinic traditions, is illustrated as a divine imperative, encapsulated in the central verse of Deuteronomy 16:20, "Justice, justice shalt thou pursue," which underscores not only the pursuit of just outcomes but also the importance of just means. By repeating the word "justice," this verse implies that justice must be actively and ethically pursued – a process in which moral ends are reached through morally sound methods. This anti-perfectionist stance in Judaism holds that achieving justice is not a straightforward attainment but an ongoing, self-reflective endeavor, where humans must continuously refine their approach to meet both divine and ethical standards.

Botwinick places justice within the context of Jewish theology, particularly the "negative theological" approach that posits God as ultimately unknowable and beyond human comprehension. Here, justice is pursued relationally and in proximity to the divine yet is never entirely captured within human frameworks. The article explores Biblical narratives, such as the *Tower of Babel* and the story of Amalek, to illustrate humanity's attempts to approach or understand the divine. Botwinick contrasts these narratives with Gnostic tendencies, which seek either to embody or intellectualize the divine fully, whereas Judaism maintains a degree of mystery surrounding God's will. Figures like Maimonides and Rabbi Akiva echo this caution against human overreach in understanding divine justice, suggesting that justice – much like knowledge of God – operates within limits accessible to human reason but ultimately lies beyond complete human grasp.

The historical roots of justice in Judaism are explored through the framework of the covenant, which binds God and humanity in a mutual relationship of commitment and ethical obligations. Botwinick revisits the dialogues between God and Abraham regarding Sodom and the binding of Isaac, two seminal events that illustrate the covenantal dynamics of divine justice. In these narratives, Abraham confronts the tension between divine commands and his sense of justice, advocating for human standards of mercy and righteousness even as he seeks to obey God. This covenantal perspective extends across generations, encapsulating both divine command and human agency in the pursuit of justice, with rituals such as the sabbatical and jubilee years emphasizing periodic social and economic reset.

The article then discusses how the Hebrew Scriptures incorporate principles of equality into the concept of justice. For example, laws governing the Sabbatical and Jubilee years (*Leviticus* 25) ensure a redistribution of resources to prevent permanent socioeconomic disparities. These cycles emphasize communal responsibility and reinforce the ideal that the land and its benefits belong to all of humanity under God's stewardship. These practices serve as a model for intergenerational justice, whereby resources and rights are preserved for future generations, not merely as a practical concern but as a core ethical and theological imperative. Through these laws, Judaism cultivates a vision of social justice that encompasses respect for both people and the environment, promoting sustained communal and ecological harmony.

Botwinick then explores justice from the mystical perspective within Judaism, where justice involves a unique mode of divine-human interaction. In Jewish mysticism, justice is conceived not only as an ethical command but as a relational experience, where humanity's efforts to enact justice can be seen as part of an ongoing dialogue with the divine. Mystical interpretations, particularly within Chassidic frameworks, approach justice as a means of bridging the earthly and divine realms. While God remains beyond human full understanding, mysticism allows for a closer encounter with the divine mystery, framing justice as an avenue through which humans fulfill both cosmic and ethical roles.

The question remains what the distance of God to humans, as held by negative theology, means for the practical application of the concept of justice. Botwinick draws on Maimonides' description of the Jewish judge, or *dayan*, as outlined in the *Hilchot Sanhedrin* (Laws Pertaining to Judicial Tribunals). The ideal judge, as Maimonides portrays, combines deep knowledge of both written and oral law with analytical and moral sensibilities, embodying a judicious skepticism and humility akin to the incomprehensibility of God himself. By embracing these qualities, the judge becomes an ethical model, reflecting Maimonides' broader philosophical view in which human knowledge of God is always indirect and limited. This "negative theological" framework suggests that just as one cannot fully grasp divine will, one should apply caution and self-restraint in human judgment. This vision extends into Botwinick's emphasis on monotheism's insistence on an egalitarian and pluralistic approach to justice, which, due to divine transcendence, cannot assert absolute hierarchical values. Justice in Judaism is therefore "blind" in a dual sense: it does not claim exclusive access to moral truth, and it requires adjudicators to prioritize integrity in their process over the certainty of outcomes.

This paradigm challenges judges to operate in a space of ethical ambiguity, where each case must be considered on its merits and where human fallibility is acknowledged. For Botwinick, the judge's role is to embody the moral courage to navigate such complexities without succumbing to the limitations of absolute knowledge. Thus, Maimonides' conception of the judge becomes a metaphor for an "ethics of uncertainty" in which humility and self-awareness replace rigid doctrinal certainty. This ethical framework urges continuous reflection and adaptation, prioritizing the pursuit of justice over the presumption of achieving a perfect or final form of justice.

## 2 The Concept of Justice from a Christian Perspective

Elisabeth Gräb-Schmidt presents justice in Christianity as a dynamic and multifaceted concept that has evolved from its classical and biblical origins into a modern imperative for social, economic, and ecological responsibility. This Christian vision of justice, founded on principles of mercy, solidarity, and a shared global order, calls for continual reassessment to meet the moral challenges of contemporary life. Justice in Christianity not only structures relationships among individuals but also between humanity and the natural world, aligning with an ecological and intergenerational responsibility. Gräb-Schmidt emphasizes that, despite historical and cultural differences, there remains a shared understanding of justice as a relational concept that upholds a universal order, one that must adapt to the challenges posed by social, economic, and ecological injustices today.

Gräb-Schmidt traces the Christian concept of justice back to Greek antiquity, where philosophers such as Plato and Aristotle viewed justice as a guiding principle for ethical and societal order. Justice was the highest of virtues, critical for individual harmony and the organization of the *polis*, or state. Plato's ideal of justice emphasized the alignment of individual abilities and societal roles to create a harmonious order, while Aristotle later distinguished between distributive and commutative justice to address the allocation of resources and fairness in interpersonal relationships. This classical understanding was influential but contrasted with the biblical perspective, which linked justice with mercy and relational responsibility beyond mere proportionality. In the Bible, justice is deeply embedded in both the Old and New Testaments, where it is intertwined with the divine qualities of mercy and love. The Hebrew term *tsedaḳa* denotes an active justice infused with compassion, guiding communal relations and advocating for the rights of the vulnerable. Prophetic literature, such as Amos and Isaiah, emphasizes God's justice as a commitment to social equity and protection for the marginalized. The New Testament reinterprets justice within the framework of salvation, where divine justice is fulfilled through Christ's sacrifice, offering a form of redemptive justice that transcends retributive measures. Paul's writings further emphasize justice as a transformative power realized through faith, guiding Christians to embody justice in service and love, especially toward those disadvantaged.

Christian concepts of justice underwent significant transformations during the medieval period and the Reformation. Thomas Aquinas synthesized Greek philosophy with Christian theology, integrating justice as one of the cardinal virtues while also emphasizing theological virtues like faith, hope, and love. Aquinas's model preserved a sense of order rooted in divine law, in which human reason and virtue could be aligned with divine justice. The Reformation brought a dramatic shift with Martin Luther's doctrine of justification by faith. Luther argued that humans could not achieve justice through their deeds alone; rather, justice is a divine gift granted through grace. This understanding of justice, centered on God's mercy rather than human merit, redefined justice as an expression of God's relational commitment to humanity, framing it as both a forensic (legal) and transformative concept. Luther's views sparked ongoing theological debate, particularly regarding the balance between faith and works in the Christian life. In modern theological discourse, a renewed interest in the Pauline concept of justice can be observed, emphasizing community and service. This re-evaluation critiques Martin Luther's forensic reading of justification, advocating for a broader understanding of justice as communal and relational.

In early modernity, the focus shifts from divine or cosmological foundations to rational and human-centered frameworks. Early modernity critiques metaphysical assumptions and instead grounds justice in human reason and freedom. This transformation sees the rise of social contract theories (e. g., Hobbes, Locke, Rousseau, Kant), which redefine justice as a system ensuring individual liberty and equality within societal structures. Justice becomes intertwined with freedom, encapsulated in the triad of liberty, equality, and solidarity. However, these developments challenge traditional foundations of justice, as the emphasis on human agency and rationality risks marginalizing theological dimensions. Despite these developments, Gräb-Schmidt notes the limits of purely rational or contractual approaches, as they often fail to address deeper issues of mercy and relational responsibility. The contractual notion of justice, while promoting equality, often lacks the compassion and relationality integral to biblical justice. Thus, she argues for a model that reconciles personal freedom with communal responsibilities and includes global solidarity, ecological care, and intergenerational justice. In modernity, freedom's connection to justice expanded through the recognition of human rights and the pluralization of values. Justice became a dynamic concept addressing global challenges like inequality and economic disparities while maintaining its grounding in individual dignity and collective responsibility. This evolution reflects the tension between freedom's self-restriction and its limitless potential, with justice serving as its guiding framework.

Gräb-Schmidt concludes by discussing the relevance of Christian justice in a globalized world. She points out that today's justice debates increasingly emphasize ecological sustainability, economic fairness, and the rights of future generations. Drawing from the Christian maxim, "Seek first his kingdom and his righteousness" (Matthew 6:33), Gräb-Schmidt advocates for a justice that is not only social but cosmic, encompassing the well-being of the entire creation. The Christian churches in Germany, for instance, have underscored this broader perspective by linking justice to solidarity and sustainability, challenging believers to address pressing global issues through a framework of justice rooted in divine mercy and communal care.

## 3 The Concept of Justice from an Islamic Perspective

As Sabri Ciftci emphasizes in his article, the concept of justice in Islam is deeply intertwined with scriptural principles, philosophical reflections, and legal traditions. Central to Islamic justice are three key scriptural concepts: *tawḥīd* (the oneness of God), *khalīfa* (man as God's vicegerent), and *maṣlaḥa* (promotion of public interest). These principles form the foundation for both individual and societal justice. *Tawḥīd* emphasises the unity and harmony of God and creation, and suggests that social justice reflects the cosmic order. *Khalīfa* grants humans free will and responsibility to enact justice on earth, while *maṣlaḥa* emphasizes collective welfare and moral goodness.

The main term for justice in the Islamic tradition is *ʿadāla* and its root already possesses the meaning of to straighten, be equal, or balance. The Qurʾān outlines various dimensions of justice, including *qisṭ* (fair share), *mīzān* (balance), and *wasaṭ* (moderation). These concepts imply that moderation and balance should be pursued. In practice, this means that justice will be realized when rulers and people act in harmony and moderation to create orderly social and political systems. Justice also relates to *ḥaqq*, signifying truth and rights, which requires equitable treatment of individuals regardless of status. Furthermore, theological constructs like *mīthāq* (primordial covenant) and *walāya* (God's care) reinforce the belief in divine justice and human obligation to uphold it.

Medieval Muslim Philosophers like al-Fārābī and al-Kindī saw justice as a balance between individual virtues and social order. The theological school Muʿtazila, known as *ahl al-ʿadl wa-t-tawḥīd* (the People of Justice and Unity), emphasized God's absolute justice (*ʿadl*) and unity (*tawḥīd*), arguing that injustice is incompatible with divine nature. They believed in human free will, holding individuals morally accountable for their actions, and rejected predestination, which they saw as inconsistent with divine justice. Their doctrine of "commanding good and forbidding evil" (*al-amr bi-l-maʿrūf wa-n-nahy ʿani-l-munkar*) made it a religious duty to promote justice and prevent wrongdoing in society.

Ciftci highlights two central dimensions of Islamic justice: political justice, focusing on leadership and governance, and social justice, emphasizing welfare and equity. Historically, political justice emerged especially from early debates on leadership after the *fitna* (civil war), leading to differing Sunni and Shīʿī doctrines on legitimate rule. Sunni theories emphasized communal consensus, while Shīʿī perspectives linked justice to divinely guided leaders. Social justice in Islam has its roots in early jurisprudential theory, particularly the principles of *sharīʿa*, which emphasize the protection of life, religion, property, and progeny. Islamic jurists like al-Ghazālī and Ibn Taymīya further developed theories of economic justice, advocating redistribution of wealth, provision of public goods, and charitable giving (*zakāt*), which became central to the welfare-oriented model of Islamic governance. Over time, social justice became a hallmark of a just ruler, aligning political authority with the principles of equity and public interest to ensure societal harmony.

Modern Islamic thinkers and theologians responded to colonialism, modernization, and socio-economic challenges by reinterpreting classical principles of justice. Reformers like Jamāl ad-Dīn al-Afghānī and Muḥammad ʿAbduh sought to reconcile Islamic principles with Western ideas, advocating for freedom, and participation of people in public affairs through elected assemblies based on the Islamic concept of *shūrā* (consultation). Constitutionalists in the modern Islamic world, such as Namık Kemal and the leaders of movements in the Ottoman Empire and Iran, argued that constitutional governance and popular sovereignty were inherently compatible with Islamic principles. They tied ideas like freedom, accountability, and justice to Islamic concepts such as *maṣlaḥa* (public interest), positioning democracy as a tool to ensure just governance. Movements like the Iranian Constitutional Revolution (1905–1911) and Egypt's ʿUrābī revolt (1879–1882) mobilized the public using Islamic justice rhetoric to challenge corruption, foreign domination, and authoritarian rule.

The Islamist theory of justice builds on classical Islamic principles while addressing modern challenges such as oppression (*ẓulm*), inequality, and socio-political decay. Thinkers like Sayyid Quṭb emphasized *tawḥīd* (divine unity) as the foundation of a harmonious, just society, critiquing Western materialism and advocating for an Islamic system that balances spiritual and material needs. Similarly, ʿAlī Sharīʿatī focused on resistance to tyranny and human agency, framing justice as central to human dignity and the fight against oppression. Ciftci highlights how Islamists reinterpret scriptural principles like *khalīfa* (vicegerency) to propose solutions rooted in individual responsibility and community solidarity. Yet a weakness of the Islamist theory of justice is its limited practical frameworks. Furthermore, the question arises how abstract principles like *tawḥīd* or resistance to *ẓulm* can be effectively operationalized to address modern socio-political complexities.

Cifci highlights the political roots of Islamic justice and argues for the compatibility of Islam and democracy. In fact, he emphasizes that democracy provides the institutional basis for fulfilling the primary responsibility of man as vicegerent of God on earth; namely, the pursuance of justice as directed in many verses in scripture. The so called Arab Spring is one of the latest manifestations of how discourses on Islamic justice can become politically consequential. During the upheavals, the Islamic justice principles were invoked by protest movements to challenge authoritarian regimes and demanded justice, freedom, and dignity. The rhetoric of Islamic justice was particularly effective in mobilizing diverse social groups, as it provided a familiar framework for advocating democratic reforms while addressing issues like corruption, inequality, and oppression.

# 4 Commonalities and Differences

## 4.1 Divine Justice and the Human-Divine Relationship in Judaism, Christianity, and Islam

In the monotheistic traditions, there is broad agreement that God embodies perfect justice. Throughout the Hebrew Bible, the New Testament, and the Qurʾān, divine justice is portrayed as a fundamental attribute, shaping the moral and ethical framework that humans are expected to emulate.[2] Yet, certain scriptural episodes appear to challenge a straightforward understanding of divine justice, raising critical questions about how human beings can comprehend the will and judgment of God. One such example is Abraham's plea for Sodom, a narrative found in the He-

2 For example, Ps 9:7–8: "The Lord reigns forever; He has established His throne for judgment. He rules the world in righteousness and judges the peoples with equity."; 2 Thess 1:6: "God is just: He will pay back trouble to those who trouble you."; Q 50:29: "And My word cannot be changed: I am not unjust to any creature."

brew Bible (Gen 18:16–33) and also reflected in the Qur'ān (Q 11:74–76; Q 29:31–32). Over time, this passage has become a *locus classicus* in theological discourse on the interplay between divine justice and human responsibility. Therefore, in this section we will use the story and the questions it raises to guide us through the theme of divine justice and the human-divine relationship. In this way, we will also be able to trace general theological issues of justice and present solutions found in the traditions of each religion.

In the Hebrew Bible, the narrative starts with the theme of covenant. Abraham and his descendants " [...] will surely become a great and powerful nation, and all nations on earth will be blessed through him. For I have chosen him, so that he will direct his children and his household after him to keep the way of the Lord by doing what is right and just, so that the Lord will bring about for Abraham what he has promised him." (Gen 18:18–19).[3] The ethical charge entrusted to Abraham's lineage contrasts with the grave sin attributed to Sodom, as God discloses the impending destruction of the city. Abraham's subsequent challenge – "Will you sweep away the righteous with the wicked? [...] Will not the Judge of all the earth do right?" (Gen 18:23–25) – positions him as an advocate, questioning the fairness of collective punishment and urging the preservation of innocent lives.

These verses have elicited a wide range of interpretations and generated profound theological inquiries. Among the most significant concerns is the covenantal framework evoked by the Abrahamic narrative. This covenant, which will be examined in detail, is understood to provide critical insight into the dynamics of divine justice in Judaism, Christianity, and Islam. Far from representing a solely legal or ritual dimension, the covenant establishes an enduring moral and spiritual bond that holds humanity accountable to divine standards. Within this covenantal context, divine justice and human responsibility emerge as central themes, linking moral conduct and social order with the overarching aim of universal moral rectification. It will be shown, however, that while the three traditions converge on the foundational role of covenant in articulating divine justice, significant theological divergences remain.

In Judaism, the covenant (*brit*) is presented as a reciprocal and enduring commitment between God and the people of Israel. Originating with Abraham and solidified through Moses at Sinai, the covenant establishes obligations that extend beyond ritual observance and into the moral sphere.[4] God's protection and blessing

---

3 Throughout this chapter, we will use the New International Version (NIV) for Bible translations; for the Qu'ān, the translation of M.A.S. Abdel Halem is used.

4 The covenant with Abraham, also called "covenant of the flesh", pertains to Israel as a family or kin group. Abraham will be father of many nations, though one nation in particular, his direct descendants inheriting Canaan. The covenant between Israel and God at Sinai is a covenant of the

of Israel are contingent upon Israel's adherence to the Torah's commandments (*mitzvot*). Emphasis is placed on the protection of the vulnerable – widows, orphans, and strangers – and on the maintenance of societal harmony. Justice (*tsedeḳ*) and righteousness (*tsedaḳah*) are intertwined, manifesting as both a legal and ethical imperative. For instance, *Deuteronomy* 16:20's instruction to "pursue justice" signifies not only a legal requirement but also a divine mandate underscoring the moral dimension of covenantal life.[5] In the case of the covenant with Abraham, God promises that not only a great nation will emerge from Abraham, but that this nation will be a source of blessing for all nations. Because the descendants of Abraham will uphold righteousness (*tsedaḳah*) and justice (*mishpat*) as their moral and ethical calling (Gen 18:18–19), this covenant is not merely a promise of land but also a moral mission to establish justice in the world. The tension between particularism (the unique covenant with Israel) and universalism (the blessing for all nations) in the covenant tradition has been widely discussed within Jewish thought. A number of Jewish theologians emphasize that the ultimate purpose of the covenant is universal redemption – the establishment of a world where all nations recognize God.[6]

Christianity reinterprets and recontextualizes the Jewish covenant through the New Covenant, established by the life, death, and resurrection of Jesus Christ (*Luke* 22:20). This covenantal framework is conceived as universal rather than ethnically particular, extending to all who believe in Christ rather than to those who adhere to the Mosaic Law. In Christian theological discourse, divine justice is reflected in God's unwavering faithfulness to the covenant despite human disobedience. Throughout the Old Testament narratives (e.g., *Amos* 5:18–20, *Hosea* 11), God's justice is intertwined with mercy, continually calling the covenant community back to right relationship. The New Testament reframes the understanding of divine justice, now seen through the lens of Christ's redemptive work. This eschatological and grace-oriented notion of justice emphasizes transformation, forgiveness, and the renewal of humanity rather than judgment based on human merit. Abraham's exemplary faith, portrayed in *Hebrews* 11:8–19, serves to illustrate the dynamic interplay between divine promise and human trust in God's justice. Paul's writings,

---

law, cf. Walzer, Michael, *In God's Shadow: Politics in the Hebrew Bible*, New Haven: Yale University Press, 2012, 1f.

5 Cf. Botwinick in this volume.

6 For example, Maimonides sees the Torah as providing a model for a universal ethical system that can benefit all nations, even though it was given specifically to Israel, cf. Kellner, Menachem/Gillis, David, *Maimonides the Universalist: The Ethical Horizons of the Mishneh Torah*, Liverpool, 2020, published online: *Liverpool Scholarship Online*, https://doi.org/10.3828/liverpool/9781906764555.001.0001 (accessed on 12.12.2024).

especially *Romans* 4:1–17 and *Galatians* 3:28–29, emphasize faith as the principle that justifies humanity before God, thereby universalizing the covenant's salvific scope. In this way, the covenant in Christianity ultimately unites divine justice with the comprehensive renewal of humanity, underscoring divine grace as the path to moral rectification.[7]

In Islam, the understanding of covenant differs significantly from the other two religions. Here the concept of covenant (*ʿahd* or *mīthāq*) appears in several forms: First, there is the primordial covenant as discussed in the Islamic tradition. It refers to a pre-temporal agreement made between God and each soul before the beginning of creation. This notion of the covenant establishes a fundamental recognition of divine authority and justice that transcends ethnic, national, and historical boundaries. This covenant is alluded to in Q 7:172,[8] where God asks the spirits of all humanity, "Am I not your Lord?" to which they respond affirmatively. In Islamic belief, this covenant represents the fundamental understanding that all humans are inherently aware of a higher power and are thus obliged to uphold this awareness throughout their existence. Any act that transgresses this awareness, including any form of sin or injustice committed by an individual, constitutes a violation of this covenant. Consequently, each soul will be held to account for its actions on the day of Judgement.[9] Subsequent covenants with the prophets – Noah, Abraham, Moses, and Muḥammad – further articulate the responsibilities of communities toward divine guidance and the ethical standards set forth in revelation (Q 33:7). The covenant with Abraham is alluded to in Q 2:124 and reinterpreted in regard to its previous scriptures. In this passage, the Qurʾān places emphasis on the notion that covenantal blessings are dependent upon righteousness, rather than solely upon lineage (Q 2:124). This universal criterion allows all humanity – beyond any particular ethnic group – to return to monotheistic faith and uphold justice.[10]

---

7 The context of Galatians is a controversy between Paul and his opponents who expect from the believers circumcision and observance of ritual regulations of Israelites, cf. Kraus, Wolfgang, "Bund NT,", published online: WIBILEX, https://www.die-bibel.de/ressourcen/wibilex/neues-testament/bund-nt (accessed on 06.12.2024).

8 This verse, also known as the "verse of covenant", is the central passage for the understanding of covenant in Sunni, Shīʿī and Sufī-circles, but interpretations vary, cf. Lumbard, Joseph, "Covenant and Covenants in the Qur'an," *Journal of Qur'anic Studies* 17,2 (2015), 1–23, here 5.

9 al-Qadi, Wadad Kadi, "The Primordial Covenant and Human History in the Qur'ān, *Proceedings of the American Philosophical Society* 147,4 (2003), 332–38.

10 In this way, the pagan people from the times of Muḥammad as well as the people of the book could return to pristine monotheism, therefore ethnic and national borders are transcended, cf. Firestone, Reuven, "Abraham and Authenticity," in: Adam J. Silverstein/Guy G. Stroumsa (eds.), *The Oxford Handbook of the Abrahamic Religions*, 2015, published online: Oxford Academic, https://doi.org/10.1093/oxfordhb/9780199697762.013.9 (accessed 07.12.2024).

In Q 57:25, divine justice is closely connected to the sending of messengers and scriptures that provide guidance so that humankind might establish justice. The Qur'ān also highlights the human tendency to neglect this covenant, despite divine reminders, and stresses that God's judgment is never unjust (Q 6:131; Q 4:40). His scales for weighing good deeds are perfectly fair, ensuring that no one will be wronged (Q 4:40). This divine justice extends to the Day of Judgment, where deeds will be weighed justly (Q 7:8; 21:47; 23:102).[11] The Qur'ān states, that by straying from this path, humans harmed themselves. A third dimension of the covenant is the personal covenant of faith and obedience each Muslim undertakes. As the Qur'ān states, when a person is unjust, he is at first unjust to himself (Q 2:57). The scholar Abū l-Faraj al-Iṣfahānī (897–967) wrote that one has to be just to himself first, before being just to others. Especially this last covenantal aspect is not only about righteous behavior or observance of Islamic law, but is a virtue of an individual character.[12]

Taken together, the covenantal traditions of Judaism, Christianity, and Islam each establish a framework in which divine justice is integral to the relationship between God and humanity. The covenant defines moral boundaries, responsibilities, and aspirations, situating justice at the core of communal ethics and personal virtue. Rather than functioning merely as a legal contract, the covenant symbolizes a transformative engagement that aims to shape societies and individuals, guiding them toward an ultimate realization of justice that mirrors the divine will.

We now turn to the second part of the narrative in *Genesis* 18. In this instance, Abraham presents a compelling argument, imploring God to act in a fair and just manner and interceding on behalf of the inhabitants of Sodom. In a prolonged dialogue, Abraham negotiates with God, striving to identify a minimum number of righteous individuals that would justify sparing the entire city. Ultimately, God agrees to spare Sodom if only ten righteous people can be found. Abraham's plea thus underscores not only the demand for justice but also the call for mercy, extending compassion to the wicked alongside the righteous. But in the end, none could be found, and God's judgement was carried out.[13] This raised complex questions regarding the severity of God's wrath and the nature of collective punishment. Religious traditions have addressed these concerns through various

11 Lumbard, "Covenant and Covenants," 10 f.

12 Ibid., 15; Mohamed, Yasien, "The Concept of Justice in Miskawayh and Isfahani," *Journal for Islamic studies* 18/19 (1998), 51–111, here 87.

13 Weiss, Shira, *Ethical Ambiguity in the Hebrew Bible: Philosophical Analysis of Scriptural Narrative*, Cambridge: Cambridge University Press; 2018, 43–91, here 45 f.; Harris, Michael J., *Divine Command Ethics: Jewish and Christian Perspectives*, Oxford: Routledge, 2003, 60 ff.

interpretive strategies, often highlighting the interplay between mercy and justice in understanding the human-divine relationship.

In Judaism, one approach to addressing the question of God's judgment over an entire community, including innocent individuals, is to suggest that they were not genuinely innocent. This interpretation, which is reflected in Rabbinic traditions, justifies their punishment.[14] More prominently, interpreters emphasize the need to balance justice with mercy. Within the Tanakh, terms that describe divine justice reveal a tension: *mishpat* underscores God as ultimate judge who punishes wrongdoing (Gen 18:18 – 33; Jer 11:20), while concepts such as *tsedakọt* ("healing acts") and depictions of God rescuing the oppressed (Isa 45:21) emphasize a redemptive dimension to divine justice. Especially the *Psalms* reflect God's saving justice regarding the innocent or Israel (Ps 35:24).[15] Rabbinic tradition grapples extensively with this tension. For example, Rabbi Levi warns that a world governed by strict justice alone cannot endure: "If You wish to have a world, there can be no strict justice, and if You wish to have strict justice, there can be no world. You seek to hold the rope from both ends; You wish to have the world and You wish to have strict justice. If You do not concede somewhat, the world will be unable to endure.'"[16] Midrashic readings, drawing on *Ezekiel* 33:11, suggest that God derives no pleasure from the death of the wicked and encourages humans to return to righteousness, following Abraham's example.[17] Similarly, the *Targum Jonathan* emphasizes the interplay of justice and mercy, noting that God allowed Abraham to intercede for Sodom, reflecting his willingness to temper judgment with compassion.[18] Many interpreters have sought to portray that although God's justice is absolute, it is intertwined with his mercy. Only the combination of justice and mercy could lead to an enduring world.[19]

Maimonides (1138 – 1204) expands on this topic by stating that the terms associated with God, such as justice (*mishpat*), mercy (*chesed*), and righteousness (*tse-*

---

14 *Bereshit Rabbah* 49:9, published online: Sefaria.org, https://www.sefaria.org/Bereshit_Rabbah.49?lang=bi (accessed on 07.12.2024).

15 Scharbert, Josef, "Gerechtigkeit," in: *Theologische Realenzyklopädie Online*, Berlin/New York: De Gruyter, 2010, https://doi.org/10.1515/tre.12_404_24 (accessed 19.11.2024).

16 *Bereshit Rabbah* 49:9.

17 *Midrash Tanchuma*, *Vayera* 8, published online: sefaria.org, https://www.sefaria.org/Midrash_Tanchuma%2C_Vayera.8.1?lang=bi&with=all&lang2=en (accessed on 26.08.2024).

18 *Targum Jonathan* on *Genesis* 18, published online: sefaria.org, https://www.sefaria.org/Targum_Jonathan_on_Genesis.18.32?lang=bi (accessed on 26.08.2024).

19 Cf. Legend of the Jews 1:1, published online: Sefaria.org, https://www.sefaria.org/Legends_of_the_Jews.1.1.5?lang=bi (accessed on 04.04.2025).

*daḳa*), are attributes of *action*, not essential attributes of God.[20] This means they describe how God relates to the world rather than defining God's nature. Through these actions, God maintains the world's moral and physical order, ensuring its sustainability. According to Maimonides, justice ensures moral order, while mercy grants space for repentance and growth. The delicate balance between these forces sustains the cosmos, preventing it from becoming uninhabitable due to human imperfection and ensures that individuals and societies can thrive, creating a sustainable moral framework.[21] Maimonides emphasizes that divine justice is absolute and omniscient, encompassing all factors that humans cannot perceive. In contrast, human justice is inherently limited by our partial understanding and subjective biases. His position reflects a traditional and widely accepted view within Judaism. There is the acceptance of divine justice as inherently unknowable yet grounded in trust in God's ultimate goodness. Divine justice in Judaism is mirrored especially in the laws and commandments which essentially serve the purpose to establish justice on earth (Ps 119:137–44), but justice is not only served by acting in accordance to God's law but also by imitating the divine quality of justice (Dtn 13:5). God's covenant with Abraham emphasizes a justice that humans are expected to emulate, making it comprehensible and applicable in human society.[22] In *Mishneh Torah* (Laws of Character Traits 1:6), Maimonides stresses the obligation to emulate God by practicing justice and mercy. This involves fostering traits like kindness, humility, and fairness in human interactions. Humans must pursue justice (*tsedeḳ*) not only through strict adherence to the law but also through actions that reflect compassion and equity, recognizing the interplay of justice and mercy as modeled by God. Maimonides introduces the concept of *lifnim mi-shurat ha-din* (acting beyond the letter of the law) in *Guide for the Perplexed* (Part 3, Chapter 53).[23] This principle calls for individuals to temper strict justice with mercy and ethical sensitivity. For Maimonides, true imitation of God involves not only upholding laws but also exceeding them in kindness and fairness.[24]

In the modern era, this question has been addressed in a variety of ways. Abraham Joshua Heshel (1907–1972) for example emphasizes the relational and compassionate aspects of God. He critiques overly legalistic interpretations of di-

**20** According to Maimonides, God's essence cannot be described, only his deeds, cf. Shapira, Haim., "The Virtue of Mercy According to Maimonides: Ethics, Law, and Theology," *Harvard Theological Review* 111,4 (2018), 559–85, https://doi.org/10.1017/S0017816018000275 (accessed on 15.12.2024).

**21** Maimonides, *Guide for the Perplexed*, Part 3, Chapters 53–54, 32 ff.

**22** Novak, David, "Divine Justice/Divine command," *Studies in Christian Ethics* 23,1 (2010), 6–20.

**23** Eisen, Robert, "Lifnim Mi-Shurat Ha-Din" in Maimonides' "Mishneh Torah," *The Jewish Quarterly Review* 89,3–4 (1999), 291–317.

**24** Shapira, "The Virtue of Mercy," 580 ff.

vine justice, proposing that God's primary attribute is *pathos* – an empathetic engagement with humanity. Heschel posits that justice and mercy are inextricably linked and both represent expressions of divine love. He postulates that God experiences suffering alongside humanity, particularly in the context of injustice, and that human beings bear a collective responsibility for moral action.[25] In contrast, Yeshayahu Leibowitz (1903–1994) presents a markedly different perspective on this matter. He addresses the subject from the perspective of *halakhic* discipline, maintaining that divine justice is fundamentally distinct from human justice because it is not constrained by human moral reasoning. He asserts that the service of God necessitates unwavering compliance with the commandments, without attempting to reconcile divine justice with human suffering. He cautions against allowing human emotions or subjective interpretations of mercy to impede the objective implementation of divine laws.[26]

Christian theology, while rooted in these earlier biblical traditions, increasingly stresses that mercy defines the very content of divine justice. The interplay of justice and mercy is already seen in the Old Testament, emphasized by passages like Ps 85:10 "Mercy and truth have met together; righteousness and peace have kissed". Divine justice is inseparable from divine mercy and love, reflecting the harmony of God's attributes in his governance of the universe.[27]

To give an example, Aquinas (1225–1274) treats justice as giving each creature its due, but mercy surpasses the strict demands of justice. He writes that "Mercy without justice is the mother of dissolution; justice without mercy is cruelty" (*Summa Theologica* I, Q21, Art 3). Divine justice, according to Aquinas, can be understood as a distributive principle, whereby all creatures are guaranteed to receive what is appropriate according to their nature and purpose. Nevertheless, this does not entitle humans to assert any rights over God, as all that they receive is derived from divine generosity. However, God's justice encompasses an internal dimension, whereby his actions remain consistent with his own nature and will. Aquinas underscores the fact that divine justice is grounded in the benevolence and wisdom of God, which distinguishes it from the concept of human justice.

---

**25** Brooks, Michael, *Good God: Suffering, Faith, Reason and Science*, London: Sacristy Press, 2024, 154 ff. See also Heschel, Abraham Joshua, *The Prophets: Two Volumes in One*, New York: Hendrickson Publishers, 2007.

**26** Rynhold, Daniel, "Yeshayahu Leibowitz," published online: Edward N. Zalta (ed.), *The Stanford Encyclopedia of Philosophy* (Spring 2019 Edition), https://plato.stanford.edu/archives/spr2019/entries/leibowitz-yeshayahu/ (accessed on 15.12.2024); Ben-Pazi, Hanoch, "Theodicy as the Justified Demands of Atheism: Yeshayahu Leibowitz Versus Emmanuel Levinas," *Modern Judaism-A Journal of Jewish Ideas and Experience* 36,3 (2016), 249–76.

**27** Cf. Gräb-Schmidt in this volume.

He posits that mercy does not negate justice but rather serves to augment it. For example, the pardoning of sins or the bestowal of gifts in excess of what is owed serves to illustrate mercy as a superior form of perfection. Every divine act is characterized by both justice and mercy, with mercy frequently preceding justice. To illustrate, the act of creation itself can be considered an act of mercy, given that no external force compelled the divine entity to create. Subsequent acts, such as the guidance of creation, reflect a justice that is both immanent and transcendent.[28]

In modern Christian thought, theologians such as Karl Barth (1886–1968), argue that God's justice cannot be separated from his love. He emphasizes that God's justice is fully revealed in Christ, who embodies divine mercy and reconciles humanity to God. For Barth, justice is not a detached principle but is manifested through covenantal faithfulness, grace, and redemption. Barth ties justice to God's character, emphasizing that it must always align with his love and grace. In the eyes of Barth, God's defining act is to turn towards humanity and to take pity on them. This mercy is the essence of his justice. Barth insists that mercy precedes justice. God's merciful act of grace in Jesus Christ defines his righteousness and reveals his justice. Mercy and justice are inseparable; one cannot exist without the other in God's nature.[29]

This Christian understanding of justice, inseparably linked to redemption and grace, differs significantly from Jewish frameworks. While Jewish thought underscores the necessity of observing the divine commandments and showing mercy by imitating the divine qualities of justice within a covenantal framework, Christian theology posits that justice cannot be achieved solely by human efforts but is ultimately a gift received through faith in Christ. Pauline theology and the subsequent doctrine of justification illustrate this shift: justice becomes something bestowed, not earned, thereby reconfiguring the understanding of human and divine roles in achieving justice.[30] In this context, Gräb-Schmidt highlights that for Martin Luther, divine justice is not only encompassed by mercy, but that God's very being is mercy. She argues that the core of the doctrine of justification is God's acting justly within his mercy. She further argues that God's ways are beyond human understanding, particularly when it comes to justice. Belief in God does not make indi-

---

**28** Skaff, Jeffrey, *Thomas Aquinas and Karl Barth: A New Conversation*, Oxford: Routledge, 2022, 15 ff.

**29** Ibid., 22 ff. and Gräb-Schmidt in this volume.

**30** "Justification by Faith" is a much disputed topic and currently scholars are debating about its different meanings, cf. Gathercole, Simon, "Justification by Faith," in: Matthew V. Novenson/R. Barry Matlock (eds.), *The Oxford Handbook of Pauline Studies*, 2022, published online: *Oxford Academic*, https://doi.org/10.1093/oxfordhb/9780199600489.013.35 (accessed on 09.12.2024).

viduals irresponsible or inclined towards a *laissez-faire* attitude, but rather obligates them to act justly and participate in the divine dispensation of justice.

In the writings of the church father John Chrysostom (349–407), the relation between law and divine grace is analyzed. He argues that the concept of justice was initially defined as the fulfillment of all commandments. However, the law, according to his view, is not seen as having the capacity to compel all humans to act justly or to make them just in their actions. Christ alone is the embodiment of justice and only he is able to fulfill all of the commandments; thus, he elevates the law to a higher plane. Since his advent, justice is attained not through human merit but through divine grace. In emulation of Abraham's example, this grace can only be received through faith.[31] As Botwinick notes in this volume, this theology gave rise to tensions between Judaism and Christianity.

Turning to Islamic perspectives on divine justice and mercy, certain conceptual parallels with Jewish thought become evident. In both traditions, divine law holds a central position in establishing justice. The emphasis on divine law and human limitation contrasts with the Christian focus, which tends to prioritize faith and universal love over legal frameworks, often equating divine justice with mercy and interpreting justice as an expression of divine love. While mercy remains central to both Jewish and Islamic understandings, it is more intricately integrated within legal and ethical contexts, ensuring that justice is neither divorced from moral accountability nor reduced solely to sentiment.

Before engaging more deeply with the interplay of justice and mercy in Islam, the Qur'ānic account of Abraham (Ibrāhīm) and the destruction of Sodom and Gomorrah (the people of Lūṭ) merits attention. In Q 11:74–76 and Q 29:31–32, Abraham's plea on behalf of the city differs notably from the biblical narrative. While the Hebrew Bible recounts Abraham's sustained negotiation, the Qur'ān alludes only briefly to his concern, depicting Abraham as forbearing, tender-hearted, and devout, yet ultimately submitting to God's irreversible and just decision. Subsequently, the Qur'ānic narrative stresses that God's decision is final and just, reflecting his omniscience and authority: "Abraham, cease your pleading: what your Lord has ordained has come about; punishment is coming to them, which cannot be turned back'" (Q 11:74–6). This more concise portrayal underscores divine omniscience and authority, leaving less space for the extensive dialogical exploration of divine justice and mercy found in the biblical text. Islamic commentators highlight Abraham's compassion for the righteous, while stressing that God's punish-

31 Merkel, Helmut, " "Gerechtigkeit," in: *Theologische Realenzyklopädie Online*, Berlin/New York: De Gruyter, 2010, https://doi.org/10.1515/tre.12_404_24 (accessed 19.11.2024).

ment rests on perfect knowledge inaccessible to human understanding.[32] In the second allusion to the episode (Q 29:31–32), Abraham addresses the angels, who had brought him the good news and informed him of their intention to destroy the city of Sodom. Abraham responds by noting that Lot, his nephew, resides there. In response, they state "We know who lives there better than you do. We shall save him and his household, except for his wife: she will be one of those who stay behind." As evidenced by this and other Qur'ānic examples, within Islamic theology, the concept of justice is closely intertwined with God's wisdom (ḥikma), particularly in the context of the moral nature and actions of God. For example, early Islamic exegesis, such as in *Tafsīr aṭ-Ṭabarī*, acknowledges Abraham's role as a prophet advocating for mercy, but ultimately underscores God's unquestionable justice, tempered by his wisdom and knowledge of human actions beyond what humans can perceive.[33]

But mercy does play a pivotal role in general in the Islamic conceptions of justice.[34] The Qur'ān frequently situates justice within a broader framework of cosmic order and mercy. *Sūrat ar-Raḥmān* (Q 55: the Lord of Mercy or most Gracious) exemplifies this: God, the Most Merciful, creates and sustains the world in a balanced manner. The imagery of the *mīzān* (balance) in Q 55:7–9 presents justice as an integral aspect of the natural order (Q 55:7–9): "He has raised up the sky. He has set the balance, so that you may not exceed in the balance: weigh with justice and do not fall short in the balance."[35] In these verses, heaven is mentioned alongside the concept of balance and thereby linked to it, allowing the conclusion that justice is regarded as a heavenly virtue. The reference to the balance of nature in the *sūra* is contrasted with that of the human being; it is their responsibility to maintain order, and with the instrument of the scale, justice is to be established in social life.[36] Given that the establishment of the heavens is referenced in the initial portion of verse 7, it is plausible that the subsequent section may pertain to the constellation of Libra. This is followed in verses 8 and 9 by the associated terrestrial scale and its "moral application".[37] Traditional exegesis often equates *mīzān* with

32 Moqbel, Tariq Hesham, *Ethics in the Qur'ān and the Tafsīr Tradition. From the Polynoia of Scripture to the Homonoia of Exegesis*, Leiden: Brill, 2024, 112 f.

33 Ibid., 116. This is also a connection drawn in Christian and Jewish sources, as for example in Maimonides and Aquinas.

34 But this topic has not been studied sufficiently in academic scholarship yet.

35 Abdel Haleem, M.A.S., Translation of the Holy Qur'ān, published online: Quran.com, https://quran.com/55?translations=85 (accessed on 01.07.2024).

36 Iqbal, Zafar, "Contemplating an Islamic Theory of Justice: Situating Tradition Amidst Modernity", *Review of Islamic Economics* 10.1 (2006): 91–121.

37 Neuwirth, Angelika, *Der Koran, Handkommentar. Frühmekkanische Suren: Poetische Prophetie*, Bd. 1, Berlin: Verlag der Weltreligionen, 2011, 107. The exhortation to give full measure also appears

*ʿadl* (justice), interpreting divine guidance – including the Qurʾān itself – as the measure enabling humanity to act justly.[38] The metaphor of justice as a balance is an important feature of the Qurʾān. That the balance between justice and mercy is central to Islamic ethics is also shown in other contexts. For instance, God's justice holds individuals accountable for their actions, but his mercy provides opportunities for repentance and forgiveness, reflecting a compassionate approach to judgment. This duality is especially significant in the concept of *tawba* (repentance), where God's justice acknowledges human sin, but his mercy allows for redemption and a return to the path of righteousness (Q 39:53): "Say, '[God says], My servants who have harmed yourselves by your own excess, do not despair of God's mercy. God forgives all sins: He is truly the Most Forgiving, the Most Merciful.'"[39]

Medieval Muslim thinkers, particularly al-Ghazālī (447–505/1055–1111), developed a sophisticated understanding of divine justice as perfectly aligned with God's wisdom (*ḥikma*). According to him, God's justice is evident in the ordered arrangement of all elements of creation, both in the macrocosm of the universe and the microcosm of the human being.[40] Al-Ghazālī argues that, through careful observation of nature, humans can recognize these divine signs, as the harmony of nature reflects the beauty of the divine presence. In the Qurʾān, God is described as having created everything in a just manner (Q 20:50). This is based on the premise that God is both merciful and generous, having granted existence to all creatures, and that he is just, having placed everything in its appropriate order (*al-mīzān*).[41] He further emphasizes that God's justice differs fundamentally from human justice. God cannot commit injustice, not because he is constrained by ex-

in other verses of the Qurʾān (7:85, 11:84, 17:35, 26:181–83), thus forming a Qurʾānic topos that can also be found in biblical literature—similarly to the admonitions concerning the just treatment of orphans and the poor (Deut 25:13–15). A further fitting parallel is found in Proverbs 11:1: "A false balance is an abomination to the Lord, but a just weight is His delight." Cf. https://corpuscoranicum.de/de/verse-navigator/sura/83/verse/1/commentary#anmerkung_verse_1-9 (accessed on 30.11.2024).

**38** aṭ-Ṭabarī, Abū Ǧaʿfar Muḥammad Ibn Ǧarīr, *Tafsīr aṭ-Ṭabarī, ǧāmiʿ al-bayān ʿan taʾwīl āy al-qurʾān*, vol. 22, al-Qāhira: Dār Hiǧr, 2001, 179; Al-Qurṭubī, Abī ʿAbdallāh Muḥammad, *al-Ǧāmiʿ li-aḥkām al-Qurʾān*, Riyāḍ: Dār ʿĀlam al-Kutub, vol. 17,154.

**39** Khalil, Atif, "Atonement, Returning, and Repentance in Islam," *Religions* 14,2 (2023), 168, published online: https://doi.org/10.3390/rel14020168 (accessed on 10.12.2024).

**40** Brockopp, Jonathan, "Justice and Injustice," in: Jane Dammen McAuliffe (ed.), *Encyclopedia of the Qurʾān*, vol. 3, 69–73, Leiden/Boston: Brill, 2003, 70.

**41** Kuşpınar, Bilal, "An Analysis of the Views of al-Ghazālī, Ibn al-ʿArabī and Mawlānā Rūmī on the Concept of Justice," *Selçuklu Medeniyeti Araştırmaları Dergisi* 1 (2016) 217–48, hier 223 f.

ternal laws, but because he created all things from nothing – not out of need, but to manifest his power.[42]

Al-Ghazālī links this cosmic justice with human responsibility – humans are entrusted with maintaining justice in their actions, reflecting divine attributes in their interpersonal dealings. While justice in Islam requires holding individuals accountable for their actions, al-Ghazālī emphasizes that God's mercy surpasses his justice. He cites the *ḥadīth* in which God declares, "My mercy prevails over My wrath." This indicates that although God is just, his dealings with creation are primarily characterized by compassion and forgiveness. The concept of imitating the divine attributes encourages believers to practice compassion, forgiveness, and fairness, moving beyond a merely legalistic understanding of justice. Al-Ghazālī emphasizes that this emulation leads to spiritual growth and the fulfillment of human potential.[43]

But there are perspectives seeking to diminish the role of mercy in conceptions of justice. One example is Daud Rahbar (1926–2013), who adopts a more critical and legalistic view. He emphasizes God's role as the sovereign judge, highlighting that divine justice is primarily concerned with upholding moral and ethical order in creation. He frames justice as a manifestation of God's authority over both individual and collective human actions. Rahbar critiques the overemphasis on mercy and insists on the primacy of justice in God's dealings with humanity. He argues that reducing divine justice to mere compassion risks undermining the ethical seriousness of human responsibility and the consequences of moral failings. Rahbar views justice as a moral imperative that not only governs divine-human relations but also demands strict adherence to ethical laws by individuals and societies. He underscores that neglecting justice leads to social and moral decay, as historically exemplified by the downfall of civilizations mentioned in the Qur'ān.[44]

In sum, Islamic notions of divine justice are closely interwoven with the ideas of law, wisdom, and cosmic harmony. While mercy consistently moderates the application of justice, allowing for human repentance and spiritual growth, the moral structure of divine justice remains intact. Thus, Islam presents a balanced framework in which mercy does not eclipse justice, but rather complements it, en-

---

**42** Orman, Sabri, "al-Ghazālī on Justice and Social Justice," *Turkish Journal of Islamic Economics* 5,2 (2018), 1–68, here 21.

**43** al-Ghazālī, *Ihyā' 'Ulūm al-Dīn*, cf. Ashfaq, Muhammad/ Hashmi, Shah Junaid Ahmad/ Khan, Abdul Ghafar, "Hermeneutics of al-Ghazzālī Concerning Mercy (al-Raḥmah) and its Social Applications: A Religio-Ethical Study," *Al-Qanṭara* 10,1 (2024), 257–70.

**44** Rahbar, Daud, *A God of Justice: A Study in the Ethical Doctrine of the Qur'ān*, 105–7. See also the discussion in Reynolds, Gabriel S., *Allah: God in the Qur'ān*, New Haven: Yale University Press, 2020, 5, where he criticizes the view as one-sided, because God is more than simply justice or mercy.

suring a comprehensive vision of divine governance that is both exacting and compassionate.

## 4.2 Social Justice in Judaism, Christianity, and Islam

As the foregoing examination has shown, the concept of covenant plays a central role in shaping understandings of divine justice across Judaism, Christianity, and Islam. Each tradition's covenant theology defines not only the community's relationship with God but also the moral and ethical obligations guiding human conduct. Although all three religions affirm that God is just, they differ in how justice and mercy interrelate. In Judaism and Islam, divine justice is often understood in tension with and tempered by mercy, ensuring that strict judgment does not render the world uninhabitable. In Christianity, by contrast, mercy profoundly defines and shapes the very notion of divine justice, often expressed as an extension of divine love. These theological distinctions inform how each tradition conceptualizes the human responsibility to pursue justice. All three emphasize the importance of cultivating both justice and compassion in earthly societies, reflecting the attributes of God as understood within their respective covenantal frameworks. In each religion, the pursuit of social justice is not solely about rectifying human inequalities or achieving social equilibrium. Rather, it entails aligning human moral order with a divinely ordained vision of righteousness, understood as a gift entrusted to humanity.

Having established these foundational theological perspectives, the discussion now turns to a more tangible dimension of justice: its manifestation in social action. One exemplary sphere where religious traditions address social justice is charity – expressed as *tsedaḳa* in Judaism, *agape* or *caritas* in Christianity, and *zakāt* and *ṣadaqa* in Islam. These acts of giving transcend mere philanthropy. They serve as concrete expressions of covenantal responsibility, moral striving, and the commitment to realize on earth a measure of the justice and mercy that define the divine-human relationship. It is through such charitable practices that religious communities attempt to mirror divine attributes, translate theological principles into social ethics, and foster a world reflecting their respective understandings of divine justice.

In Judaism, the general imperative to pursue justice – often understood as adherence to the commandments and the ethical demands of the law – is complemented by the principle of *imitatio dei* (Lev 19:2; Deut 13:5; *Shabbat* 133b). This principle requires individuals to emulate the attributes of God, including divine justice, mercy, and compassion, thereby extending the theological foundation of justice into practical ethical action.[45] The framework for Jewish social justice draws on several key roots. Among them, especially human dignity (Gen 1:26–27) is emphasized: each person is created in the image of God, endowing all human beings with inherent worth. This commitment to human dignity extends compassion and moral consideration not only to fellow humans, but also to animals and the environment. Another key-principle is loving-kindness (*chesed*): The principle of *chesed* emphasizes love of the neighbor and active benevolence toward others. It is closely related to Abraham's advocacy for Sodom, as demonstrated previously, and underscores that true compassion involves selfless acts not motivated by the expectation of any reward. Furthermore, the "ways of peace" are interpreted in rabbinic literature as the imperative to foster justice and fairness in dealings with non-Jews. This principle promotes harmonious relations and mutual respect between communities.[46]

The concept of charity (*tsedaḳah*), literally meaning "righteousness," exemplifies these principles in tangible form. *Deuteronomy* 15:7–11 commands generosity toward those in need, framing it as a moral duty rather than a voluntary benevolence. Unlike "acts of loving-kindness", which can be extended to anyone – rich or poor, living or deceased – *tsedaḳah* specifically targets the living poor as a means of ensuring a just society.[47] Rabbinic literature views charity both as a commandment (*mitzvah*) and a virtuous act with potential spiritual benefits, although Babylonian rabbinic sources tend to emphasize its practical social value rather than its atoning power. Rules regarding donors and recipients were detailed: everyone must give, even those dependent on charity themselves.[48] Because the rabbis conceptualized charity as an act with both earthly and heavenly dimensions, they established a two-way relationship between donors, recipients, and God. Charity is

---

45 Hellinger, Moshe, "Judaism," in: Michael D. Palmer/Stanley M Burgess (eds.), *The Wiley-Blackwell Companion to Religion and Social Justice*, 170–89, Oxford: John Wiley & Sons, 2012, 172.

46 The other roots are: "You shall not stand idly by" (Lev 19:16): This command stresses the obligation to intervene against injustice, mandating active protection of the vulnerable and the oppressed; as well as "loving the stranger" (Dtn 10:19), commanding empathy and care for outsiders and foreign residents, cf. Schwarz, Rabbi Sid, "Judaism and Social Justice: Five Core Values from the Rabbinic Tradition," *Religions: A Scholarly Journal* 2012,2 (2012), 18–29.

47 "Ẓedakah," in: Michael Berenbaum/Fred Skolnik (eds.), *Encyclopaedia Judaica*, 487, vol. 21, Detroit, MI: Macmillan Reference USA, 2007, published online: *Gale eBooks* https://link.gale.com/apps/doc/CX2587521442/GVRL?u=muenster&sid=bookmark-GVRL&xid=557a4432 (accessed on 12.12.2024).

48 Posner, Raphael/Ben-Sasson, Haim Hillel/Levitats, Isaac, "Charity," in: Michael Berenbaum/Fred Skolnik (eds.), *Encyclopaedia Judaica*, 569–75, vol. 4, Detroit, MI: Macmillan Reference USA, 2007, published online: *Gale eBooks*, https://link.gale.com/apps/doc/CX2587504163/GVRL?u=muenster&sid=bookmark-GVRL&xid=3ef21f37 (accessed on 12.12.2024); Gray, Alyssa M., *Charity in Rabbinic Judaism*, London: Routledge, 2019, 199 ff.

considered particularly meritorious when the donor and recipient are unknown to one another.[49]

Over time, Jewish thinkers like Maimonides amplified charity's role as a means to establish a just and humane social order, moving away from its earlier association with divine atonement. In his *Mishneh Torah*, Maimonides framed *tsedaḳah* as an obligation of justice, emphasizing the ethical duty to redistribute resources for societal equity. Maimonides categorized charity into eight ascending levels, focusing on the giver's intent and the recipient's dignity, where he included charity given begrudgingly as the lowest form. In the subsequent three levels, he distinguished between three forms of charitable giving: (1) voluntary giving to the poor, though not in a generous manner; (2) giving to the poor only after being asked; and (3) giving to the poor before being asked. Therefore, he ordered these levels of charity by including thoughts of compassion and kindness. He listed "self-sufficiency" as the highest form, including offering employment, loans, or partnerships to help the recipient become self-reliant. He argued that the highest form of charity is one that helps recipients achieve independence, preserving their dignity and reducing their reliance on future aid. Maimonides integrated *tsedaḳah* into a broader vision of an ethical life, aligning it with the ideal of "walking in God's ways" by imitating divine compassion. Acts of *tsedaḳah* contribute to the social harmony and redemption of society, reflecting Jewish values of justice and righteousness.[50]

There is disagreement in Jewish Theology over the recipients of charity and also the amount one should give.[51] As to the question of the recipients there is the question of giving also to non-Jews. In Jewish tradition, while charity (*tsedaḳah*) primarily prioritizes fellow Jews, there are clear precedents and mandates for aiding non-Jews. The Talmud and later rabbinic texts establish that charity to non-Jews is required "for the sake of peace".[52] This principle fosters harmonious relationships between Jewish and non-Jewish communities. Examples include car-

49 Gray, *Charity in Rabbinic*, 199 ff.

50 Maimonides, "Gifts to the Poor," trans. Joseph B. Meszler, Williamsburg, Virginia, 2003, published online: sefaria.org, https://www.sefaria.org/Mishneh_Torah%2C_Gifts_to_the_Poor.1?ven=Gifts_for_the_Poor,_Trans._by_Joseph_B._Meszler,_Williamsburg,_Virginia,_2003&lang=bi (accessed on 12.12.2024); Kalmanson, Leah, "Jewish Perspectives on Charity," in: Jennifer A. Thompson/Allison B. Wolf, *Applying Jewish Ethics: Beyond the Rabbinic Tradition*, 51–65, Lanham: Lexington Books, 2022, 52 f.

51 Broyde, Michael J., "The Giving of Charity in Jewish Law: For What Purpose and Toward What Goal?," in: Yossi Prager (ed.), *Toward a Renewed Ethic of Jewish Philanthropy*, 241–74, New York: Yeshiva University Press, 2010.

52 *Mishnah Gittin* 5:8; *Shulchan Arukh, Yoreh Deah* 254, 256, published online: sefaria.org, https://www.sefaria.org/Mishnah_Gittin?tab=contents (accessed on 12.12.2024).

ing for the non-Jewish poor and assisting with their burial expenses. The ethical obligation is rooted in broader Jewish values of justice and kindness. However, Jewish law often balances particularistic priorities (helping Jews first) with universalist ethics, which allow for extending aid to non-Jews when addressing significant needs. For example, some contemporary interpretations of *tsedaḳah* suggest allocating funds both to Jewish and non-Jewish causes, emphasizing the importance of addressing global poverty irrespective of religion.[53]

Contemporary Jewish practices integrate charity into broader themes of *tikkun olam* (repairing the world), blending theological and ethical dimensions in ways that reflect evolving societal values.[54] Furthermore, the professionalization and institutionalization of charitable activities, alongside global philanthropic initiatives, demonstrate the evolving nature of Jewish social engagement.[55] In this manner, *tsedaḳah* remains a dynamic expression of Jewish social ethics and an enduring instrument for advancing justice and compassion within and beyond the Jewish community.

In both Christianity and Judaism, the concept of social justice is grounded in the belief that all creation possesses an inherent dignity (Gen 1:26–27). The New Testament intensifies these claims, as exemplified in *Matthew* 25:40, where service to the marginalized is equated with serving Christ himself. Building upon the biblical command to "love your neighbor as yourself" (Lev 19:18), the Christian understanding of neighborly love includes the entire human family, as illustrated in the parable of the *Good Samaritan* (*Luke* 10:25–37).[56] The early Christian community's emphasis on solidarity and care for the poor is evident in passages like *Luke* 4:18–19 and *James* 2:5, which call for prioritizing the needs of the vulnerable. Thus, Christian social teaching encourages not only compassionate responses to immediate suffering but also long-term commitment to addressing structural inequalities, fostering participation, and promoting inclusive well-being (*Acts* 2:44–45; 1 Cor 12:12–26). Stewardship of creation is likewise a significant concern, rooted in the *Parable of the Talents* (Matt 25:14–30), which underscores accountability

53 Kats, Yaʿaḳov, *Exclusiveness and Tolerance*, Oxford et al.: Oxford Univ. Press, 1961, 32 ff.; there is an example also from the Mishna stating that Jews should give to Jews and Gentiles alike and the Babylonian Talmud extends this idea. In modernity, Rabbi Soloveitchik argues for example for giving charity regardless of religion, cf. Kollar, Nathan R./Shafiq, Muhammad (eds.), *Poverty and Wealth in Judaism, Christianity, and Islam*, New York: Palgrave Macmillan US, 2016, 253, 256.

54 Rosenthal, Gilbert S., "Tikkun ha-Olam: The Metamorphosis of a Concept," *The Journal of Religion* 85,2 (2005), 214–40.

55 Posner/ Ben-Sasson/ Levitats, "Charity," https://link.gale.com/apps/doc/CX2587504163/GVRL?u=muenster&sid=bookmark-GVRL&xid=3ef21f37 (accessed on 12.12.2024).

56 Burgess, Stanley M., "Christianity," in: Michael D. Palmer/Stanley M Burgess (eds.), The Wiley-Blackwell Companion to Religion and Social Justice, 46–60, Oxford: John Wiley & Sons, 2012, 47 f.

for the responsible use of resources and the pursuit of sustainability for future generations.[57]

Turning to the practice of charity, Christianity employs the concept of *agape* – unconditional, selfless love – as its fundamental guiding principle (1 Cor 13).[58] Unlike *tsedaḳah* in Judaism, which primarily focuses on ensuring justice through obligatory support for the poor, Christian charity often frames support for the needy as a direct response to divine grace and a reflection of God's sacrificial love for humanity. Early Christian theologians such as the church father Basil the Great (around 330–79) exemplified this approach, urging the wealthy to share their goods and live alongside the poor (Matt 19:16–22). Charity in Christianity manifests in various forms, including almsgiving, hospitality, communal sharing of resources (*Acts* 2:44–47), and even voluntary poverty, modeled by monastic communities that relinquished personal possessions in imitation of Christ's own humility. Self-denial and voluntary poverty were seen as the highest forms of devotion in the early Christian community.[59] In comparison to early Rabbinic Judaism, which institutionalized charitable practices through weekly funds (*kuppah*) and food distributions (*tamhui)* after the destruction of the Temple, early Christianity also established communal norms for caring for widows, orphans, and the marginalized. Both religions thus recognize charity as essential for communal cohesion and support of vulnerable populations, though their theological emphases differ. While Judaism tends to stress adherence to divine commandments and structured obligations, Christianity often presents charity as the outflow of divine love, personal devotion, and transformation through grace.[60]

During the medieval period, institutional forms of charity became more common within Christianity, giving rise to hospitals, orphanages, and philanthropic networks. Thomas Aquinas's theological reflection further refined the concept of charity (*caritas*), treating it as a theological virtue directly infused by God's grace. For Aquinas, charity establishes friendship with God and neighbor, aiming at eternal beatitude and transforming human relationships into reflections of di-

57 Of course, these are just general examples for the sake of comparing it to the other religious scriptures. It should be noted that principles and definitions of social justice are debated in scholarship as well as between the different currents of Christianity, cf. Hiebert, Dennis "The Recurring Christian Debate about Social Justice," in: Dennis Hiebert (ed.), *The Routledge International Handbook of Sociology and Christianity*, 440–52, vol. 1, London: Routledge, 2024.

58 Jackson, Timothy P., *The Priority of Love*, Princeton, NJ: Princeton University Press, 2002, 29 ff.

59 Burgess, Stanley M., "Christianity," in: Michael D. Palmer/Stanley M Burgess (eds.), *The Wiley-Blackwell Companion to Religion and Social Justice*, 46–60, Oxford: John Wiley & Sons, 2012, 47 f.

60 Bird, Frederick B., "A Comparative Study of the Work of Charity in Christianity and Judaism," *The Journal of Religious Ethics* 10,1 (1982), 144–69.

vine fellowship. This true happiness, created through charity, transcends worldly goods and culminates in eternal communion with God. Loving God compels one to love others, as all humanity shares the same divine source and destiny. Aquinas argues that charity transforms every human being into a "neighbor" deserving of love. Charity reaches its perfection in loving one's enemies, reflecting God's love for humanity even in sin. This radical love demonstrates the transformative power of divine grace. Furthermore, he developed an order of charity, in which the closeness to God, the closeness to self, and closeness to others is systemized. His hierarchical ordering of charity bears a certain resemblance to Maimonides' gradations of giving, yet Aquinas focuses on the spiritual love inspiring charitable acts, whereas Maimonides emphasizes legal and ethical obligation.[61]

Christianity recognizes no boundaries of religion or ethnicity when it comes to aiding those in need. Jesus' command to love all people, including enemies (Matt 5:44–45), affirms a universal moral responsibility, while Aquinas argues that the highest virtue of charity mirrors God's universal and impartial love.[62]

Modern Christian thought, influenced by movements such as liberation theology, has expanded the scope of charity to include advocacy for systemic change. This shift underscores the need to address not only immediate material needs but also to tackle structural injustices that perpetuate poverty and exclusion. In contemporary Christianity, therefore, charity encompasses both personal acts of mercy and collective efforts to shape more just social and economic orders.[63]

In Islam, the overarching principle guiding human responsibility for establishing justice is the concept of human beings as God's vicegerents (*khalīfa*) on earth. The Qur'ān (e.g., Q 6:165; 27:62) characterizes humans as successors on earth, entrusting them with stewardship and the duty to maintain just social and environmental orders (Q 2:30). Within this framework, social justice entails preserving the balance (mīzān) commanded in the Qur'ān (Q 55:7–9).

Comparisons with Jewish and Christian teachings reveal three principal dimensions of social justice in Islam: dignity, equality, and well-being. As in *Genesis*, the Qur'ān (Q 17:70; 49:13) affirms the inherent dignity and equality of all human

61 Wadell, Paul J., "Charity: How Friendship with God Unfolds in Love for Others'" in: Kevin Timpe/Craig A. Boyd (eds.), *Virtues and Their Vices*, Oxford, 2014; published online: *Oxford Academic*, https://doi.org/10.1093/acprof:oso/9780199645541.003.0018 (accessed on 13.12); Calmer, Seth, "*Ma'alot Tsedaqah* and *Ordine Caritatis:* Orders of Charitable Priority in Maimonides and Aquinas," *Journal of Ecumenical Studies* 47,2 (2012), 167–84.

62 Ibid.

63 West, Gerald, "The Bible and the Poor: A New Way of Doing Theology," in: Christopher Rowland (ed.), *The Cambridge Companion to Liberation Theology*, 159–82, *Cambridge Companions to Religion*, Cambridge: Cambridge University Press, 2007.

beings, rejecting any notion of superiority based on race, ethnicity, or wealth.[64] This view of human equality underlines the necessity of treating all individuals fairly and without discrimination. Social justice further involves ensuring the well-being of society's most vulnerable members. As the Qur'ān repeatedly emphasizes (Q 2:177; 51:19), care for the poor, orphans, widows, and travelers constitutes a central pillar of a just community. Justice also requires proactive participation in improving society, advocating for what is right, and rectifying injustice.[65] The concept of brotherhood (Q 49:10) reinforces these communal obligations, fostering unity and ethical solidarity.[66]

Among the most frequently addressed themes related to social justice in the Qur'ān is charity, often expressed through *zakāt* and *ṣadaqa.* Although used broadly and somewhat interchangeably in the Qur'ān, these terms evolved distinct legal and ethical nuances over time. *Ṣadaqa* generally refers to voluntary charitable giving, while *zakāt* is a prescribed obligation and one of the Five Pillars of Islam. Etymologically linked to righteousness – akin to the Hebrew *tsedaḳah* – *ṣadaqa* may include not only monetary assistance but also moral support, kind words (Q 2:263), and voluntary service (Q 9:79). As in Judaism, discreet giving is encouraged (Q 2:271). The Qur'ān (Q 9:60) specifies categories of recipients, including the poor, debtors, and travelers in need, ensuring a comprehensive framework for the equitable distribution of resources. Beyond merely alleviating poverty, *ṣadaqa* aims to foster general well-being and economic stability within society.[67]

*Zakāt,* derived from the root *z-k-w* (purity, growth), is associated with piety and moral refinement (Q 2:177). It involves purifying one's wealth by sharing it and thereby promoting societal welfare. The Qur'ān employs metaphors to illustrate this principle (Q 2:265), and frequently couples the command to give *zakāt* with worship (Q 98:5). The obligation to pay *zakāt,* linked to earlier prophets such as Abraham and Jesus (Q 19:31; 21:73), was institutionalized early in Islamic history. Under the Prophet Muḥammad and the early Caliphate, *zakāt* was systematically collected and distributed through the *bayt al-māl* (public treasury). Over

---

**64** Asim, Qari, "Social Justice in Islam," in: Ann Marie Mealey/Pam Jarvis/Jonathan Doherty, Jan Fook (eds.), *Everyday Social Justice and Citizenship*, vol. 1, 57–66, London: Routledge, 2018.

**65** Qutub, Amal/Khan, Nazir/Qasqas, Mahdi, "Islam and Social Justice," in: Norma Jean Profitt/Cyndy Baskin (eds.), *Spirituality and Social Justice: Spirit in the Political Quest for a Just World*, 131–53, Toronto/Vancouver: Canadian Scholars, 2019.

**66** Brockopp, "Justice," 70.

**67** Nanji, Azim, "Almsgiving," in: Jane Dammen McAuliffe (ed.), *Encyclopedia of the Qur'ān*, vol. 1, 64–70, Leiden/Boston: Brill, 2003, 65.

time, however, the integration of the alms tax into broader fiscal systems diminished its spiritual character.[68]

In discussing social justice, al-Ghazālī's perspective is instructive. He defines injustice as any harm inflicted upon individuals or groups – whether in contracts, transactions, or personal relations. Simply refraining from harm meets only the minimum standard of justice, while striving for *iḥsān* (benevolence) surpasses it. Benevolence involves generous giving without expectation of return and refraining from exploitative economic practices.[69] For al-Ghazālī, *zakāt* represents a crucial instrument of socioeconomic balance, blending religious, moral, and social dimensions. He notes that the obligation to pay *zakāt* persists even when poverty is absent, reflecting the principle that just wealth distribution serves as a perpetual societal safeguard. Debates arose among jurists regarding whether the wealthy bear additional obligations to assist the needy beyond their *zakāt* dues. Some, like as-Sarakhsī, argue that the poor hold a right to further support.[70]

Despite the theological differences observed in the works of Aquinas and al-Ghazālī, certain parallels emerge. Both Aquinas and al-Ghazālī see a link between charity and human happiness, viewing charitable acts as a means to spiritual refinement and alignment with the divine will. Al-Ghazālī considers acts of charity as part of the external and internal disciplines needed to purify the heart and align oneself with God's will. Charity transcends mere obligation (as in *zakāt*) to reflect higher virtues like selflessness and love of God, which lead to ultimate happiness. Aquinas views charity as both a spiritual act and a practical expression of love for God and humanity. It serves as a means to align the human will with divine will, thereby achieving beatitude (perfect happiness in union with God).[71]

As in Judaism and Christianity[72], Islamic charity extends beyond communal or religious boundaries. Historical examples and prophetic traditions indicate that assistance should be offered to individuals regardless of their faith, reflecting an inclusive ethical vision.[73] In modern times, the state-administered collection of *zakāt* has declined in many regions and returned to individual practice. Some contemporary efforts to reintroduce *zakāt* into formalized structures, such as Pakistan's 1979

---

**68** Ibid., 69.

**69** *Ihyā*, II, 74–75, cf. Orman, "al-Ghazālī on Justice," 37, 54.

**70** Orman, "al-Ghazālī on Justice," 37.

**71** Shah, Rania, "Saint Thomas Aquinas and Imam al-Ghazali on the attainment of happiness," *The International Journal of Religion and Spirituality in Society* 6,2 (2015), 15–29.

**72** A monograph focusing on comparing charity in the three religions by also observing the respective historical circumstances is Frenkel, Miriam/Lev, Yaacov (eds.), *Charity and Giving in Monotheistic Religions*, Berlin/Boston: De Gruyter, 2009.

**73** Nanji, "Almsgiving," 69.

Zakāt Fund, have met with resistance, including from groups that emphasize the spiritual and voluntary nature of almsgiving. Consequently, modern philanthropic endeavors often encourage voluntary giving through foundations and charitable organizations aimed at addressing global poverty and suffering.[74]

Concluding the discussion, several points warrant reflection. The examination of covenantal theology and divine justice in Judaism, Christianity, and Islam has demonstrated that each tradition envisions justice as an essential component of the divine-human relationship. These theological frameworks inform not only beliefs about God's nature but also human ethical responsibilities, particularly regarding the vulnerable and marginalized. Social justice, as seen through the examples of charity, emerges as a concrete expression of religious ideals, bridging spiritual commitment and social engagement.

However, certain critical observations must be noted. First, while the three monotheistic faiths present comprehensive and often inspiring paradigms of justice and moral responsibility, a persistent gap exists between these principles and their realization in historical and contemporary contexts. Religious understandings of justice can be influenced by political, cultural, or social factors, resulting in inconsistent applications and, at times, contradictions between doctrine and practice. This has been demonstrated in the analysis conducted by Sabri Ciftci, particularly with regard to Islamist conceptualizations of justice, as exemplified by Quṭb. Quṭb's work underscores an abstract notion of Islamic law, yet lacks a clear delineation of the means through which his vision of social justice might be actualized.

Second, although Judaism, Christianity, and Islam each affirm the universal significance of justice and human dignity, the practical extension of these ideals beyond the boundaries of the faith community has not always been seamless. Even as all three traditions provide theological grounds for inclusive charity and assistance to those outside their communities – often exemplified by relief efforts during natural disasters – instances remain in which aid and compassion have been shaped by confessional affiliations or instrumentalized to serve missionary aims.[75]

Finally, the use of religious ideals to advance political or institutional power has, in certain periods of history, undermined the credibility of these moral visions. The rhetoric of justice, mercy, and universalism has occasionally been employed to justify conquest, colonialism, or other forms of domination. Such co-op-

---

74 Ibid., 70.

75 Silverstein, Adam J./Stroumsa, Guy G. (eds.), *The Oxford Handbook of the Abrahamic Religions*, 2015, published online: *Oxford Academic*, https://doi.org/10.1093/oxfordhb/9780199697762.001.0001 (accessed on 14.12.2024).

tation complicates the moral authority of these religious traditions, posing challenges for those who seek to apply their teachings sincerely and equitably.[76]

These critiques underscore that while theological concepts of justice and charity possess a rich potential to guide ethical action, their authentic implementation requires continual critical self-examination, openness to internal and external scrutiny, and willingness to address historical legacies and current inequalities. It is in the sustained effort to reconcile religious ideals with lived reality that the transformative promise of these traditions, in matters of justice, may be most fully realized.

76 See, for example, Atalia Omer/Joshua Lupo (eds.), *Religion, Modernity, and the Global Afterlives of Colonialism*, USA: University of Notre Dame Press, 2024; Daggers, Jenny, *Postcolonial Theology of Religions: Particularity and Pluralism in World Christianity*, London: Taylor & Francis, 2013.

# List of Contributors

**Aryeh Botwinick** is Professor of Jewish Studies in the College of Liberal Arts at Temple University. He received his Ph.D. from the Inter-Disciplinary Program in Political Philosophy at Princeton University. His research interests focus on the relationship between Western monotheism and Western secularism and the continuity of logical structure between key interpretations of monotheism and key readings of philosophical skepticism and liberalism. His publications include *Emmanuel Levinas and the Limits to Ethics: A Critique and a Re-Appropriation* (Routledge 2014). He received the *College of Liberal Arts Award for Excellence in Teaching* in 2008.

**Elisabeth Gräb-Schmidt** is Professor of Systematic Theology and Director of the Institute for Ethics at the Faculty of Protestant Theology at the University of Tübingen. She studied theology at the universities of Göttingen, Heidelberg, Berkeley, and Mainz, and received her doctorate from the Johannes Gutenberg University in Mainz in 1992. Her research interests focus on the relationship between ethics and technology and on theories of religion in secular contexts. She is currently the editor of the *Zeitschrift für Evangelische Ethik* (Journal for Protestant Ethics) and the *Zeitschrift für Theologie und Kirche* (Journal for Theology and Church). Her most recent publication is *Das Böse* (Evil) (Leipzig 2024).

**Sabri Ciftci** is a professor and Michael W. Suleiman Chair in the Department of Political Science at Kansas State University. He is also the founding director of the Middle East Studies minor. Ciftci is primarily a scholar of Islam and democracy, Muslim political attitudes, Arab public opinion, and Turkish politics. His most recent projects examine religion and state-building in MENA and historical origins of Turkish foreign policy. Ciftci is the author *of Islam, Justice, and Democracy* (2021, Temple University Press) and co-author of *Beyond Piety and Politics* (2022, Indiana University Press). He has also widely published in such journals as *Comparative Political Studies*, *Political Research Quarterly*, and others.

**Catharina Rachik** is currently a research associate at the Friedrich-Alexander-Universität Erlangen-Nürnberg (FAU) where she coordinates the book-series "Key Concepts in Interreligious Discourse". Before she joined the Bavarian Research Center for Interreligious Discourses she has been research associate and coordinator in the Center for Islamic Theology at the University of Münster. She received her M.A. in Islamic Studies at the University of Münster and is writing her dissertation on Moses in the Qurʾān. Her research focuses on Qurʾānic Studies and Tafsīr (classical and modern), the Qurʾān in Late Antiquity, as well as on the field of Islamic art. Her publications include "Der Exodus im Qurʾān," in: Carolin Neuber (ed.), *Der immer neue Exodus*, Stuttgart, 2018.

**Georges Tamer** holds the Chair of Oriental Philology and Islamic Studies and is founding director of the Bavarian Research Center for Interreligious Discourses at the Friedrich-Alexander-Universität Erlangen-Nürnberg. He received his Ph.D. in Philosophy from the Free University Berlin in 2000 and completed his habilitation in Islamic Studies in Erlangen in 2007. His research focuses on Qurʾānic hermeneutics, philosophy in the Islamic world, Arabic literature and interreligious discourses. His publications include: *Zeit und Gott: Hellenistische Zeitvorstellungen in der altarabischen Dichtung und im Koran*, 2008; *Hermeneutical Crossroads: Understanding Scripture in Judaism, Christianity and Islam in the Pre-Modern Orient* (2017), *Islamic Philosophy and the Crisis of Modernity* (2024), *Handbook of Qurʾānic Hermeneutics*, 7 volumes (2023–).

# Index of Persons


ʿAbduh, Muḥammad 115, 137–139, 141, 148, 189
Abraham 17–19, 21, 34, 40, 79 f., 183 f., 190–197, 199 f., 204, 209
Adıvar, Halide Edib 143
al-Afghānī, Jamāl ad-Dīn 116, 137–139, 141, 189
ʿAlī b. Abī Ṭālib 125
Amos 65, 186, 192
Anselm of Canterbury 70
Apel, Karl-Otto 96
Arendt, Hannah 40, 84
Aristotle 61, 63 f., 67, 186
Atatürk, Mustafa Kemal 144
Augustine 71 f.

Barth, Karl 77, 85, 93, 198

Cain 79 f., 157
Camus, Albert 76
Cicero 71, 78
Crone, Patricia 124, 128, 155

Epstein, Yechiel Michel 12

al-Fārābī, Abū Naṣr Muḥammad 119 f., 123, 134, 189
Freud, Sigmund 108

al-Ghannūshī, Rāshid 122, 145, 162–164
al-Ghazālī, Abū Ḥāmid 120, 130, 136, 189, 201 f., 210

Habermas, Jürgen 89, 96, 99
Hauerwas, Stanley 100
Hobbes, Thomas 5, 40, 86, 90, 187
Höffe, Otfried 99
Hosea 65, 192

Ibn Ḥanbal, Aḥmad 127
Ibn Khaldūn 134, 144
Ibn Miskawayh, Muḥammad 121
Ibn Taymīya 130, 133–136, 138, 174, 189
al-Iṣfahānī, Rāghīb 120, 194

Jesus 34, 64, 66, 74, 78 f., 92, 169, 192, 198, 208 f.
al-Jīlānī, Shaikh ʿAbd al-Qādir 18
Job 64, 79 f., 83–85
John of Salisbury 71 f.

Kafka, Franz 103
Kant, Immanuel 83, 86 f., 91, 99, 102 f., 105, 108, 187
Kemal, Namık 116, 142–145, 158, 189
Khomeinī, Ayatollah Rūḥollāh 116, 128, 165
Kierkegaard, Søren 103

Lactantius 83
Leibniz 74, 83 f.
Locke, John 86, 187
Luther, Martin 71–75, 85, 92 f., 103–105, 107, 187, 198

Maimonides 1, 5, 11, 16 f., 40–54, 184–186, 192, 195 f., 200, 205, 208
Marcion 4, 8, 68
Matthew 66, 79, 188, 198, 206
Mawdūdī, Abū l-Aʿlā 116, 158, 162 f., 166
Melanchthon 75
Moses 6, 16, 20–23, 25 f., 34, 43, 45 f., 52, 191, 193
Muʿāwiya I 125
Muḥammad 120, 125, 136, 138, 141, 145, 151, 154, 159 f., 163, 193, 201, 209

Naftali ʻTsevi Yehudah Berlin (Netziv) 6 f.
an-Naim, Abdullahi Ahmed 122, 146, 166
Nietzsche, Friedrich 5, 40, 83
Nussbaum, Martha 63, 100 f., 108

Oakeshott, Michael 8–10, 40

Paul 9, 31–34, 36, 64–66, 74, 92 f., 106, 168 f., 187, 192 f., 208


https://doi.org/10.1515/9783110561692-006

Pieper, Joseph 110
Pinchas 25–27
Plato 44, 61–63, 82, 186

Quṭb, Sayyid 116, 118, 122, 146–159, 161–164, 166, 168, 173, 189, 211

Rabbi Akiva 11–15, 17, 41, 56, 184
Rabbi Eliezer 12 f.
Rabbi Meir 11
Rashi 4, 19–21, 24, 29, 49, 52
Rawls, John 86, 96, 98 f., 101, 105, 108, 123, 146, 152, 155, 167
ar-Rāziq, ʿAlī ʿAbd 144
Riḍā, Rashīd 138
Rousseau, Jean-Jacques 86, 187

Sen, Amartya 63, 100, 167
Sharīʿatī, ʿAlī 116, 128, 145 f., 148, 155–164, 166, 168, 170, 173, 190
Smith, Adam 97, 123, 149, 167, 170

Ṭabāṭabāʾī, Mīrzā Seyyed Muḥammad 143
Thomas Aquinas 67, 69 f., 110, 187, 198, 207, 210

Ulpian 62, 82
ʿUmar b. al-Khaṭṭāb 132

Volozhiner, Reb Chaim 22 f., 36–39

Walzer, Michael 21, 96, 99 f., 119, 192
Weber, Max 73
Wiesel, Elie 84

# Index of Subjects


action 2, 10, 20, 22 f., 26 f., 32 f., 36, 38 – 41, 52, 54, 56, 61 f., 65 – 68, 70 – 76, 80 f., 83 – 85, 87, 91, 93 f., 96, 98 – 100, 104, 106 – 109, 120, 128 f., 161 – 164, 173, 183, 189, 193, 196 f., 199 – 204, 212
*ʿadāla* 117, 144, 188
agency 61, 70 f., 75, 81, 108, 139, 142, 146 f., 149, 156, 158, 161, 163, 168, 175, 185, 187, 190
*aḳedah* 18 f.

circle of justice 130 f., 143
community 6, 13, 19 f., 22 f., 25 – 27, 30, 32, 35, 37, 40, 43, 47, 49, 52, 62, 65, 70, 72, 89, 92 – 95, 98, 100, 109 f., 115, 122, 124 – 127, 132, 138, 142, 145, 148, 150 f., 153 – 155, 160 – 164, 167, 169, 174 – 176, 187, 190, 192, 195, 203, 206 f., 209, 211
commutative justice 67 f., 186
constitutionalism 139 – 142
cosmology 54, 76, 87, 95, 166
– cosmological 69, 77, 80, 88, 102, 110, 166, 187
cosmos 7 f., 59, 80, 86, 108, 115, 164, 196
covenant 1, 19, 21 – 26, 66 – 68, 94, 118, 169, 183 f., 188, 191 – 194, 196, 203

*debitum* 75 f.
deification 78
democracy 39, 63, 88, 99, 115, 121 – 123, 133 f., 136, 138 – 141, 145 f., 150, 153, 162 – 165, 168, 170 – 174, 176 f., 189 f.
dignity 59, 86, 88, 90, 94, 100, 103, 108 – 110, 122, 128, 139, 143, 146, 150, 156, 163, 167, 172, 176 f., 188, 190, 204 – 206, 208, 211
*dikaiosýne* 67, 89
distributive justice 152 f., 167, 170
divine command 17, 19, 55, 184 f., 194, 196
– divine commandments 22, 32 f., 37, 40, 198, 207
divine justice 17, 121, 165, 183 f., 187 – 199, 201 – 203, 211

economy (economics/economical) 97 f., 109, 136
equality 27 – 30, 59, 63 f., 66 – 68, 86, 88, 96, 98 – 101, 105 f., 118, 121, 149 – 151, 153, 158 – 160, 175, 185, 187, 208 f.

*fiqh* 123, 129, 133, 174
*fitna* 124, 128, 189
freedom 19, 51 f., 56, 60 – 62, 66, 70, 74, 83, 85 – 91, 93, 95 – 110, 123, 137, 140 – 145, 148 – 151, 153, 158 – 160, 167 – 171, 175 f., 187 – 190
free will 37, 115 f., 120, 126, 138, 146, 158, 161, 166, 168, 175 f.

gift 25, 62, 66 f., 70, 73 f., 105, 110, 187, 198, 203, 205
Gnosticism 4, 7 – 9
grace 70 – 73, 75, 77 f., 80, 83 f., 101, 187, 192 f., 198 f., 207 f.

*halakhah* 13,
human-divine relationship 1, 191, 195
human free will 188 f.
humanity 59, 65 – 68, 70 f., 74, 76 f., 80 f., 83 – 88, 91, 94 – 96, 99, 101 – 103, 107 – 111, 115, 148, 151, 157, 161, 165, 167, 169, 183 – 187, 191 – 194, 197 f., 201 – 203, 207 f., 210
human nature 42, 84, 152, 161
human rights 59 f., 85, 87 f., 90, 100, 107 f., 187

*iḥsān* 115, 210

judge 1, 11, 17, 40 – 46, 48 – 52, 54, 63, 65, 68, 77, 117, 139, 183, 185 f., 190 f., 195, 202
judgement 65, 68, 72, 74, 80, 82 – 85, 97, 105, 108, 133, 193 f.
justification 20, 31 – 33, 44, 54, 60 f., 71 – 75, 77 f., 82 f., 85, 91 f., 94, 103 – 105, 109, 115, 126, 129 f., 134, 174 f., 187, 198

*khalīfa* (vicegerency) 115 f., 118, 120, 145 – 147, 167, 175, 177, 188, 190, 208


https://doi.org/10.1515/9783110561692-007

law 9, 11 – 14, 19 – 22, 25, 27 – 34, 40 – 43, 45 f., 48 – 54, 56, 65 f., 69, 71 – 75, 80 – 82, 85 – 91, 93, 95, 99, 102 f., 107 f., 110, 115 f., 118, 123, 125, 129 – 135, 137 – 139, 142, 144, 146 f., 152 – 156, 161 – 163, 166 – 169, 171, 183, 185, 187, 192, 194, 196 f., 199, 202 f., 205 f., 211
liberty 59, 74, 86, 88 – 91, 102, 187

*maṣlaḥa* 115 f., 118, 120, 131, 133, 169
mercy 19, 65 – 68, 71 f., 75, 77, 80, 82 – 85, 89, 93, 95, 101 f., 109 f., 149, 170, 183, 185 – 188, 192, 194 – 203, 208, 211
*mishpat* 67, 192, 195
*mīzān* 117, 188, 200 f., 208
morality 9, 26, 73, 84, 119 f., 183
Muʿtazila 119, 127, 189

negative theology 1, 4, 9, 12, 19, 38, 40, 42 f., 46, 49 f., 185

order 4, 18 f., 24 f., 36 f., 44, 47 f., 53, 59, 61 – 66, 69 – 72, 74 – 78, 80 – 83, 86 – 91, 94, 98, 100 – 102, 105, 108 f., 116 – 118, 121, 125 – 127, 129 f., 134 f., 137, 140, 147 – 149, 151, 154, 156 – 161, 163, 165 – 167, 173 – 177, 183, 186 – 189, 191, 196, 200 – 203, 205, 208

plurality 90, 102, 106
political justice 81, 99, 115 f., 120 f., 123 – 126, 132, 135, 137 – 139, 141 f., 144 – 147, 162, 167, 170 – 172, 175, 177, 189

predestination 189

Rabbinic authority 45, 47
reformists 138 f.
revivalism 163

*sharīʿa* 123, 131, 133 f., 137, 141, 154, 164, 189
Shīʿa 116, 124 f., 128, 161
*shūrā* 139, 145, 189
social justice 62, 65, 68, 79, 81, 83, 109, 115 – 118, 121 – 124, 129 – 135, 138, 142 – 157, 159, 161, 165, 167 f., 170 – 174, 176 f., 184 f., 188 f., 202 – 204, 206 – 211
social welfare 129, 133, 139, 141 f., 145, 151, 153, 162
soul 19, 39, 61 – 63, 79, 158, 167, 193
*suum cuique* 62 – 64, 82

*tawḥīd* 115 f., 119 f., 145 f., 148, 150, 156 – 159, 163, 165 f., 175, 188 – 190
theodicy 60, 64, 75, 82 – 85, 197
*theosis* 78 f.
Tower of Babel 3 – 11, 56, 184
*tsedeḳ* 2, 41, 192, 196

virtue 2, 24, 42, 61, 64 – 67, 69 f., 72 f., 81, 94, 110, 119 f., 122, 132 – 134, 157 f., 163, 168, 186 f., 189, 194, 196, 200, 207 f., 210

*zakāt* 81, 131 f., 152, 189, 203, 209 – 211
*ẓulm* 117 f., 128, 145 f., 156, 165, 189 f.

www.ingramcontent.com/pod-product-compliance
Lightning Source LLC
LaVergne TN
LVHW051940060925
820435LV00015B/109